The Gift of Wisdom
According to St Thomas Aquinas
Shown in the Life of St Thérèse of Lisieux

The Gift of Wisdom
According to St Thomas Aquinas
Shown in the Life of St Thérèse of Lisieux

God's Little Martyr of Love

Denise Clare Oliver

Claritas Spiritual Theology®

Published 2022 by
Claritas Spiritual Theology®
London
claritas-st.com

No part of this publication may be reproduced, stored in a retrieval system or transmitted in any form or by any means, electronic, mechanical, photocopying, recording or otherwise, without the written permission of the publisher.

© 2022 Denise Clare Oliver

All rights reserved

ISBN: 978-1-8384876-0-7

Cover Design and Photography
by Dr Denise Clare Oliver

To my loving parents,
William Edward & Dulcie Oliver

CONTENTS

ACKNOWLEDGEMENTS	xiii
ABBREVIATIONS	xv
INTRODUCTION	1

1. THE GIFTS OF THE HOLY SPIRIT AND THE SUPERNATURAL ORGANISM — 21

The Gifts of the Holy Spirit	21
The Supernatural Organism	27
The Difference Between the Gifts and the Virtues	35
The Operation of the Gifts of the Holy Spirit	43
Operating and Cooperating Grace	44

2. THE GIFT OF WISDOM — 49

Wisdom as a Gift and Wisdom as a Virtue	51
Experiential Knowledge - A Taste, Love, Delight	59
Enlightens the Intellect and Enkindles the Affections and the Will	68
The Gift of Wisdom is Only Present in those who are in the State of Grace	70
Charity is Perfected by the Gift of Wisdom; Nevertheless, Charity is Higher than this Gift	72
Towards a Deeper Understanding of Judgment through the Gift of Wisdom	81

The Gift of Understanding	83
The Gift of Knowledge	84
The Gift of Wisdom	86
The Gift of Wisdom and Infused Contemplation	87
The Gift of Wisdom is Both Speculative and Practical	92
Three Stages in the Spiritual Life	95
Wisdom is in all who have Sanctifying Grace, though it is Present in Different Degrees	102
The Seventh Beatitude Corresponds to the Gift of Wisdom	106
The Effects of the Gift of Wisdom	114
Connaturality with Divine Things	115
The Gift of Wisdom Judges and Orders All Things According to Divine Rules	116
The Gift of Wisdom Gives the Soul Certitude	117
Through the Effect of the Gift of Wisdom, a Person can Reach a Heroic Degree of Charity	118
The Gift of Wisdom Gives the Soul a Desire to Suffer in Conformity to Christ; It Makes the Bitter Sweet and the Labour Rest	120
Peace	122
Through the Gift of Wisdom, Man Attains to the Sonship of God and is Conformed to His Image	123
Experience of the Indwelling of The Trinity	124
The Gift of Wisdom – A Truly Ineffable Gift	126

3. THE CHILDHOOD YEARS AND THE LIFE OF ST THÉRÈSE 127

Sickness and Struggles in Her Early Years 133

Entrance into Carmel 141

4. THE GIFT OF WISDOM IN THE LIFE OF ST THÉRÈSE – ACORDING TO CERTAIN EFFECTS OF THIS GIFT 147

Introduction 147

Confidence and Certitude in God's Mercy 156

Infused Contemplation 161

Mystical State 165

Experiences of Infused Contemplation 171

Concomitant Phenomena 176

Secrets 187

St Thérèse's Little Way – A Perfect Preparation for Infused Contemplation and the Operation of the Gift of Wisdom 207

Experiencing the Indwelling through the Operation of the Gift of Wisdom 212

The Gift of Wisdom Perfects Charity 220

Ordering Others According to Divine Rules - The Charism of Wisdom 224

Conclusion 235

5. THE FULL FLOWERING OF THE GIFT OF WISDOM IN THE LIFE OF ST THÉRÈSE   237

The Lover and the Beloved   237

Suffering – Conformity to Christ   239

Suffering Becomes Sweet and Desirable   240

The Cross is Salutary for Believers but Seems Foolish to the Eyes of the World   244

The Benefits a Soul can Receive Through Suffering   246

Progression from Suffering with Tears to Desiring Suffering and Finally Finding Joy in Suffering   249

    First Communion – Thérèse Receives the Desire to Suffer   250

    Confirmation – Thérèse Receives the Strength to Suffer   252

    Christmas Grace – Thérèse Receives the Desire to Suffer for Souls   254

    After Entering Carmel   256

    Act of Oblation   265

Quasi-Experiential Knowledge of Divine Mercy – Contemplation and the Gift of Wisdom   272

Living on Love   275

The Desire to be a Victim of Love Suffices   281

A Way of Trust and Confidence that can Lead to the Heights of Perfection   284

Vocation of Love/ The Little Doctrine   286

Thérèse's Little Way was Given to Her Through a Knowledge of Love	288
Thérèse's One Desire was to Love God and to Make Him Loved	291
Christian Perfection and the Way of Abandonment	295
Thérèse Believes all Souls Can Follow Her Little Way	297
6. GOD'S LITTLE MARTYR OF LOVE	301
Martyrdom of Love	301
First Motive Cause of Martyrdom	306
Transforming Union	310
The Desire to Die as a Martyr of Love and the Gift of Wisdom	315
Desire for Martyrdom Fulfilled	317
True Love for Jesus and the Authentic Desire for Martyrdom	321
Longing to Die to be with Christ	322
The Flame of Love Within the Heart of Thérèse	329
CONCLUSION	339
BIBLIOGRAPHY	347

ACKNOWLEDGEMENTS

A huge expression of gratitude is due to Dr Christina Pal for her editorial expertise, helpful suggestions, and constant generosity and encouragement during the whole writing process of this work. Also special thanks to Rev. Fr Frederick Miller who first introduced me to the theology of the seven gifts of the Holy Spirit, and to Rev. Fr Luke Buckles, OP who moderated this work when it was first published as a doctoral dissertation in 2013. Many thanks to Dr Colin Harte who kindly helped with proofreading of the completed work. Finally, many thanks to all my colleagues and friends in Rome, and all who prayed for the completion of this project.

ABBREVIATIONS

Works by St Thomas Aquinas

Comp. Theol.	Compendium Theologiae
In Psalm.	In Psalmos Davidis Expositio
In Sent.	Scriptum Super Libros Sententiarum Petri Lombardi
ST	Summa Theologiae
Super Ep. ad Col.	Super Epistolam S. Pauli ad Colossenses lectura
Super Ep. ad Gal.	Super Epistolam S. Pauli ad Galatas lectura
Super Ep. ad Hebr.	Super Epistolam S. Pauli ad Hebraeos Expositio
Super Ep. ad Phil.	Super Epistolam S. Pauli ad Philipenses lectura
Super Ep. ad Rom.	Super Epistolam S. Pauli ad Romanos Expositio
Super Ioan.	Super Evangelium S. Ioannis lectura
Super Is.	Expositio super Isaiam ad litteram
Super Matt.	Super Evangelium S. Matthaei lectura
Super I Ep. ad Cor.	Super I Epistolam S. Pauli ad Corinthios Expositio
Super I Ep. ad Thess.	Super I Epistolam S. Pauli ad Thessalonicenses lectura

Works by St Thérèse of Lisieux

GC I	General Correspondence, Vol. I
GC II	General Correspondence, Vol. II
LC	Last Conversations
Plays	The Plays of St Thérèse of Lisieux
PN	The Poetry of St Thérèse of Lisieux
Prayers	The Prayers of St Thérèse of Lisieux
Ms A	Autobiographical manuscript, dedicated to Mother Agnès of Jesus (1895)
Ms B	Letter to Sister Marie of the Sacred Heart, autobiographical Manuscript (1896)
Ms C	Autobiographical manuscript, dedicated to Mother Marie de Gonzague (1897)

INTRODUCTION

The Angelic Doctor of the Church, St Thomas Aquinas, says that "the goodness of the grace of one [person] is greater than the goodness of the nature of the whole universe."[1] This is because by the gift of God's grace we are given a participation in the Divine life, (2 Peter, 1:4); in other words, we share in the very life of God. This gift of sanctifying grace is the most precious gift that we can receive in this life.

We all need the gift of sanctifying grace – not only because our nature has been wounded by original sin and is in need of God's healing touch, but also because without this grace, we are incapable of living in friendship with God and reaching eternal life. Prior to original sin, Adam and Eve enjoyed sanctifying grace, and consequently, all of their thoughts and actions were able to be ordered towards God; they were able to love God above all things. Yet, they were free to choose the good or to choose evil. In choosing the latter, Adam and Eve chose not to trust God, they rejected His friendship, and hence, grace was lost, the light of reason was dimmed, and the will was wounded. After the fall, man wandered far from God.

The good news is that through the grace of Christ, we receive healing and transformation – we are

---

[1] St Thomas Aquinas, *Summa Theologiae*, translated by the Fathers of the English Dominican Province (New York: Benziger Brothers, Inc., 1948), I-II, q. 113, a. 9, ad 2. Henceforth cited as *ST*.

"internally perfected for the exercise of virtue"[2] – the light of faith transforms, heals, and perfects our understanding, and charity unites us to God. Because of sanctifying grace which we receive in baptism, we are cleansed of all sin, and we become beloved sons and daughters of the Father. Since we are baptised into the mysteries of our Lord's death and resurrection, we are spiritually born again. Sanctifying grace, which God infuses into the soul through the sacrament of baptism, changes us ontologically, and we receive the indwelling of the most Holy Trinity. God also infuses into our souls the theological and moral virtues, and the seven gifts of the Holy Spirit. None of these gifts – grace, the virtues, and the seven gifts – can be merited; they are given out of God's profound love for us. Through sanctifying grace and the theological virtue of charity received in baptism, we become friends of God, and as we advance in the spiritual life, our friendship with God continues to grow.

The aim of the present work is to focus on one of the seven gifts of the Holy Spirit, namely the gift of wisdom. This book is divided into two parts – the first part examining the teaching of the Angelic Doctor, St Thomas Aquinas, regarding the gift of wisdom, and the second part showing the operation of this gift in the life of another Doctor of the Church, St Thérèse of Lisieux.

In Part one (I), the first chapter will look closely at

---

[2] St Thomas Aquinas, *The Light of Faith: The Compendium of Theology*, translated by Cyril Vollert (St. Louis, MO: B. Herder Book Co., 1958; reprint, Manchester, NH: Sophia Institute Press, 1993), ch. 143.

the changes which take place in the soul as a result of receiving sanctifying grace. We shall begin with a description of the graced soul, and then give an overview of how the gift of wisdom fits into the whole supernatural organism. Chapter two follows with an analysis of St Thomas Aquinas' teaching on the gift of wisdom. We shall examine the ontological nature of this gift, the connatural knowing and judgment through the operation of this gift, and the effects of the gift of wisdom, including its perfecting effect on charity.

In Part two (II), following a short biography of the life of St Thérèse of Lisieux (chapter three), we will examine the effects of the gift of wisdom operating in Thérèse's life (chapters four, five, and six). The goal of this work is not to prove that the gift of wisdom was operating in the life of St Thérèse – the gifts of the Holy Spirit are always highly operative in all those who reach a high degree of sanctity. Rather, the aim is two-fold. First, a close examination of the theology of St Thomas Aquinas regarding the gift of wisdom will show *how* the gift of wisdom can be recognised in the life of a soul that is in the state of grace and open to the working of the Holy Spirit. To this end, *italics* have been used for the purpose of highlighting key words and phrases – both in the section expounding St Thomas' teaching and also in the section about the life of St Thérèse – in order to point out more clearly the manifestations of the gift of wisdom. Second, by applying the teaching of St Thomas regarding the gift of wisdom, I will demonstrate that this gift had a profound effect on St Thérèse's whole spiritual life and gave her the inspiration for her *Little Way*. It is precisely through the operation of this gift that St Thérèse was brought to the point of desiring to suffer for the salvation of souls, and ultimately to imitate her cruciform Lord by dying as a martyr of love.

At the outset, it is important to dispel certain false images of the Angelic Doctor. St Thomas gives us solid principles for understanding the whole supernatural organism and the mystical life; but there is a common misunderstanding that St Thomas is not really a theologian, but rather a philosopher, a kind of "Christian Aristotle."[3] In response, it can be said that St Thomas is a Master of the Sacred Page[4] and a theologian par excellence who has from a "supernatural point of view used Aristotle for the defense and explanation of the divine truths of faith."[5] St John Paul II explains:

> In an age when Christian thinkers were rediscovering the treasures of ancient philosophy, and more particularly of Aristotle, Thomas had the great merit of giving pride of place to the harmony which exists between faith and reason. Both the light of reason and the light of faith come from God, he argued; hence there can be no contradiction between them ... Thomas recognized that nature, philosophy's proper concern,

---

[3] Reginald Garrigou-Lagrange, OP, *Christian Perfection and Contemplation*, translated by Sister Mary Timothea Doyle, OP (Rockford, IL: Tan Books and Publishers, Inc., 2003), 48.

[4] Jean-Pierre Torrell, OP, *Saint Thomas Aquinas: The Person and His Works*, vol. I, translated by Robert Royal (Washington D.C.: Catholic University of America Press, 1996), 54-74.

[5] Garrigou-Lagrange, *Christian Perfection and Contemplation*, 48.

could contribute to the understanding of divine Revelation.[6]

St Thomas has found and used whatever is good and whatever is true – from whatever source, including the pagan philosopher Aristotle – for the service of the Gospel. The work of St Thomas can be somewhat misunderstood if it is read with the preconceived notion that he will only provide a dry, technical, philosophical work. Here, too, we can reply by pointing out that St Thomas has used philosophical terminology – since philosophy is the handmaiden of theology – in order to expound the truth of God's Self-Revelation as clearly and precisely as is humanly possible. The fact is that he has prepared with great care and precision the keys that can open many doors into the truths of the faith.[7] His works are extremely transparent and they have not been clouded by his personal prejudice or opinions; they demonstrate that he is open to all that is true.[8] They are alive with the truths of God, His love for all souls, and how God is working in the life of each individual. St Thomas' writings are speculative but also very practical – as sacred doctrine is both speculative and practical[9] – and he explains the truths of the Catholic faith in a most brilliant and systematic way. St Thomas "marvellously synthesized the knowledge of the philosopher and

---

[6] St John Paul II, *Fides et Ratio*, 43.
[7] Jacques Maritain, *The Range of Reason* (New York: Charles Scribner's Sons, 1953), 214.
[8] Benedict Ashley, OP, *Thomas Aquinas: The Gifts of the Spirit* (New York: New City Press, 1995), 9.
[9] *ST* I, q. 1, a. 4.

that of the theologian, and the gift of wisdom raised him to the highest degree of infused contemplation."[10]

Even though it is not the aim of this book to show that the gift of wisdom was operating to a high degree in the lives of St Thomas and St Thérèse (since this reality is presupposed in the present work), it is certainly worth mentioning some of the comments that popes have made down through the centuries regarding the wise and important doctrine of both St Thomas Aquinas and St Thérèse of Lisieux. Many popes have spoken of the importance of the work of St Thomas. The following are just a few examples of their declarations concerning the role of St Thomas as a teacher and guide for all who seek a clearer understanding of the truths of the faith. According to John XXII (1316-1334):

> He enlightened the Church more than all the other Doctors; in his books a man gains more in one year than in the teaching of others during the whole of his life.[11]

Later, in the sixteenth century, St Pius V (1566-1572), in declaring St Thomas a Doctor of the Church, describes him as "the most brilliant light of the Church."[12] In the eighteenth century, Benedict XIII (1724-1730) writing to the Order of Preachers

---

[10] Garrigou-Lagrange, *Christian Perfection and Contemplation*, 1.
[11] John XXII, as quoted in Pius XI, *Studiorum Ducem* 10.
[12] Cf. Ronald McArthur, "St. Thomas and the Formation of the Catholic Mind," in *The Ever-Illuminating Wisdom of St. Thomas Aquinas*, The Wethersfield Institute (San Francisco: Ignatius Press, 1999), 136.

emphasises that they should "pursue with energy [their] Doctor's works, more brilliant than the sun and written without the shadow of error."[13] Almost two centuries later, Leo XIII (1878-1903) recommends:

> Among the Scholastic Doctors, the chief and master of all towers Aquinas, who ... because 'he most venerated the ancient doctors of the Church, in a certain way seems to have inherited the intellect of all' ... he is rightly and deservedly esteemed the special bulwark and glory of the Catholic faith. With his spirit at once humble and swift, his memory ready and tenacious, his life spotless throughout, a love of truth for its own sake, richly endowed with human and divine science, like the sun he heated the world with the warmth of his virtues and filled it with the splendor of his teaching. Moreover, the Angelic Doctor... single-handed... victoriously combated the errors of former times, and supplied invincible arms to put those to rout which might in aftertimes spring up."[14]

He gives the following advice to teachers and Universities:

> We exhort you, venerable brethren, in all earnestness to restore the golden wisdom of St. Thomas, and to spread it far and wide for the defense and beauty of the Catholic faith, for the good of society, and for the advantage of all the sciences. Let carefully selected teachers endeavor to implant

---

[13] Cf. McArthur, "St. Thomas and the Formation of the Catholic Mind," 136.
[14] Leo XIII, *Aeterni Patris*, 17-18.

the doctrine of Thomas Aquinas in the minds of students, and set forth clearly his solidity and excellence over others. Let the universities already founded or to be founded by you illustrate and defend this doctrine, and use it for the refutation of prevailing errors. [15]

Then, in the early twentieth century, St Pius X (1903-1914) declares:

> Indeed, those principles of wisdom useful for all time, which the holy Fathers and Doctors passed on to us, have been organized by no one more aptly than by Thomas, and no one has explained them more clearly.[16]

Further, in *Pascendi Dominici Gregis* he recommends that: "Professors remember that they cannot set St. Thomas aside, especially in metaphysical questions, without grave detriment."[17]

While St Thomas' intellectual and systematic works may be well known, his greatness as a teacher and guide for the spiritual life often goes unnoticed. However, there is no other theologian who has shown so clearly that the Christian life ought to be one lived in conformity to Christ and guided by the Holy Spirit – without doubt, St Thomas lived and taught a "spirituality of truth."[18] St Thomas illuminates the

---

[15] Leo XIII, *Aeterni Patris*, 31.
[16] St Pius X, Apostolic Letter *In praecipius* to the Roman Academy of St. Thomas, I, 124.
[17] St Piux X, *Pascendi Dominici Gregis*, 45.
[18] Benedict Ashley, *The Gifts of the Spirit*, 7. St Thomas was naturally gifted; he also received a high degree of the gift of wisdom. We know this because he had a profound "supernatural instinct" by which he was able to discover in all things the "divine

mind of the reader, and he offers an "objective, cohesive and penetrating grasp of what is intelligible in God, in His graces, and of the essential components of the divinely transformed human person."[19] St Thomas has articulated clearly and precisely the distinction between what belongs to the natural order and what belongs to the supernatural order;[20] he has also expounded the principles of mystical theology.[21] In writing to the editor of *La vie spirituelle*, Benedict XV (1914-1922) writes:

> In our day many neglect the supernatural life and cultivate in its place an inconsistent and vague sentimentalism. Hence it is absolutely necessary to recall more often what the fathers of the Church, together with Holy Scripture, have taught us on the subject, and to do so by taking St Thomas Aquinas especially as our guide, because he has so clearly set forth their doctrine on the elevation of the supernatural life.[22]

Following St Pius X and Benedict XV, Pius XI (1922-

---

aspect by which they were related to God." There is not any other way to explain this divine instinct other than that the gift of wisdom was operating in St Thomas' life to an "eminent degree." Cf. Antonio Royo, OP, and Jordan Aumann, OP, *The Theology of Christian Perfection* (Dubuque, Iowa: The Priory Press, 1962), 422.
[19] Wojciech Giertych, OP, "Why are there so few Thomist Saints?" in the February-March Special Issue, *A Joint Project of the Journal Angelicum and the Angelicum-STOQ* (Rome, 2009): 989.
[20] Garrigou-Lagrange, *Christian Perfection and Contemplation*, 58.
[21] Garrigou-Lagrange, *Christian Perfection and Contemplation*, 80.
[22] Cf. Garrigou-Lagrange, *Christian Perfection and Contemplation*, 4. "Benedict XV congratulated the editor of *La vie spirituelle* for making this doctrine known."

39) in his encyclical *Studiorum Ducem* declares: "Thomas should be called not only the Angelic, but also the Common or Universal Doctor of the Church..."[23] He refers to the wisdom which St Thomas received from above:

> This wisdom, therefore, which comes down from, or is infused by, God, accompanied by the other gifts of the Holy Ghost, continually grew and increased in Thomas, along with charity, the mistress and queen of all the virtues. Indeed it was an absolutely certain doctrine of his that the love of God should ever continually increase in accordance with the very words of the commandment: "Thou shalt love the Lord, thy God, with thy whole heart;" for the whole and the perfect are one same thing...[24]

In the same document, Pius XI extols St Thomas for demonstrating with the witness of his life the profound connection between the intellectual life and divine intimacy:

> In dealing orally or in writing with divine things, he provides theologians with a striking example of the intimate connection which should exist between the spiritual and the intellectual life. For just as a man cannot really be said to know some distant country, if his acquaintance is confined merely to a description of it, however accurate, but must have dwelt in it for some time; so nobody can attain to an intimate knowledge of God by mere scientific investigation, unless he also dwells in the most intimate association with God. The aim of the whole theology of St. Thomas is to bring us into

---

[23] Pius XI, *Studiorum Ducem*, 11.
[24] Pius XI, *Studiorum Ducem*, 8.

> close living intimacy with God. For even as in his childhood at Monte Cassino he unceasingly put the question: "What is God?"; so all the books he wrote concerning the creation of the world, the nature of man, laws, the virtues, and the sacraments, are all concerned with God, the Author of eternal salvation ... according to Thomas, by far the most important benefit to be derived from sacred studies, is that they inspire a man with a great love for God and a great longing for eternal things.[25]

Further, Piux XI underscores the great relevance of St Thomas' theology concerning both the virtues and the gifts. This theology is essential for understanding moral theology, asceticism, and mysticism; in other words, he gives us the principles by which to understand the whole of spiritual theology:

> His eminence in the learning of asceticism and mysticism is no less remarkable; for he brought the whole science of morals back to the theory of the virtues and gifts, and marvelously defined both the science and the theory in relation to the various conditions of men, both those who strive to attain Christian perfection and fullness of spirit, in the active no less than in the contemplative life. If anyone, therefore, desires to understand fully all the implications of the commandment to love God, the growth of charity and the conjoined gifts of the Holy Ghost, the differences between the various states of life, such as the state of perfection, the religious life and the apostolate, and the nature and value of each, all these and other articles of ascetical and mystical theology, he must have recourse in

---

[25] Pius XI, *Studiorum Ducem*, 12-13.

the first place to the Angelic Doctor.[26]

In the work of St Thomas, we constantly discover new hidden treasures and see that "doctrinal mysticism is nothing else but the full flowering of speculative theology, just as experimental mysticism is the normal and full development of the grace of the virtues and of the gifts in a truly faithful, interior soul."[27] There are many more testimonies from popes over the centuries, from St Thomas' death up to the present. St John Paul II, in his encyclical *Fides et Ratio*, emphasises that "the Church has been justified in consistently proposing Saint Thomas as a master of thought and a model of the right way to do theology."[28] And concerning the *Summa Theologiae*, St John Paul II says:

> From the first pages of his *Summa Theologiae*, Aquinas was keen to show the primacy of the wisdom which is the gift of the Holy Spirit and which opens the way to a knowledge of divine realities. His theology allows us to understand what is distinctive of wisdom in its close link with faith and knowledge of the divine. This wisdom comes to know by way of connaturality; it presupposes faith and eventually formulates its right judgement on the basis of the truth of faith itself.[29]

---

[26] Pius XI, *Studiorum Ducem*, 21.
[27] Reginald Garrigou-Lagrange, OP, *The Love of God and the Cross of Jesus*, vol. I, translated by Sister Jeanne Marie (St. Louis, MO: B. Herder Book Co., 1948), 25.
[28] St John Paul II, *Fides et Ratio*, 43.
[29] St John Paul II, *Fides et Ratio*, 44.

Benedict XVI reiterates the sentiments of his predecessor concerning the theology of St Thomas:

> ..."the Church has been justified in consistently proposing St. Thomas as a master of thought and a model of the right way to do theology." It is not surprising that, after St. Augustine, among the ecclesiastical writers mentioned in the *Catechism of the Catholic Church* St. Thomas is cited more than any other, at least 61 times! He was also called the *Doctor Angelicus* ... because of his virtues and, in particular, the sublimity of his thought and the purity of his life.[30]

Finally, Pope Francis encourages us to have recourse to the teaching of St Thomas Aquinas: "I earnestly ask that we always recall a teaching of Saint Thomas Aquinas and learn to incorporate it in our pastoral discernment."[31]

The successors of St Peter have also had much to say about the thirty-third Doctor of the Church, St Thérèse of Lisieux. Before recounting their praise of this great Saint, it is important to acknowledge that a superficial glance at St Thérèse may seem to indicate that she has nothing in common with the Angelic Doctor. And one may even think that another Saint – more similar to St Thomas – may have been a better choice for the present work. In other words, one may think that another Saint (more prolific in his or her writing) could provide a clearer manifestation of the working

---

[30] Benedict XVI, "St Thomas Aquinas," General Audience, 2 June 2010.
[31] Pope Francis, *Amoris Lætitia*, 304.

of the gift of wisdom. In response, it should be stated that the writings of St Thérèse of Lisieux are indeed very simple; yet they are packed with wisdom and knowledge. Everyone who desires to grow in his or her relationship with God can follow St Thérèse's *Little Way*. By showing how the gift of wisdom was operating in her life, both the relevance of St Thomas' teaching and the greatness of God's little Saint will be made evident. The lives of St Thomas and of St Thérèse seem very different; yet they are also similar – similar by the fact that God's gift of grace was poured out upon their lives and they both received a high degree of the gifts of the Holy Spirit, including the gift of wisdom. St Thérèse did not have advanced theological training; however, there is no doubt that God was teaching her in the depths of her soul – the gift of wisdom was operating throughout her short life. André Combes in his book *The Spirituality of St Thérèse (An Introduction)* remarks that he believes the genius of St Thérèse concerning things spiritual is no less complete and fundamental than the genius of St Thomas in his teaching "concerning the work of divine grace, which consists, not in destroying or supplanting nature, but in restoring and perfecting it."[32]

These two Doctors of the Church are indeed different in regard to their written works. St Thomas, over a period of nearly twenty-two years, wrote more

---

[32] André Combes, *The Spirituality of St. Thérèse (An Introduction)*, translated by Monsignor Philip E. Hallet (Dublin: M.H. Gill and Son, Ltd., 1950), 160. According to Combes, "The grounds of St. Thérèse's marvellous spiritual peace and balance seem to justify us in comparing her genius in spiritual science with the genius of St. Thomas Aquinas in metaphysics and theology."

than eight million words. In his theology he looked for the "essence of things, searching for their deepest metaphysical foundation. He tried to find within the revealed truth, that which is most central, most essential."[33] The *prooemium* to St Thomas' *Summa Theologiae* tells us that "his work has a maternal function (it is to generate, nourish, defend and strengthen faith)."[34] As has been stated above, even though St Thérèse had no formal theological training, God was teaching her in the very depth of her soul.[35] Her works are few; but they still contain "over 1,000 biblical quotations: more than 400 from the Old Testament and over 600 from the New."[36] As Bl. Marie-Eugène of the Child Jesus says, "There is no doubt that Thérèse is a great spiritual theologian."[37] Her writings include her autobiography, letters, poetry, prayers, and some short plays for the recreation of the sisters of her convent.

St Thérèse had wisdom beyond her age precisely

---

[33] Giertych, "Why are there so few Thomist Saints?" 988-989.

[34] Giertych, "Why are there so few Thomist Saints?" 989.

[35] Bl. Marie-Eugène of the Child Jesus says: "If we can define spiritual theology as that science which orders all things in the light of God and his Christ and directs man's steps wisely to his last end, then there is no doubt that Thérèse is a great spiritual theologian. Her gaze penetrated God to such depths, and she saw with such pure clarity the path leading to Him, that she was able to express her discoveries in the simple language of a child. She possessed the science of salvation to a high degree and was able to impart it with rare perfection." Bl. Marie-Eugène of the Child Jesus, *Under the Torrent of His Love: Thérèse of Lisieux a Spiritual Genius*, translated by Sister Mary Thomas Noble, OP (New York: Alba House, 1994), 99.

[36] St John Paul II, *Divini Amoris Scientia*, 9.

[37] Bl. Marie-Eugène, *Under the Torrent of His Love*, 99.

because God was teaching her through the gift of wisdom; this is evident from a very early age. St Thérèse shows us a simple road, which can lead to the heights of sanctity. Pius XI points out that in the life of St Thérèse "the gift of wisdom appears in a lofty degree for the direction of souls thirsting for the truth and wishing, above all human conceptions, to live by the Word of God."[38] St John Paul II in his apostolic letter *Divini Amoris Scientia* says:

> [St Thérèse's] teaching not only conforms to Scripture and the Catholic faith, but excels ("eminent") for the depth and wise synthesis it achieved. Her doctrine is at once a confession of the Church's faith, an experience of the Christian mystery and a way to holiness. Thérèse offers a mature synthesis of Christian spirituality: she combines theology and the spiritual life; she expresses herself with strength and authority, with a great ability to persuade and communicate, as is shown by the reception and dissemination of her message among the People of God ...we can rightly recognize in the Saint of Lisieux the charism of a Doctor of the Church, because of the gift of the Holy Spirit she received for living and expressing her experience of faith, and because of her particular understanding of the mystery of Christ. In her are found the gifts of the new law, that is, the grace of the Holy Spirit, who manifests himself in living faith working through charity.[39]

St John Paul II provides an informative list of popes

---

[38] Reginald Garrigou-Lagrange, OP, *The Three Ages of the Interior Life*, vol. II (Rockford, IL: Tan Books and Publishers, Inc., 1989), 439.
[39] St John Paul II, *Divini Amoris Scientia*, 7.

who have noted the greatness of St Thérèse. In a homily given on 19 October 1997, he recalled those popes and said that the Magisterium, in addition to recognising the holiness of St Thérèse, has also highlighted "the wisdom of her doctrine." St Pius X received the first Italian edition of the *Story of a Soul* – he extolled the many fruits that were a result of her spirituality and said that St Thérèse was "the greatest saint of modern times." When Benedict XV declared Thérèse a Servant of God he "praised the knowledge of divine realities which God granted to Thérèse in order to teach others the ways of salvation."[40]

When St Thérèse was beatified and then canonized by Pius XI, he recommended the spirituality of Thérèse and made special reference to the "divine enlightenment" that she had received. In 1954, consecrating the Basilica in Lisieux, Ven. Pius XII, proclaimed that the message of Thérèse "penetrated to the heart of the Gospel." St John XXIII had made several visits to Lisieux before he was elected pope; he then continued to show devotion to St Thérèse during his pontificate. During the time of the Second Vatican Council, the witness and doctrine of St Thérèse were often recalled by the Council Fathers. St Paul VI, in a letter to the Bishop of Bayeux and Lisieux, extolled the message and example of St Thérèse. He offered St Thérèse as an example and encouraged teachers, pastors, educators and theologians to study her doctrine. St John Paul II described a visit that he made to Lisieux in June 1980 as "unforgettable" – he said:

---

[40] St John Paul II, *Divini Amoris Scientia*, 10.

One can say with conviction about Thérèse of Lisieux that the Spirit of God allowed her heart to reveal directly to the people of our time the fundamental mystery, the reality of the Gospel ... Her "little way" is the way of "holy childhood." There is something unique in this way, the genius of St. Thérèse of Lisieux. At the same time there is the confirmation and renewal of the most basic and most universal truth. What truth of the Gospel message is really more basic and more universal than this: God is our Father and we are his children?[41]

Most importantly, St John Paul says that St Thérèse of Lisieux is ultimately a Doctor of the Church "precisely because she is an expert in the *scientia amoris*."[42] And Benedict XVI re-echoes the words of St John Paul II, encouraging all the faithful to take advantage of the treasure of St Thérèse's doctrine:

> My beloved predecessor described her as an "expert in the *scientia amoris*" ...Thérèse expresses this science, in which she saw the whole truth of the faith shine out in love, mainly in the *story of her life*, published a year after her death with the title *The Story of a Soul* ... I would like to invite you to rediscover this small-great treasure, this luminous comment on the Gospel lived to the full! *The Story of a Soul*, in fact, is a marvellous *story of Love*, told with such authenticity, simplicity and freshness, that the reader cannot but be fascinated by it![43]

---

[41] St John Paul II, *Divini Amoris Scientia*, 10.
[42] St John Paul II, *Novo Millennio Ineunte*, 42.
[43] Benedict XVI, "St. Thérèse of Lisieux," General Audience, St Peter's Square, 6 April 2011.

Finally, Pope Francis highlights the example of St Thérèse who was "humble, small, confident in God, and meek... a child who is guided by the love and tenderness of the Father" and who, "so humble and so trusting in God, has been named Patroness of the missions, because her example makes people say: we want to come with you."[44]

---

[44] Pope Francis, *L'Osservatore Romano*, Weekly ed. in English, n. 41, 9 October 2013.

1

THE GIFTS OF THE HOLY SPIRIT AND THE SUPERNATURAL ORGANISM

Before examining St Thomas Aquinas' doctrine concerning the gift of wisdom, and then applying it to the life of St Thérèse, it is important to look briefly at how the gifts of the Holy Spirit (including the gift of wisdom) fit into the whole supernatural organism. This will include an explanation of how the virtues and the gifts differ, how grace is working in connection with the gifts of the Holy Spirit, and how the gifts play a major role in our growth in holiness. Understanding the action of the gifts together with the virtues will provide a foundation from which to understand the gift of wisdom and how it operates, as well as how it facilitates one's growth in the spiritual life.

The Gifts of the Holy Spirit

The Divine revelation on the seven gifts of the Holy Spirit is found in Isaiah 11:2:

> And the spirit of the Lord shall rest upon Him: the spirit of wisdom, and of understanding, the spirit of counsel, and fortitude, the spirit of knowledge, and of godliness, and He shall be filled with the spirit of the fear of the Lord.[1]

This text, given its Christian interpretation, is referring to Jesus the Messiah; however, its meaning has been extended by the Church to all the faithful because of the "universal principle of the economy of grace"[2] which St Paul teaches: "For those whom he foreknew he also predestined to be conformed to the image of his Son, in order that he might be the firstborn among many brethren," (Rom 8:29). In other words, if there is something in Christ that is communicable, then it is also found in the members of Christ. The seven gifts of the Holy Spirit are "communicable perfections"[3] and they are necessary for salvation.[4] Therefore, members of Christ participate in the sevenfold gift of the Holy Spirit, the fullness of which Christ possesses as Head of the Church. Through these gifts, we are transformed into the

---

[1] Is. 11:2-3 (Douay Rheims). Note the words of this translation signifying the gifts of the Holy Spirit most closely resemble the words used in *CCC* 1831. Reginald Garrigou-Lagrange explains that the "Hebrew text does not mention the gift of piety, but the Septuagint and the Vulgate do. Since the third century, tradition affirms this sevenfold number. Moreover, in the Hebrew text of Isaias, fear is named a second time in verse 3, and in the Old Testament the terms 'fear of God' and 'piety' have almost the same meaning" Reginald Garrigou-Lagrange, OP, *Three Ages of the Interior Life*, vol. I (Rockford, IL: Tan Books and Publishers, Inc., 1989) 66, footnote #1.
[2] Royo & Aumann, *Theology of Christian Perfection*, 75.
[3] Royo & Aumann, *Theology of Christian Perfection*, 75.
[4] *ST* I-II, q. 68, a. 2.

image and likeness of Christ. In so far as we live according to Christ and do not offer any resistance to the working of grace, we grow more and more into Christ's image. We become a witness and living impression of Him Who is Head and "archetype, to whom we ought to be configured."[5]

It can be known with certainty from Divine revelation found in Scripture and Tradition that all souls who are in a state of grace have the seven gifts. Over the centuries the theology of the seven gifts of the Holy Spirit has gone through a rather slow development. The existence of the gifts has been admitted universally, apart from the rare exception; today all theologians accept the existence of the seven gifts of the Holy Spirit, but there is still discussion regarding their exact nature and function.[6] The Council of

---

[5] Ven. Juan Arintero, OP, *The Mystical Evolution in the Development and Vitality of the Church*, vol. I, translated by Jordan Aumann, OP (St Louis, MO: B. Herder Book Co., 1949), 229. St Thomas says that Christ has these gifts according to their most excellent use, as they will be used in heaven (*Super Is.*, cap. 11, Cf. Benedict Ashley, *Thomas Aquinas: The Gifts of the Spirit*, 90).

[6] Royo & Aumann, *Theology of Christian Perfection*, 77. Royo and Aumann remark, "On the question of the existence of the gifts of the Holy Ghost, the teaching of theologians interests us only as a witness to the tradition of the Church, since they could not create a doctrine which treats of supernatural realities ... there are some theologians of great authority who maintain that the existence of the gifts of the Holy Ghost is an article of faith. Although the Church has not expressly defined this point, if we consider the constant teaching of the Fathers of the Church through the centuries, the mind of the Church in her liturgy and in the administration of the sacraments, the unanimous consent of theologians, and the sense of all the faithful through the world, it would seem that one has sufficient basis for saying that this is a

the Roman Synod held under St Damasus in 382 speaks of the seven gifts of the Holy Spirit affirming that indeed Christ had the seven gifts.[7] St Augustine in his *Commentary on the Sermon on the Mount* also speaks of the seven gifts of the Holy Spirit, showing how they correspond with the beatitudes. The Fathers of the Church and the scholastic theologians, including St Thomas, insist upon the seven-fold gift of the Holy Spirit.[8] Torrell points out that the "gifts of the Holy Spirit occupy a high place in Thomas's teaching and it is important to see their role in the spiritual life of the Christian."[9] St Thomas continually returns to the study of the seven gifts in order to obtain an even deeper grasp of their metaphysical reality. There is an evident development in his thought from the *Sentences* to the *Prima Secundae of the Summa Theologiae* to the *Secunda Secundae*.[10]

---

truth of faith proposed by the ordinary magisterium of the Church. Those who would not dare to say this much will at least affirm that it is a theological conclusion that is most certain and *proxima fidei*" (*Theology of Christian Perfection*, 77-78).

[7] Royo & Aumann, *Theology of Christian Perfection*, 76.

[8] Royo & Aumann, *Theology of Christian Perfection*, 78.

[9] Jean-Pierre Torrell, OP, *Saint Thomas Aquinas*, vol. 2, *Spiritual Master*, translated by Robert Royal (Washington, D.C.: The Catholic University of America Press, 2003), 207.

[10] Torrell, *Saint Thomas Aquinas*, vol. 2, *Spiritual Master*, 212. Edward D. O'Connor gives one possible interpretation of the development of St Thomas's thought on the seven gifts of the Holy Spirit: "St Thomas's theory developed in three phases. In the first (that of the commentary of the *Sentences*), the Gifts are represented as a superhuman mode of action in human life, proportionate to man's supernatural destiny. No one before Thomas had ever characterized the Gifts in this way, and Thomas was never to abandon it. However, the way he explained this superhuman mode, by reference to the divine standard or measure of the

operation of the Gifts, was soon to be replaced. The second phase (that of the 1a 2ae) is characterized by a new way of explaining the superhuman mode of the Gifts, namely, by the prompting of the Holy Spirit. Although the notion of inspiration of the Holy Spirit was familiar in Christian thought, no one had ever used it as distinctive of the Gifts. Here is Thomas's most original and influential contribution to this theology. It began to win adherers from the moment of its publication, and has become by far the most common teaching today. The third phase (2a 2ae) freed the interpretation of various particular Gifts (especially Knowledge, Wisdom and Understanding) from the uncongenial biases that had been imposed on them by the pressures of Augustinian rhetoric and scholastic systematization. The assumption that the *Sacrum Septenarium* constitutes a complete, coherent system, in which each Gift corresponds to a particular sector of the moral life, is abandoned. What remains is the notion of qualities by which the moral life of man is divinized in its mode through the variegated operation of the Holy Spirit." Edward D. O'Connor, CSC., "The Gifts of the Holy Spirit," appendix 4 to *Summa Theologiae*, vol. 24 (London: Blackfriars, 1974), 130. In the *Sentences,* the "exposition of the Gifts was governed by the principle that they make man act in a superhuman mode," (appendix 4, 118). In the *Summa* there is the "notion of movement *(motio)* or prompting *(instinctus)* by the Holy Spirit . . . the two expositions are fundamentally compatible. The commentary contrasts the human *mode of action* with one that is superhuman and in fact divine; the *Summa* contrasts a human *principle of movement* with one that is divine. The latter gives the ultimate grounds for the former. The earlier approach was that of a moralist and psychologist, observing the contrast between two ways of acting; the latter is that of a theologian and metaphysician, designating the ultimate source of these two ways," (appendix 4, 118-119). He says however, that it is "not enough ... to explain the difference between the commentary on the *Sentences* and the *Summa* by saying that they teach the same doctrine from different points of view. They are, indeed, compatible; but the *Summa* represents a great refinement of and advance upon the commentary. This advance consists precisely in the generalized doctrine of the prompting of the Spirit, which gives a better

Following St Thomas, the Dominican tradition has always been interested in the study of the Spirit's seven-fold gift.[11]

Concerning the gifts of the Holy Spirit, the *Catechism of the Council of Trent* explains, "These gifts of the Holy Ghost are for us, as it were, a divine source whence we draw the living knowledge of the precepts of Christian life."[12] Leo XIII in his encyclical *Divinum Illud Munus* says of the gifts of the Holy Spirit:

> By means of them the soul is furnished and strengthened so as to obey more easily and promptly His voice and impulse. Wherefore these gifts are of such efficacy that they lead the just man to the highest degree of sanctity; and of such excellence that they continue to exist even in heaven, though in a more perfect way.[13]

St John Paul II in his encyclical *Dominum et Vivificantem* says:

> By becoming "the light of hearts," that is to say the light of consciences, the Holy Spirit "convinces concerning sin," which is to say, he makes man realize his own evil and at the same time directs him toward what is good. Thanks to the multiplicity of the Spirit's gifts, by reason of which he is invoked as the "sevenfold one," every kind of human sin can be reached by God's saving power.

---

explanation than one can find in the commentary for the superhuman mode of the Gifts" (appendix 4, 123).

[11] Benedict Ashley, *The Gifts of the Spirit*, 85.

[12] *Catechism of the Council of Trent*, Part I, chap. 9, § 3: "I believe in the Holy Ghost," as quoted in Garrigou-Lagrange, *Three Ages of the Interior Life*, vol. I, 67-68.

[13] Leo XIII, *Divinum Illud Munus*, 9.

> In reality – as Saint Bonaventure says – by virtue of the seven gifts of the Holy Spirit all evils are destroyed and all good things are produced.[14]

Finally, the present *Catechism of the Catholic Church* says that the seven gifts "complete and perfect the virtues of those who receive them,"[15] and that the "moral life of Christians is sustained by the gifts of the Holy Spirit. These [gifts] are permanent dispositions which make man docile in following the promptings of the Holy Spirit."[16]

The Supernatural Organism

St Thomas teaches:

> Since the last end of rational creatures exceeds the capacity of their nature and since whatever conduces to the end must be proportionate to the end according to the right order of providence, rational creatures are given divine aids that are not merely proportionate to nature but that transcend the capacity of nature.[17]

In order for us to be able to reach God, and ultimately the beatific vision, the natural capacity of our soul (the natural organism) is not sufficient; we also need the whole supernatural organism. Eternal beatitude is not something that can be reached with-

---

[14] St John Paul II, *Dominum et Vivificantem*, 42.
[15] CCC 1831.
[16] CCC 1830.
[17] St Thomas Aquinas, *Comp. Theol.*, ch. 143.

out God's assistance. Such happiness is beyond the capacity of human nature.[18] Therefore, in order for us to reach beatitude, Divine assistance is required. Because perfect happiness is beyond the natural capacity of all human beings, God gives us something by which we can one day reach final beatitude. In other words, it is necessary that we receive from God something which raises us beyond the capacity of our natural principles, so that we can act for this supernatural end; human nature must be, in some way, raised to a supernatural level.[19] The gift of sanctifying grace raises the soul to a supernatural level; grace surpasses everything that can be achieved by way of human nature. When we have sanctifying grace within our soul we are "partaking of the Divine Nature,

---

[18] Garrigou-Lagrange, *Three Ages of the Interior Life*, vol. I, 51. St Thomas says "Now man's happiness is twofold ...One is proportionate to human nature, a happiness, to wit, which man can obtain by means of his natural principles. The other is a happiness surpassing man's nature, and which man can obtain by the power of God alone, by a kind of participation of the Godhead, about which it is written (2 Peter 1:4) that by Christ we are made 'partakers of the Divine nature.' And because such happiness surpasses the capacity of human nature, man's natural principles which enable him to act well according to his capacity, do not suffice to direct man to this same happiness. Hence it is necessary for man to receive from God some additional principles, whereby he may be directed to supernatural happiness, even as he is directed to his connatural end, by means of his natural principles, albeit not without Divine assistance" (*ST* I-II, q. 62, a. 1).

[19] Torrell, *Saint Thomas Aquinas*, vol. 2, *Spiritual Master*, 180. St Thomas writes, "Nothing can act beyond its species, since the cause must always be more powerful than its effect. Now the gift of grace surpasses every capability of created nature, since it is nothing short of a partaking of the Divine Nature, which exceeds every other nature" (*ST* I-II, q. 112, a. 1).

which exceeds every other nature."[20] This gift of grace "is the effect of God in His creature which surpasses all other effects."[21] Through this gift of grace, we enter into the Trinitarian life of God, not as strangers but as sons and daughters of God.[22] Grace is a pure gift from God which is given out of His intense love for us; it is an utterly gratuitous gift bestowed on us because of the merits of Christ's death on the Cross.[23]

To grow in the perfection of the Christian life one must have sanctifying grace within one's soul; sanctifying grace is the very principle that elevates the soul to the order of the supernatural. Grace respects

---

[20] *ST* I-II, q. 112, a. 1. The Latin name for sanctifying grace is *gratia gratum faciens*; it is "the grace of adoption." See St Thomas Aquinas, *Super Ep. ad Rom.*, cap. 1, lec. 3, n. 46: "gratiam gratum facientem, quae est gratia adoptionis" and *ST* I-II, q. 111, a. 1.

[21] Marie-Michel Labourdette, OP, *Cours de Théologie morale, de la grâce*, vol. VI, I-II, q. 109-114 (Toulouse : Studium Saint Thomas d'Aquin, 1958-1962), 99. "Ainsi la grâce est un don qui dépasse tout don naturel; c'est un effet de Die en sa créature; qui dépasse tous ses autres effets." St Thomas says that when a person is in a state of grace, God is present in a special way, "wherein God is said to be present as the object known is in the knower, and the beloved in the lover" (*ST* I, q. 43, a. 3).

[22] Labourdette, *Cours de Théologie morale, de la grâce*, 99: "Pour le juste, l'intériorité de Dieu s'est ouverte, il est introduit au plan de la vie intime de Dieu, de sa vie trinitaire, il entre, si on peut dire, dans la famille des Personnes divines, non comme un étranger, mais comme un fils de la Maison."

[23] Benedict XVI, *Spe Salvi*, 35. St Thomas explains, "God's love is the cause of goodness in things and is not called forth by any preexisting goodness, as our love is" (*Comp. Theol.*, ch. 143). Garrigou-Lagrange points out that no one has more clearly affirmed the "absolute gratuity of the life of grace" than St Thomas Aquinas (*Christian Perfection and Contemplation*, 58).

human nature, perfects it, and at the same time, works through it.[24] In order for an act to be truly supernatural and meritorious so as to contribute to growth in the spiritual life, that act must be one that springs from an "inner principle, which is the life of grace."[25] Grace is the principle of supernatural and meritorious actions.[26] It is a supernatural habit which God infuses into the very essence of the soul, and together with it He infuses the supernatural virtues and the seven gifts of the Holy Spirit into the faculties of the soul, thus making it possible for us to perform supernatural acts. St Thomas says:

> God infuses into man, over and above the natural faculty of reason, the light of grace whereby he is internally perfected for the exercise of virtue, both as regards knowledge, inasmuch as man's mind is elevated by this light to the knowledge of truths surpassing reason, and as regards action and affection, inasmuch as man's affective power is raised by this light above all created things to the

---

[24] Jordan Aumann, OP, *Christian Spirituality in the Catholic Tradition* (London: Sheed and Ward, Ltd., 1985), 132.

[25] Ven. Arintero, *Mystical Evolution in the Development and Vitality of the Church*, vol. I, 198. St Thomas says that "our works are meritorious ... according as they proceed from free-will in so far as we do them willingly" (*ST* I-II, q. 114, a. 6).

[26] Cf. *ST* I-II, q. 109, a. 6. St Teresa of Avila says, "just as all the streams that flow from a crystal-clear fount are also clear, the works of a soul in grace, because they proceed from this fount of life, in which the soul is planted like a tree, are most pleasing in the eyes of both God and man." St Teresa of Avila, *Interior Castle, The Collected Works of St Teresa of Avila*, translated by Kieran Kavanaugh, and Otilio Rodriguez, (Washington, D.C.: ICS Publications, 1980), I Mansions, ch. 2, 2, 288-289.

love of God, to hope in Him, and to the performance of acts that such love imposes.[27]

God gives us "certain forms and supernatural qualities, whereby we may be moved by Him sweetly and promptly to acquire eternal good;"[28] at baptism we not only receive the gift of sanctifying grace, we also receive the infused virtues and the seven gifts of the Holy Spirit. Grace is infused into the very essence of our soul and the virtues and gifts are infused into the faculties of our soul. As St Thomas says, sanctifying grace "perfects the essence of the soul,"[29] and the infused virtues and gifts perfect the powers of the soul "in reference to their actions."[30] The faculties of our soul, which are the principle of human actions, are also the subjects of the gifts and the virtues.[31]

There is an analogy between the natural organism and the supernatural organism. The essence of the soul is not something which is "immediately operative;" in other words, it needs faculties through which to operate, namely, the intellect and the will.[32] Likewise, at the supernatural level, grace perfects the essence of the soul, but we also need operative habits in order to act at a supernatural level. Hence, along with sanctifying grace, we receive the operative habits of the infused virtues and the seven gifts of the Holy

---

[27] St Thomas Aquinas, *Comp. Theol.*, ch. 143. St Thomas says, "Knowledge of the supernatural end is in us only from the Holy Spirit" (*Super Ep. ad Gal.*, cap. 5, lec. 4, 308).
[28] *ST* I-II, q. 110, a. 2.
[29] *ST* III, q. 62, a. 2.
[30] *ST* III, q. 62, a. 2.
[31] Cf. *ST* I-II, q. 68, a. 4.
[32] Royo & Aumann, *Theology of Christian Perfection*, 54.

Spirit.[33] In order for our faculties and powers to operate in a way that will lead us to our ultimate end, which is happiness with God, our faculties and powers also need to possess something which exceeds the "proportion of human nature."[34] The seven gifts of the Holy Spirit and the infused virtues confer a "certain special perfection ordained to the powers' proper actions."[35]

With sanctifying grace as the principle, God infuses into the soul the virtues and gifts.[36] These divine aids are "infused at the root of our being;"[37] this means that the activity of God in the life of a soul is not just some kind of external intervention that helps with daily pursuits. Rather it is a "creative presence introduced at the root of existence."[38] God's grace works within the very substance of one's being, and "acts even at the level of our natural inclinations."[39] This supernatural life, which permeates one's whole being, makes it possible for all activities to become

---

[33] Garrigou-Lagrange, *Three Ages of the Interior Life*, vol. I, 51.

[34] *ST* I-II, q. 51, a. 4.

[35] *ST* III, q. 62, a. 2.

[36] Garrigou-Lagrange, *Three Ages of the Interior Life*, vol. I, 51.

[37] Marie-Dominique Chenu, OP, *Aquinas and His Role in Theology*, translated by Paul Philibert (Collegeville, MN: The Liturgical Press, 2002), 47: "Divine life is built up in us according to the framework of our nature, even as it surpasses our nature ontologically. We can say that grace is within us after the fashion of a (*super*) nature; that is to say, after the fashion of a principle most interior to ourselves, most our own, at the same time that it is divine. It is the dynamic force of grace that makes us capable of living communion with God."

[38] Chenu, *Aquinas and His Role in Theology*, 50.

[39] Servais Pinckaers, OP, *Sources of Christian Ethics*, translated from the third edition by Sr Mary Thomas Noble (Edinburgh: T&T Clark, 1995), 453.

supernaturalized.[40]

God could have ordained that our natural faculties be elevated to the supernatural order by constantly giving us actual graces; however, this would be difficult for our "psychological structure" because there would be a huge disproportion between our natural faculties and the supernatural act that would take place. Therefore, God gives us these infused operative habits so that we can advance towards our supernatural goal in a way that we will not experience as a violent motion, but in a way that is connatural.[41] St Thomas explains:

> It is not fitting that God should provide less for those He loves, that they may acquire supernatural good, than for creatures whom He loves that they may acquire natural good. Now He so provides for natural creatures that not merely does He move them to their natural acts but He bestows on them certain forms and powers which are the principles of acts, in order that they may of themselves be inclined to these movements, and thus the movements whereby they are moved by God become natural and easy to creatures … Much more, therefore does He infuse into those He moves towards the acquisition of supernatural good certain forms or supernatural qualities whereby they may be moved by Him sweetly and promptly to acquire eternal good.[42]

---

[40] Gabriel of St Mary Magdalen, OCD, *Divine Intimacy*, translated from the 7th Italian Edition by the Discalced Carmelite Nuns of Boston (Boston: published by Msgr. William. J. Doheny, 1981), 9.
[41] Royo & Aumann, *Theology of Christian Perfection*, 55.
[42] *ST* I-II, q. 110, a. 2.

For this reason, God gives us the habits of the virtues and the gifts. If God did not infuse the virtues and gifts into the soul at baptism, then we would have to receive transient graces in order to perform various acts. We would not be able to perform acts with any kind of ease, or in a way that is connatural, as is the case when an act is performed by way of the virtues and gifts.[43]

Of all the supernatural treasures which are infused into the soul at baptism along with sanctifying grace, the greatest of these is the theological virtue of charity. By way of charity, we also enter into a relationship with God, which St Thomas describes as friendship. Jesus says to his disciples: No longer do I call you servants, for the servant does not know what his master is doing; but I have called you friends, (Jn,

---

[43] John of St Thomas, *The Gifts of the Holy Ghost*, translated from the Latin by Dominic Hughes, OP. (New York: Sheed and Ward, 1951), 45-46. O'Connor writes, "To call the Gifts *habitus* is only to declare in precise Aristotelian terms a point that was implicitly acknowledged by more or less all who had written on the subject ... But Thomas's use of the term was more than a mere explicit declaration of what others had assumed. Since he denied that the Gifts were virtues, there was a certain need for him to maintain that they were at any rate *habitus*. Much more important, however, is the fact that he had defined the Gifts by the prompting of the Holy Spirit. This immediately poses the question, whether the Gifts are abiding endowments, or reduced entirely to the transitory, intermittent, impulses coming from the Spirit. In affirming that the Gifts are abiding dispositions, Thomas is keeping his theory in accord with the traditional understanding of the Gifts. He is also adhering to an important principle of his theology of grace, that God equips the soul to respond connaturally to his action, even when the action is supernatural" ("The Gifts of the Holy Spirit," appendix 4 to *Summa Theologiae*, 124).

15:15). St Thomas explains that "this was said to them by reason of nothing else but charity. Therefore friendship is charity."[44] On the natural level, we do not have the capacity to enter into this kind of friendship with God; His invitation and His grace are needed. To deny this would be to say the soul has no need of God's grace.[45]

The Difference Between the Gifts and the Virtues

St Thomas explains that both the infused virtues and the seven gifts of the Holy Spirit are habits. He takes Sacred Scripture as his guiding principle when he considers the gifts of the Holy Spirit as *habitus*; he quotes John 14:17 which states, "He shall abide with you, and shall be in you." St Thomas explains, "Now the Holy Ghost is not in a man without His gifts. Therefore His gifts abide in man ... they are not merely acts or passions but abiding habits ... the gifts of the Holy Ghost are habits whereby man is perfected to obey readily the Holy Ghost."[46] Moreover, in Isaiah,

---

[44] *ST* II-II, q. 23, a. 1.
[45] Fabio Giardini, "The Growth Process of Christian Prayer Life," *Angelicum* 69 (1992): 399.
[46] *ST* I-II, q. 68, a. 3. According to papal theologian Wojciech Giertych, "That all the gifts are permanent habits rooted in both the intellectual and appetitive powers, making man docile to the promptings of the Spirit, is an original theory of Aquinas which he did not propose from the beginning of his teaching career." Wojciech Giertych, *The New Law as a Rule for Acts*, Dissertatio ad Lauream in Facultate S. Theologiae apud Pontificiam Uni-

it can be seen that the seven gifts of the Holy Spirit are given in a "permanent fashion."[47] For these reasons, St Thomas says that both the virtues and the seven gifts of the Holy Spirit are *habits*.[48] These habits are infused into the soul by God; hence the name "infused habits."[49]

> Both the virtues and the gifts are abiding habits, but they differ considerably in the way they are moved. St Thomas again takes Scripture as his guiding principle: Accordingly, in order to differentiate the gifts from the virtues, we must be guided by the

---

versitatem S. Thomas de Urbe, Romae, 1989, 245.

[47] John of St Thomas, *The Gifts of the Holy Ghost*, 45.

[48] Pinckaers writes: "[A]mong the interior principles are located the *habitus*, which received St Thomas's special attention. These are stable dispositions that develop the power of our faculties and render us capable of performing actions of high quality. They are not to be confused with our ordinary understanding of habits – psychological mechanisms that diminish the moral commitment to an action. The *habitus* as St Thomas intended it is a principle of progress and resourcefulness through full commitment. It is through these *habitus* or stable dispositions that we acquire mastery over our actions and become entirely free" (*Sources of Christian Ethics*, 225). St Thomas clearly states that the gift of wisdom is a habit. He writes, "[I]t is written (Ecclesiasticus 15:5): 'God filled him with the spirit of wisdom and understanding.' Now wisdom and understanding are habits. Therefore some habits are infused into man by God" (*ST* I-II, q. 51, a. 4.) Royo and Aumann remark that "Saint Thomas studies the metaphysical nature of the gifts of the Holy Ghost by asking whether they are habits, in order to determine the proximate genus in the essential definition of the gifts" (*Theology of Christian Perfection*, 79). John of Saint Thomas says, "The gifts are habits or dispositions of the intellect and the will. They dispose these faculties to follow the impulse of the Holy Ghost, who regulates and delimits the objects of the gifts" (*The Gifts of the Holy Ghost*, 63).

[49] *ST* I-II, q. 50, a. 2.

> way in which Scripture expresses itself, for we find there that the term employed is "spirit" rather than "gift." For thus it is written (Isaiah 11:2-3): "The spirit ... of wisdom and of understanding ... shall rest upon him," etc.: from which words we are clearly given to understand that these seven are there set down as being in us by Divine inspiration. Now inspiration denotes motion from without. For it must be noted that in man there is a twofold principle of movement, one within him, viz. the reason; the other extrinsic to him, viz. God.[50]

The infused virtues are directed by and under the control of human reason illumined by faith, and hence they are always under a human mode of operation. In the case of the gifts, it is the Holy Spirit who is the

---

[50] *ST* I-II, q. 68, a. 1: "Now it is evident that whatever is moved must be proportionate to its mover: and the perfection of the mobile as such, consists in a disposition whereby it is disposed to be well moved by its mover. Hence the more exalted the mover, the more perfect must be the disposition whereby the mobile is made proportionate to its mover: thus we see that a disciple needs a more perfect disposition in order to receive a higher teaching from his master. Now it is manifest that human virtues perfect man according as it is natural for him to be moved by his reason in his interior and exterior actions. Consequently man needs yet higher perfections, whereby to be disposed to be moved by God. These perfections are called gifts, not only because they are infused by God, but also because by them man is disposed to become amenable to the Divine inspiration." See O'Connor, for his treatment of the development from the *Sentences* to the *Summa Theologiae* concerning the "concept of a superhuman mode of activity [and] the notion of movement (*motio*) or prompting (*instinctus*) by the Holy Spirit" (appendix 4, to the *Summa Theologiae*, 118).

"unique motor cause."[51] The Holy Spirit is the "primary mover" when the gifts are operating; therefore, the gifts have a Divine mode of operation and not a human mode.[52] St Thomas says, "Now the habit of a virtue qualifies a person to act well. If it enables him to act well in a human mode, it is called a virtue. But if it qualifies one for acting well, above the human mode, it is called a gift."[53] St Thomas insists that "the gifts are habits perfecting man so that he is ready to follow the promptings of the Holy Ghost."[54]

The seven gifts of the Holy Spirit are "perfections of man, whereby he becomes amenable to the promptings of the Holy Ghost."[55] The soul is easily led to

---

[51] Jordan Aumann, *Spiritual Theology* (London: Sheed and Ward, 1980), 92-93.

[52] Jordan Aumann, "Mystical Experience, the Infused Virtues and the Gifts," *Angelicum* 58 (1981): 39.

[53] St Thomas Aquinas, *Super Ep. ad Gal.*, cap. 5, lec. 6 no. 329: "Habitus autem virtutis perficit ad bene agendum. Et si quidem perficit ad bene operandum humano modo, dicitur virtus. Si vero perficiat ad bene operandum supra modum humanum, dictur donum." St Thomas says that the Holy Spirit "moves us to act and work well. For the word 'spirit' indicates a certain impulse" (*Super Ioan.*, cap. 14, lec. 4, n. 1916).

[54] *ST* I-II, q. 68, a. 4. St Thomas uses the word *instinctus* above all to describe the prompting that a person receives from the Holy Spirit when he describes the gifts of the Holy Spirit. It "occurs sixteen times in 1a2ae, 68." Edward D O'Connor, CSC, "The Gifts of the Holy Spirit," appendix 5 to *Summa Theologiae*, vol. 24 (London: Blackfriars, 1974), 140.

[55] *ST* I-II, q. 68, a. 3. The Thomistic Lexicon defines *instinctus, us, m.*, as *instigation* or *impulse*. Roy J. Deferrari, Mary Inviolata Barry, and Ignatius McGuiness, OP, *A Lexicon of St. Thomas Aquinas* (Baltimore: The John D. Lucas Printing Co., 1948), 570. O'Connor points out that "Thomas's preferred term for the action of the Holy Spirit to which the Gift makes men docile is *instinctus*...Thomas chose the term in preference to another which was available to

follow the inspirations of the Holy Spirit because God has placed within the soul these habitual, stable, dispositions.⁵⁶ The difference between the infused virtues and the seven gifts of the Holy Spirit is clearly manifested when the gifts are defined as

---

him, namely *inspiratio,* inspiration. The choice seems to have been quite deliberate for where his master, Albert, spoke of the *inspirationes* of the Holy Spirit in connection with certain Gifts, he, already in the commentary on the *Sentences,* adopted *instinctus.* The choice is all the more striking in that inspiration was a term well established in theological usage, whereas instinctus as a noun had received comparatively little use in any context," (appendix 5, 131). O'Connor bases his study primarily on St Thomas' use of the word *instinctus* in the *Summa Theologiae* and remarks that "After a minute examination of the way Thomas uses these terms, my conclusion is that *instinctus* was chosen in order not to specify in any way whatsoever the nature of the Holy Spirit's action. *Inspiratio,* the term traditionally set for the action of spirits upon man, designated a type of action. In virtue of the same analogy which has led men to speak of immaterial beings as spirits, because they were pictured as something like the wind this term represented the action of such beings as analogous to blowing. *Instinctus,* however, does not designate a type of action at all. It refers to that by which an action is provoked or elicited. In present context, it does not designate the action of the Holy Spirit directly, but only indirectly, as that which somewhat initiated the human act under consideration. Moreover, it is free from all association with which the term *inspiratio* had been coloured by a long theological tradition about divine (and diabolical) inspirations. Hence, when a man is said to act by the *instinctus* of the Holy Spirit, all that this means, so far as the force of the *word* itself is concerned (we are not concerned with *doctrine*), is that the action was brought about by the influence of the Holy Spirit. Nothing whatsoever is specified about the nature of the influence, or the form it has taken, e.g., whether it was an impulse, invitation, illumination, strengthening or the like" (appendix 5, 131-132).
⁵⁶ Antoine Gardeil, OP, *The Gifts of the Holy Ghost in the Dominican Saints* (Milwaukee: The Bruce Publishing Company, 1937), 31.

habits which God gives in order that we can be moved by the inspirations of the Holy Spirit.[57] Human reason commands the virtues to act, whereas in the case of the seven gifts of the Holy Spirit "the position of the human mind is of one moved rather than of a mover."[58] The seven gifts make us conformable to the promptings of the Holy Spirit and ready to be moved by Him at any time.[59]

One would think that because "sanctifying grace and the infused virtues are substantially supernatural … in accordance with the axiom *operatio sequitur esse*, that the operations of the infused virtues would likewise be supernatural."[60] However, this line of thinking does not take into account the fact that the infused virtues operate according to a human mode. "The infused virtues provide the supernatural power, but the acts that proceed from the infused virtues are in the human mode of operation."[61] This is not the case with the seven gifts of the Holy Spirit which have a supernatural mode of operation; for they are not only substantially supernatural. In other words, they are not just supernatural "in their essence" – as are the infused theological and moral virtues – but they are also supernatural in their "mode of action." Hence, we can say that the gifts are "doubly supernatural."[62]

---

[57] *ST* I-II, q. 68, a. 1, ad 3.

[58] *ST* II-II, q. 52, a. 2, ad 1.

[59] Anscar Vonier, OSB, *The Spirit and the Bride* (London: Burns, Oates and Washbourne, Ltd., 1935), 164-165.

[60] Aumann, "Mystical Experience, the Infused Virtues and the Gifts," 49. *Operatio sequitur esse* means *operation follows being*.

[61] Aumann, "Mystical Experience, the Infused Virtues and the Gifts," 49.

[62] Garrigou-Lagrange, *Christian Perfection and Contemplation*, 38.

The seven gifts of the Holy Spirit operate only when God wishes and the soul seconds the Divine impulse by putting no obstacle in the way.[63] It is important to note that when God operates through the gifts, He does not circumvent our free will. Our actions remain conscious and free. Nevertheless, it is always the Holy Spirit who decides to act on the soul whenever and however He wills. In other words, even though it is the Holy Spirit Who has moved us when the gifts are operating, it does not mean that we lose the ability to act freely or to gain merit, because we must also second the motion of the Holy Spirit.[64] In fact, the person who is most open and docile to the action of the Holy Spirit will always be the most free. Everything depends on God's grace; however, God "not only respects, but supports the free character of his movement."[65]

God gives us the seven gifts of the Holy Spirit so that we can reach happiness in this life, and perfect happiness in the next. The seven gifts of the Holy Spirit are given to assist the virtues and "to help the virtues (*in adiutorium virtutum*) to attain their final goal."[66] The gifts of the Holy Spirit, as St Thomas says,

---

[63] Royo & Aumann, *Theology of Christian Perfection*, 87.
[64] Aumann, *Spiritual Theology*, 92-93. Pinckaers says that St Thomas would "use the expression *instinctus Spiritus Sancti* to describe the action of the Holy Spirit through his gifts at the heart of the Christian life, (I-II, q. 68)" (*The Sources of Christian Ethics*, 358).
[65] Torrell, *Saint Thomas Aquinas*, vol. 2, *Spiritual Master*, 215.
[66] Torrell, *Saint Thomas Aquinas*, vol. 2, *Spiritual Master*, 214.

are "necessary for salvation."[67] They lead the soul to eternal life and assist us in overcoming "difficulties which exceed the power of human reason and the virtues."[68] The seven gifts help us with our imperfections and it is the Holy Spirit Who finally lifts our focus away from self and up to God.[69] Even the theological virtues, which surpass human nature[70] and perfect reason, need the help of the gifts. They help to perfect the theological virtues and to safeguard the soul from "all folly, ignorance, dullness of mind and hardness of heart."[71] However, St Thomas explains that just because the gifts help the theological virtues, it does not mean that the seven gifts are higher than the theological virtues. The theological virtues always "remain superior to the gifts since they are their roots."[72] Nevertheless, the gifts do surpass the virtues in regard to their mode of operation because when the gifts operate one has been "moved by a

---

[67] *ST* I-II, q. 68, a. 2. Torrell points out that St Thomas explains how the gifts are necessary for salvation and are not just reserved for a privileged few. He says, "We must emphasize how far this position is from all elitism. Life under the regime of the gifts is not a game preserve restricted to a small number of people. Nothing could be further from Thomas's thinking, since he affirms with the greatest of clarity that the gifts are necessary to salvation" (*Spiritual Master*, vol. 2, 213). Aumann explains that the seven gifts of the Holy Spirit as well as the infused virtues are always given to everyone at Baptism "with sanctifying grace and form part of the supernatural organism." They are habits, which are always present as long as a person remains in the state of grace (*Spiritual Theology*, 93).

[68] John of St Thomas, *The Gifts of the Holy Ghost*, 272.

[69] Vonier, *The Spirit and the Bride*, 165-166.

[70] *ST* I-II, q. 62, a. 1, ad 1.

[71] *ST* I-II, q. 68, a. 2, ad 3.

[72] Torrell, *Saint Thomas Aquinas*, vol. 2, *Spiritual Master*, 214-215.

higher principle."[73] Hence, we draw closer to God and advance in charity "by works of virtue, and above all by the works of the gifts."[74]

The Operation of the Gifts of the Holy Spirit

The seven gifts of the Holy Spirit are of great importance for growth in the spiritual life. We need not only the infused virtues, but also the extra help and assistance of the gifts of the Holy Spirit. The gifts of the Holy Spirit are of the supernatural order and operate according to a supernatural mode. As such, it is impossible that they would be put into operation by a purely natural impulse, because the natural order can never determine the "operations of the supernatural order. Nor is it possible that the supernatural powers actuate themselves, because a habit can be actuated only by the power and action of the agent which caused it."[75] In order for both the infused virtues and gifts to operate there is always the need for an actual grace. To have sanctifying grace and the habits of both the infused virtues and the gifts is not sufficient; an actual grace is always needed in order for us to make acts of virtue and for the gifts to operate.

---

[73] *ST* I-II, q. 68, a. 2, ad 1.
[74] *ST* I-II, q. 69, a. 1.
[75] Royo & Aumann, *Theology of Christian Perfection,* 42.

Operating and Cooperating Grace

In addition to sanctifying grace, in order for the infused virtues and the seven gifts of the Holy Spirit to be able to operate, God also gives us actual graces, which move us "to will and act."[76] Actual graces are needed in order for us to make acts of the infused virtues and for operations of the seven gifts of the Holy Spirit. Actual graces can be divided into *operating* and *cooperating* graces. When we make an act of virtue (infused virtue), the will is moved and also "moves itself."[77] God has first moved the will by giving us an actual grace; we then decide whether we are going to make an act of virtue. If we do, there is an act which is commanded by the will.[78] God then assists us in this act by "strengthening the will interiorly" and by giving us the outward capacity to act. It is in this respect that we can speak of co-operating grace. "He operates that we may will; and when we will, He co-operates that we may perfect."[79] St Paul speaks of co-operating grace in his Epistle to the Philippians when he says: "For it is God who worketh in you, both to will and to accomplish." (Phil 2:13). "For God not only infuses but he also moves

---

[76] *ST* I-II, q. 111, a. 2. St Thomas says that God moves a person to willing the good "as in the case of those whom He moves by grace" (*ST* I-II, q. 9 a. 6. ad 3). He says, "For the Holy Spirit stirs up and turns the affections to right willing" (*Super Ep. ad Gal.*, cap. 5, lec. 4, n. 308).

[77] Reginald Garrigou-Lagrange, OP, *Grace*, translated by the Dominican Nuns, Corpus Christi Monastery, California (St. Louis, MO: B. Herder Book Co., 1952), 172.

[78] *ST* I-II, q. 111, a. 2.

[79] *ST* I-II, q. 111, a. 2. Here St Thomas is quoting St Augustine.

us to use the graces infused well, and this is called cooperating grace."[80] Our acts of virtue remain free and meritorious and help us to grow in the spiritual life and advance towards our final goal, perfect happiness with God in heaven.

The seven gifts of the Holy Spirit are habits which remain in the soul as long as we are in a state of sanctifying grace. The gifts require actual graces to put them in to motion. The difference between the gifts and the infused virtues is that God is the sole mover when there is an operation of the gifts. When the will is moved by God and then also moves, this operation is attributed to both God and man; but when the movement is attributed only to God, this kind of actual grace is referred to as an *operating grace*.[81] When we perform acts with the infused virtues, we deliberate whether we are going to perform a work of virtue, even if this deliberation and decision lasts only a moment. We decide for example, to perform an act of charity. With the operation of the seven gifts there is no deliberation, the movement is attributed to the Holy Spirit alone.

When there is an operation of one of the seven gifts, it is the Holy Spirit Who acts; we are not moving ourselves. However, this does not mean that we are not free; we remain free and merit when the gifts are operating because we second the Divine motion and

---

[80] St Thomas Aquinas, *Super I Ep. ad Cor.*, cap. 15, lec. 1, n. 909: "Deus enim non solum infundit gratiam, qua nostra opera grata fiunt et meritoria, sed etiam movet ad bene utendum gratia infusa, et haec vocatur gratia cooperans."
[81] *ST* I-II, q. 111, a. 2.

do not put any obstacles in the way.[82] Therefore the operations which proceed from the gifts "are vital, free, and meritorious, and yet the will does not, properly speaking, move itself to perform them, as it moves itself by deliberation in a human manner, but is specifically moved by the Holy Ghost."[83]

An analogy which aptly illustrates the distinction between the action of the virtues and the action of the gifts is that of a boat. The gifts are represented by the sail of the boat, and the Holy Spirit is the wind which blows and moves the sail. When the wind blows, we can think of this as an actual operating grace; and we can think of the sail as the habit of the gift which needs to receive an actual grace in order for there to be an operation of the gift. When the wind blows, the boat skims along very rapidly and reaches its destination. On the other hand, without the wind, an oarsman would have to row with difficulty, despite the presence of the sail. This represents what it can be like when we are acting through the virtues; it is difficult, and we need the help of one of the seven gifts. The action of the Holy Spirit through the gifts can be likened to a favourable wind which comes along and catches the sail; and the boat reaches its destination with ease. Hence, there is a vast difference between an act which is performed by means of the infused virtues and one that is performed by means of the seven gifts of the Holy Spirit.[84] When the Holy Spirit

---

[82] Cf. *ST* I-II, q. 68, a. 3, ad 2.
[83] Garrigou-Lagrange, *Grace*, 171-172.
[84] Cf. John of St Thomas, *The Gifts of the Holy Ghost*, 57, and Bl. Marie-Eugène of the Child, OCD, Jesus, *I Want to See God*, vol. I (Notre Dame, IN: Christian Classics, 1953), 339.

"fills the soul interiorly, and measures it by His rule, then without labour and in a new-found freedom of the heart the soul moves rapidly like a sail filled with a breeze."[85]

The gifts of the Holy Spirit are crucial for growth in the spiritual life. With sanctifying grace as the life-giving principle, actual graces (operating and co-operating), and the virtues and the gifts of the Holy Spirit, we will grow in holiness and move closer to our final end, perfect happiness in heaven. Heaven is far beyond and above any person's natural goodness; we need the life of grace which starts here on earth and finds its perfection in heaven.

---

[85] John of St Thomas, *The Gifts of the Holy Ghost*, 57.

2

THE GIFT OF WISDOM

With the supernatural organism including the seven gifts of the Holy Spirit having been explained, the groundwork has been laid for moving onto the focus of this book, which is the gift of wisdom. In this chapter, following the teaching of the Angelic Doctor St Thomas Aquinas, as it is set forth in the *Summa Theologiae* II-II, q. 45, the gift of wisdom and its effects will be examined and explained. When considering any topic that is contained in the *Summa Theologiae*, it is always important to have an understanding of where St Thomas has placed it in the overall structure of his work. His *Summa* is "in many ways comparable to the great architectural structure of his generation."[1] The precision and harmony of the structure all work together, thus making the *Summa Theologiae* a work that can be compared to a great Gothic Cathedral. One cannot fully understand any question or section of the *Summa* without an awareness of where it fits into the overall work.[2]

The *Summa Theologiae* consists of three parts. One way of understanding the order of these parts is to see that in the *prima pars* (first part, I) Aquinas considers God and His creation, in the *secuna pars* (second part, II) he considers the human person's movement back to God, and finally in the *tertia pars* (third part, III), he

---

[1] Pinckaers, *The Sources of Christian Ethics*, 229.
[2] Pinckaers, *The Sources of Christian Ethics*, 220.

contemplates Christ, who leads us to the Father.[3] The *secunda pars* is divided into two parts. In the *prima secundae* (first part of the second part, I-II), St Thomas considers the acts of the human person. He discusses these acts in so far as they are free voluntary acts. He then discusses the passions of the soul, and the habits in general (good and bad), virtues and vices, and finally "he discusses the exterior principles that influence human activity: law and grace."[4] In the *prima secundae*, St Thomas is describing the "general structures of Christian action."[5] The whole moral system of St Thomas focuses on the virtues and the seven gifts of the Holy Spirit as the means by which man can attain ultimate happiness – union with God. St Thomas deals with sin "only as the negation of virtue and [sees] legal precepts and obligations as aids to virtue."[6] It is in this section (I-II) that St Thomas speaks of the gifts of the Holy Spirit in general. In the *secunda secundae* (second part of the second part, II-II), St Thomas examines each of the seven gifts of the Holy Spirit individually and looks at them in more detail, coordinating them with their corresponding virtues and beatitudes.

St Thomas' exposition concerning the gift of wisdom is situated in the *secunda secundae*, adjacent to his discussion on the theological virtue of charity. In Thomistic terms, the gift of wisdom can be defined as

---

[3] Torrell, *Saint Thomas Aquinas*, vol. 1, *The Person and His Works*, 148.
[4] Torrell, *Saint Thomas Aquinas*, vol. 1, *The Person and His Works*, 149.
[5] Yves Congar, OP, *I Believe in the Holy Spirit*, vol. III, translated by David Smith (New York: The Seabury Press, 1983), 123.
[6] Pinckaers, *The Sources of Christian Ethics*, 227.

> a supernatural habit, inseparable from charity, by which we judge rightly concerning God and divine things through their ultimate and highest causes under a special instinct and movement of the Holy Ghost, who makes us taste these things by a certain connaturality and sympathy.[7]

When St Thomas discusses the gift of wisdom, he begins by explaining that wisdom "considers the highest cause [and] by means of that cause we are able to form a most certain judgment about other causes."[8] Through the gift of wisdom a person judges of Divine things, and supernatural knowledge is coordinated and unified.[9]

Wisdom as a Gift and Wisdom as a Virtue

In order to be able to understand something of the supernatural order it is helpful to first look at something which is comparable in the natural order. In the case of the gift of wisdom it is helpful first to look at the intellectual virtue of wisdom which is radically different from the gift of wisdom; nevertheless it has certain things in common and can therefore help one to understand the gift which bares the same name. St Thomas accepts the teaching of Aristotle

---

[7] Royo & Aumann, *Theology of Christian Perfection*, 418.
[8] *ST* II-II, q. 45, a. 1.
[9] Martinez, *Sanctifier*, 185.

that wisdom considers the highest causes and that its main activities are to contemplate that reality, to make judgments as a result of this contemplation, and to put things in order.[10] According to Aquinas, "wisdom is called an intellectual virtue, so far as it proceeds from the judgment of reason: but it is called a gift, according as its work proceeds from the Divine prompting."[11] Both the gift of wisdom and the virtue of wisdom are intellectual habits and they are both "concerned with the attainment of truths through their supreme causes."[12] When things are considered according to their highest causes, then, as St Thomas says, "by means of that cause we are able to form a most certain judgment about other causes"[13] and set all things in order.

Our intellectual knowledge is not isolated; rather there is unity, a coordinated knowledge in that every science "coordinates the knowledge that belongs to it and unifies it in the causes and principles that it studies."[14] If we consider the study of medicine, and a doctor who is said to be wise in his field, he is wise because he considers the "highest cause" in this branch of knowledge and by means of this highest cause he can "judge of all other matters by that cause"[15] and put them in order. Hence, he is said to

---

[10] Thomas R. Heath, OP, "The Gift of Wisdom," appendix 4 to *Summa Theologiae*, vol. 35 (London: Blackfriars, 1972), 200-201.
[11] *ST* I-II, q. 68. a. 1, ad 4.
[12] John of St Thomas, *The Gifts of the Holy Ghost*, 126.
[13] *ST* II-II, q. 45, a. 1.
[14] Luis M. Martinez, *The Sanctifier*, translation by Sister M. Aquinas, OSU (Boston: Pauline Books and Media, 1985), 185.
[15] *ST* II-II, q. 9, a. 2.

be "wise in that genus."[16]

Or we can take the example of the architect, who "plans the form of the house;" he arranges and judges things in light of the form of the house, which is the higher principle. In other words, he plans the form which the house should take and then judges and arranges, for example, how the wood should be trimmed and the size of the stones; he orders things so that they go together to make the form of the house.[17] He designs the entire house, which means the whole structure of the house "depends on him."[18] He is a wise architect, wise in his branch of knowledge. In employing this example, St Thomas is following St Paul, who says, "As a wise architect, I have laid the foundation" (1 Cor 3:10).[19] However, just because a person is wise in a particular genus, it does not mean he or she is wise absolutely speaking; for it is only the person who knows the highest cause of all things who is truly wise.[20] A person is said to be wise absolutely when he or she "knows the cause which is absolutely

---

[16] *ST* II-II, q. 45, a. 1.

[17] *ST* II-II, q. 45, a. 1. See also *ST* I, q. 1, a. 6.

[18] St Thomas Aquinas, *Super Ep. ad Rom.*, cap. 8, lec. 2. n. 621: "...In arte aedificatoria dicitur sapiens, non ille qui scit dolare ligna et lapides, sed ille qui concipit et disponit convenientem formam domus: ex hoc enim totum artificium dependet."

[19] *ST* I, q. 1, a. 6. See also *ST* II-II, q. 45, a. 1.

[20] *ST* II-II, q. 45, a. 1. St Thomas says: if "certitude of the judgment is derived from the highest cause, the knowledge has a special name, which is wisdom: for a wise man in any branch of knowledge is one who knows the highest cause of that kind of knowledge, and is able to judge of all matters by that cause: and a wise man absolutely, is one who knows the cause which is absolutely highest, namely God" (*ST* II-II, q. 9, a. 2).

highest, namely God."[21] And even though the knowledge we can have about God through wisdom is little, "it is preferable to all other knowledge."[22] Hence, it is the truly wise person who considers the cause of all things, "the Supreme Cause, which is God."[23] When one sees God as the first cause, one is said to be wise in the strictest sense.[24]

Wisdom coordinates the knowledge obtained about God through reasoning. This kind of knowledge of God and His existence can be reached by reason alone; for example, Socrates, Plato, and Aristotle were philosophers who came to a knowledge of God through metaphysical discourse.[25] There is however a higher type of wisdom. The person who, guided by faith and through the use of reason, deduces certain conclusions from the revealed truth of Divine revelation is said to possess "theological wisdom."[26] Theology looks at the truths of the faith which have been revealed (and what has been drawn from those principles) in a way that is both speculative and

---

[21] *ST* II-II, q. 9, a. 2.
[22] *ST* I-II, q. 66, a. 5, ad 3. St Thomas says: "There is one absolute Wisdom elevated above all things, that is, the divine Wisdom, by participating in which all wise persons are wise" (*Super Ioan,* cap. 1, lec. 1, n. 33). People become wise "according to divine wisdom, which is the true wisdom" (*Super I Ep. ad Cor.,* cap. 3, lec. 3, n. 178).
[23] *ST* I-II, q. 66, a. 5.
[24] St Thomas Aquinas, *Super Ep. ad Rom.,* cap. 8, lec. 2. n. 621: "Ad cuius intellectum sciendum quod sapiens simpliciter dicitur qui cognoscit causam altissimam ex qua omnia dependent. Causa autem suprema simpliciter omnium Deus est."
[25] Robert Edward Brennan, OP, *The Seven Horns of the Lamb: A Study of the Gifts Based on Saint Thomas Aquinas* (Milwaukee: The Bruce Publishing Company, 1966), 80.
[26] Royo & Aumann, *Theology of Christian Perfection,* 419.

practical.²⁷ It often uses propositions from metaphysics in order to judge and understand the nature of certain truths; it uses "natural propositions," but this is "merely to apprehend and judge the nature of truths."²⁸ Both metaphysics and theological wisdom involve discursive reasoning and a person attains this intellectual wisdom by human effort. But there is a wisdom which is higher than both of these kinds of wisdom – the gift of wisdom – in which judgment is not the result of a discursive process.²⁹ It is this third kind of wisdom, the gift of wisdom, which "pre-eminently deserves the name wisdom."³⁰

When St Thomas discusses the gift of wisdom, he begins by explaining that wisdom considers the highest cause and "by means of that cause we are able to form a most certain judgment about other causes."³¹ So far, this sounds the same as the intellectual virtue of wisdom; however the judgment which happens through the operation of the gift of wisdom happens as a result of connatural knowing. Hence, the way knowledge is received through the

---

[27] *ST* I, q. 1.
[28] John of St Thomas, *The Gifts of the Holy Ghost*, 143.
[29] *ST* I, q. 1, a. 6, ad 3. In the corpus I, q. 1, a. 6, and I, q. 1, a. 6, ad 3. St Thomas speaks of three kinds of wisdom.
[30] Jacques Maritain, *The Range of Reason*, 214. Maritain notes "three wisdoms recognized by Saint Thomas, metaphysical wisdom, theological wisdom and the wisdom of contemplation, this last, which operates in the superhuman way of the Gift of Wisdom and is rooted in the living faith, pre-eminently deserves the name wisdom ... which faith alone however does not suffice to produce, since this experience depends also upon love and the gifts of the Holy Spirit."
[31] *ST* II-II, q. 45, a. 1.

virtue of wisdom and the gift of wisdom differs greatly. St Thomas explains that "rectitude of judgment is twofold: first, on account of perfect use of reason, secondly, on account of a certain connaturality with the matter about which one has to judge."[32] He says:

> It belongs to the wisdom that is an intellectual virtue to pronounce right judgment about Divine things after reason has made its inquiry, but it belongs to wisdom as a gift of the Holy Ghost to judge aright about them on account of connaturality with them.[33]

He gives the example of chastity. If a man has learned moral science (ethics) then he will be able to judge correctly by the power of his reason. However, if he has practised the habit of chastity he is able to judge through a certain connaturality towards it.[34] In comparing the intellectual virtue of wisdom and the gift of wisdom – when they judge of Divine things – the intellectual virtue judges through speculative inquiry and the gift of wisdom judges "on account of a connaturality with them."[35] Both the virtue and the gift involve right judgment; and in both cases, the right judgment is concerning Divine things. The distinguishing factor is the modality of the judgment. In the case of the virtue, the judgment happens "after reason has made inquiry,"[36] which involves study,

---

[32] *ST* II-II, q. 45, a. 2. See also *ST* I, q. 1, a. 6, ad 3.
[33] *ST* II-II, q. 45, a. 2.
[34] John of St Thomas, *The Gifts of the Holy Ghost*, 125.
[35] *ST* II-II, q. 45, a. 2.
[36] *ST* II-II, q. 45, a. 2.

discourse, human effort, and speculation. In the case of the gift, the right judgment does not come as the result of a discursive process; rather, it is accounted for by a certain *connaturality*.[37] Thus, through the operation of the gift of wisdom, a person does not come to know of Divine things through a "metaphysical discourse, but with what is known in affection as knowable and lovable in accord with an interior taste and experience."[38] It is a "knowledge which is in the intellect not by virtue of conceptual connections and by way of demonstration,"[39] but on account of a connaturality with Divine things. Therefore, it is possible for a person who has never studied theology, but who is faithful to God and advanced in the spiritual life, to have a profound understanding of Divine mysteries. Intimate friends often intuitively know the heart and thoughts of one another. In a similar but far superior way, as a result of a person's friendship with God and through the operation of the gift of wisdom, a person can have a deep understanding of the things of God. He or she may not be able to articulate the truths of the faith very well; the things that he or she understands are known by way of the heart, as if they were second nature to that person.[40] This is connatural knowing; in other words, it is received on account of a certain

---

[37] *ST* II-II, q. 45, a. 2.
[38] John of St Thomas, *The Gifts of the Holy Ghost*, 143.
[39] Maritain, *The Range of Reason*, 22.
[40] St Teresa of Avila says that God can make a "little old woman wiser… in this science," even wiser than a person who is very learned (*Life*, ch. 34, 12, 298).

connaturality[41] with God and Divine things. This way of knowing comes "from the very depths of love."[42] Through the gift of wisdom, a person receives a "simple and loving knowledge of God and His works"[43] This happens because of the soul's union with "spiritual truths; the soul is, as it were, made connatural to things divine."[44] Thus even in the study of theology, knowledge acquired discursively through the intellectual virtue of wisdom cannot be compared to the connatural knowledge that is received through the operation of the gift of wisdom and that "flows from a child-like encounter in faith and love with God."[45]

Therefore the gift of wisdom differs from wisdom which is an acquired virtue; for "the latter is attained by human effort, whereas the former is 'descending from above' (James 3:15)."[46] The virtue of wisdom is directed by, and under the control of reason; therefore, it is always under a human mode of operation.[47] On the other hand, as explained above, when the gift of wisdom is operating, judgment does not happen from any knowledge that one derives from studying or discursive reasoning about causes, but rather from a union and connaturality with the supreme cause, namely God.[48] So when speaking of wisdom as a gift

---

[41] *ST* II-II, q. 45, a. 2.

[42] Martinez, *Sanctifier*, 152-53.

[43] Garrigou-Lagrange, *Three Ages of the Interior Life,* vol. II, 310.

[44] John of St Thomas, *The Gifts of the Holy Ghost*, 125.

[45] Giertych, "Why are there so few Thomist Saints?" 998.

[46] *ST* II-II, q. 45, a. 1, ad 2.

[47] Aumann, *Spiritual Theology*, 92-93.

[48] John of St Thomas, *The Gifts of the Holy Ghost,* 125. St Thomas says, "Now whatever can be known about God, which pertains to

one is speaking of something supremely higher. For the judgment which happens as a result of the operation of the gift of wisdom comes from the Holy Spirit, and a person judges and orders "all things according to Divine rules."[49] When one knows of Divine things through the operation of the gift of wisdom, this is the highest kind of wisdom one can have. This kind of knowing is what St John of the Cross calls "mystical theology which is known through love and by which one not only knows but at the same time experiences."[50]

Experiential Knowledge – A Taste, Love, Delight

The connatural knowing that happens as a result of the operation of the gift of wisdom is referred to by different names: *connatural knowledge, experimental knowledge*, or *quasi-experimental knowledge* of God.[51] (In

---

wisdom God knows in himself and exhaustively" (*Super Ep. ad Col.*, cap. 2, lec. 1, n. 81).

[49] *ST* II-II, q. 45, a. 1.

[50] St John of the Cross, OCD, *The Spiritual Canticle* in St John of the Cross, *The Collected Works*, translated by Kieran Kavanaugh, OCD and Otilio Rodriguez, OCD (Washington, D.C.: ICS Publications, 1991), prologue, 1, 409. [All works of St John of the Cross are cited from this volume.]

[51] See Deferrari, *A Lexicon of St. Thomas Aquinas*. *Quasi* means "*as if, just as, as it were.*" *Experimentalis* means "*concerned with experience, experimental.*" [As has been explained in the Introduction, these key words are italicized here because they express the key aspects of the operation of this gift which will be identified later in Part II – in the life of St Thérèse.]

this context, *experimental* and *experiential* are synonymous.) St Thomas uses the term *quasi-experiential* rather than just *experiential* because it expresses more clearly the "affective experience ... since it is experience in an analogous sense."[52] This *quasi-experiential* knowledge is a "knowledge that is accompanied by love."[53] In the "ancient phrase of the great mystic, the pseudo Dionysius 'Man suffers from God,' his heart melts under the great fire of God's familiarity."[54]

---

[52] John F. Dedek, "Quasi Experimentalis Cognitio: A Historical Approach to the meaning of St Thomas," *Theological Studies*, vol. 22, n. 3 (September 1961), 384-385: "To our knowledge, St Thomas was the first to use such restrictive expressions as *quasi, quodammodo,* and *quaedam* in connection with the just man's experimental knowledge of God. His contemporaries and immediate predecessors ... spoke of this knowledge which is accompanied by *sapor* as experimental but never as quasi-experimental. St Thomas, however, was more precise. For *experientia* in its proper sense signifies for Thomas an act of the senses, and from this it is transferred to designate an act of the intellect. But St Thomas also takes *experientia* in a qualified sense (*experientiam quandam*) to stand for an affective experience, an act of the appetite delighting in its object ... Thus, St Thomas qualifies the affective experience: he does not call it simply *experientiam* but *experientiam quandam*, since it is experience in an analogous sense (*secundum quamdam similitudinem*), not in the proper sense in which it is used to refer to an act of sense cognition, nor in the sense in which it is commonly transferred to designate an act of the intellect."
[53] Wojciech Giertych, OP, *The New Law as a Rule for Acts*, 234. Dedek in his article "Quasi experimentalis cognition," highlights this by referring to *Summa Theologiae* I, q. 64, a. 1. St Thomas points out "that experimental knowledge is properly called wisdom, since it joins knowledge to a kind of taste. This understanding is quite in line with his understanding of wisdom; for, according to Thomas, proper to wisdom is not merely speculative but affective knowledge, that is, knowledge which leads to love" ("Quasi Experimentalis Cognitio," 380).
[54] Vonier, *The Spirit and the Bride*, 191.

St Thomas quoting Dionysius says: "Hierotheus is perfect in Divine things, for he not only learns, but is patient of, Divine things."[55] The Latin text says *non solum discens, sed et patiens divina* – which can be translated *not only learning, but suffering Divine things*. This indicates something passive,[56] something which is received. It is not forced, but given and received, something that is experienced, (although the experience may be very subtle); it is something that gives a spiritual taste.[57] This way of knowing God is very intimate and gives the soul a "taste, love, delight, or internal contact of the will with spiritual things."[58] Consequently, a person is able to say, "Taste and see that the Lord is sweet,"[59] and by way of the gift of wisdom the soul really does taste, because it knows God and tastes the goodness of God through an "experience of the heart."[60]

St Thomas describes why the analogy of taste is used when referring to spiritual things, rather than

---

[55] *ST* II-II, q. 45, a. 2.

[56] Dedek points out that in *De Veritate* q. 26, a. 3, ad 18m, "St Thomas explicitly states that 'Hierotheus' experience of divine things was an affective act ... Hence it is that the just man's knowledge of the goodness of God is said to be affective or experimental knowledge, because it is joined to an affective experience of love and spiritual taste" ("Quasi experimentalis cognitio," 381).

[57] *Sapio, -ere* means *to taste or savour*. See Deferrari, *A Lexicon of St. Thomas Aquinas*.

[58] John of St Thomas, *The Gifts of the Holy Ghost*, 125.

[59] Ps 33:9 (Douay Rheims Catholic Bible). This verse is often rendered as "Taste and see that the Lord is good!" (Ps 34:8 RSV-CE).

[60] Gabriel of St Mary Magdalen, *Divine Intimacy*, 937.

other sense analogies. He points out that all human experiences come through the senses, and this happens in different ways. If the experience comes through the sense of sight, hearing, or smell, then this can happen at a distance, in comparison to that of taste and touch, which come in such a way that the object of the senses is much closer. A further distinction can be made by highlighting the difference between taste and touch because touch senses the outside of the object, whereas taste senses the inside.[61] God is so close to us; in fact, He is in us. The three Persons of the Blessed Trinity dwell within the soul who is in a state of grace, and hence in Scripture the experience of Divine goodness is called *tasting*. Now in the corporeal world we first see and then taste; however in the case of the spiritual world, the experience is first tasted and then seen. Examining this order, St Thomas remarks that in spiritual matters, the soul must first taste before it can see. Here, tasting can be understood as a kind of experiential knowing, while seeing is more of an intellectual knowing. Because spiritual realities are beyond the capacity of the senses (through which the human intellect receives data), through the gift of wisdom, God gives the soul an experience of His sweetness through which the soul can see and know. The text of Psalm 33 invites the

---

[61] St Thomas Aquinas, *In Psalm.*, 33, n. 9: "Secundo ponit experientiae effectum, *et videte quoniam*. Dicit ergo, *gustate et videte* et cetera. Experientia de re sumitur per sensum; sed aliter de re praesenti, et aliter de absente: quia de absente per visum, odoratum et auditum; de praesente vero per tactum et gustum; sed per tactum de extrinseca praesente, per gustum vero de intrinseca."

disciple to first taste and then see how sweet is the Lord.[62]

For St Thomas, the analogy of taste is the most certain sense for the human being – because it is more immediate and intimate (objectively) than all the other senses.[63] Hence taste is the best sense analogy to describe a connatural knowing of God and the most appropriate sense analogy to describe the gift of wisdom.

---

[62] St Thomas Aquinas, *In Psalm.*, 33, n. 9: "Deus autem non longe est a nobis, nec extra nos, sed in nobis: Hier. 14: *tu in nobis es domine*. Et ideo experientia divinae bonitatis dicitur gustatio: 1 Pet. 2: *si tamen gustatis quam dulcis* et cetera. Prov. Ult.: *gustavit et vidit, quoniam bona est negotiatio ejus*. Effectus autem experientiae ponitur duplex. Unus est certitudo intellectus, alius securitas affectus. Quantum ad primum dicit, *et videte*. In corporalibus namque prius videtur, et postea gustatur; sed in rebus spiritualibus prius gustatur, postea autem videtur; quia nullus cognoscit qui non gustat; et ideo dicit prius, *gustate*, et postea, *videte*. Quantum ad secundum dicit, *quoniam suavis est Dominus*. Sap. 12: o quam bonus et suavis est Domine spiritus tuus in nobis. Ps. 30: quam magna multitudo dulcedinis tuae." Gabriel of St Mary Magdalen says: "the gift of wisdom ... lets us taste [God's mysteries] and gives us a delightful knowledge of them. This is the *savory knowledge* ... the untranslatable '*dulce sapere*' invoked by St Thomas in the *Adoro Te Devote*; it is the precious gift which the Holy Spirit offers us in these words ... (Ps. 33:9) 'Taste and see that the Lord is sweet'" (*Divine Intimacy*, 937).

[63] Jacobus M. Ramirez, *De Donis Spiritus Sancti deque Vita Mystica* (Madrid: Instituto de Filosofia "Luis Vives", 1974), 322: St Thomas says that taste is better in humans than among other animals, whose sense of hearing and smell is better.

Connatural Knowing and Charity

We shall now examine the connatural knowing (i.e., tasting) which comes as a result of the operation of the gift of wisdom and the soul being united to God through the theological virtue of charity. In St Thomas' teaching on the seven gifts of the Holy Spirit, he highlights the intimacy of God's action in the life of the believer and the savour and sweetness that can be experienced.[64] This experience of *connaturality*[65] comes from the union that the soul has with God through the theological virtue of charity. There is no other way that the soul could have such an intimate closeness with God than through friendship with Him in charity.[66] The theological virtues have God as their object and direct the soul to God.[67] However, through the theological virtue of faith alone, the soul does not reach this loving union with God which enables it to taste of the Divine. The theological virtue of charity "attains to God immediately as He is in Himself, intimately uniting [the soul] to Him."[68] Charity gives a spiritual taste to the knowledge of the gift of wisdom; it is charity that adds an "affective

---

[64] Torrell, *Saint Thomas Aquinas*, vol. 2, *Spiritual Master*, 207.

[65] In his treatment of the gifts of the Holy Spirit, the word *connatural* (Latin: *connaturalis, e,* adj.) for St Thomas means: "agreeing with the nature of a thing"; the noun *connaturality* (Latin: *connaturalitas, atis,* f.) means: "natural inclination, natural attraction to something, natural inclination or attraction." See Deferrari, *A Lexicon of St. Thomas Aquinas*.

[66] Martinez, *Sanctifier*, 186-187.

[67] *ST* I-II, q. 66, a. 6; *ST* I-II, q. 62, a. 1, ad 2.

[68] John of St Thomas, *The Gifts of the Holy Ghost*, 129.

experience of spiritual sweetness and delectation."[69] Hence, knowledge which is received through the gift of wisdom is an "affective knowledge, that is, knowledge which leads to love." St Thomas "expressly identifies... 'affective' and 'experimental,' as synonymous"[70] when he says that

> knowledge of God's will or goodness is affective or experimental and thereby a man experiences in himself the taste of God's sweetness, and complacency in God's will, as Dionysius says of Hierotheos ... that "he learnt divine things through experience of them." It is in this way that we are told to prove God's will, and to taste His sweetness.[71]

The gift of wisdom helps us relish Divine things by a "connatural attraction [effected] by charity."[72] The person in the state of grace can have a knowledge of God's goodness which is "affective or experimental knowledge, because it is joined to an affective experience of love and spiritual taste."[73] St Thomas describes this as a "delight, which follows immediately upon the knowledge itself in act."[74] This cannot be true for the person who is not in a state of sanctifying

---

[69] Dedek, "Quasi Experimentalis Cognitio," 381.
[70] Dedek, "Quasi Experimentalis Cognitio," 380.
[71] *ST* II-II, q. 97, a. 2, ad 2.
[72] Bl. Marie-Eugène, *I Want to See God*, 345.
[73] Dedek, "Quasi Experimentalis Cognitio," 381.
[74] St Thomas Aquinas, *In Sent.*, III, d. 35, q. 2, a. 1, qc. III, ad 1: "Ad primum ergo dicendum, quod saporem sapientia importat quantum ad dilectionem praecedentem, non quantum ad cognitionem sequentem, nisi ratione delectationis, quae ipsam cognitionem in actu exequitur."

grace. On the other hand, the person who is not in a state of grace could receive the type of knowledge that is given, for example, through prophecy. St Thomas teaches that in order that a man may prophesy it is not absolutely necessary that he be morally good. Even a person in the state of mortal sin can prophesy. This kind of knowledge (received through prophecy), however, is an inferior kind of "supernatural knowledge" in comparison to the type of knowledge that one can possess only when one is in a state of grace. The more God raises a person to share in this superior type of knowledge, the greater the necessity for the "agreement between love and knowledge ... to the point that the perfection of knowledge cannot be achieved without love."[75] This *connatural knowing* is "an *experiential knowledge* of God, in which He is united to the soul in its very depths and gives Himself to it."[76] In other words, this type of knowledge, which

---

[75] Serge-Thomas Bonino, OP, "The Role of the Apostles in the Communication of Revelation according to the *Lectura super Ioannem.* of St. Thomas Aquinas," translated by Teresa Bede and Matthew Levering, in *Reading John with Saint Thomas Aquinas: Theological Exegesis and Speculative Theology,* edited by Michael Dauphinais and Matthew Levering (Washington, D.C.: The Catholic University of America Press, 2005), 327.

[76] John of St Thomas, *The Gifts of the Holy Ghost,* 127. Dedek remarks that "medieval writers preceding St. Thomas used the term 'experimental knowledge' to designate the kind of knowledge which is coupled with an affective experience of love and spiritual taste. Experiential knowledge was conceived of as knowledge that is joined to charity and to the affective experiences that go with charity" ("Quasi Experimentalis Cognitio," 374). "The notion of experiential knowledge was also put to use by medieval theologians in their discussions of the gift of wisdom. The reason for this is easy to understand, since wisdom was conceived of not as sheer knowledge but as knowledge that is

is connatural and experimental, is a result of love; it is a knowledge which is very precious.

Through the seven gifts of the Holy Spirit a person has a certain connaturality toward Divine things.[77] There is a certain connaturality that is typical of all of the seven gifts; however, this is particularly true in the case of the gift of wisdom.[78] In fact, the hallmark of this gift is *connatural knowing*; this is one of its main aspects.[79] Even though all the gifts have a certain connaturality, it is only through the gift of wisdom that we can have a delightful connatural experience of God which is sweet. This gift has an influence on the other gifts of the Holy Spirit by bringing to them a kind of subtle taste.[80] Whereas the other six gifts of the Holy Spirit "perceive, judge or act on things distinct from God, the gift of wisdom is primarily concerned with God himself."[81] It is in fact the gift of wisdom that gives the theological virtues and the moral virtues their "ultimate perfection and makes them truly divine. Perfected by the gift of wisdom, charity extends the divine influence to all the other virtues, because charity is the form of all the other virtues."[82]

---

coupled with love and taste" ("Quasi Experimentalis Cognitio," 372).

[77] John of St Thomas, *The Gifts of the Holy Ghost*, 45.

[78] Royo & Aumann, *Theology of Christian Perfection*, 420; see also Martinez, *Sanctifier*, 187-188.

[79] The gift of wisdom "makes us taste [God and divine things] by a certain connaturality." Royo & Aumann, *Theology of Christian Perfection*, 418.

[80] Bl. Marie-Eugène, *I Want to See God*, 355.

[81] Royo & Aumann, *Theology of Christian Perfection*, 419-420.

[82] Royo & Aumann, *Theology of Christian Perfection*, 425. Charity has God as its object and end and therefore it moves all the "other

In a certain way the gift of wisdom directs the other six gifts of the Holy Spirit, just as charity "which is intimately united with it, directs all the virtues."[83]

Enlightens the Intellect and Enkindles the Affections and the Will

A lot has been said so far about connatural experience through the gift of wisdom. Another aspect which is essential to the gift of wisdom needs to be clarified – the special prompting that is given by the Holy Spirit. Charity provides the connatural experience for the gift of wisdom; however, it is necessary to distinguish the gift of wisdom from the theological virtue of charity. It is inadequate simply to say that the gift of wisdom is like charity because it is described as a taste or savour. The act of the gift of wisdom is in the intellect, and through the gift of wisdom the intellect knows and judges; this is accompanied by a kind of taste, which has previously been described and comes as a result of a person being united to God through the theological virtue of charity which is in the will; thus a person experiences a loving and intimate union with God and judges of Divine things.[84] Hence charity is not the same as the gift of wisdom because "wisdom

---

virtues to act. For the habit to which the end pertains always commands the habits to which the means pertain" (*ST* I-II, q. 114, a. 4, ad 1).

[83] Martinez, *Sanctifier*, 303. St Thomas says that "the excellence of the gifts corresponds with the order in which they are enumerated" (*ST* I-II, q. 68, a. 7).

[84] John of St Thomas, *The Gifts of the Holy Ghost*, 54-55.

The Gift of Wisdom

is substantially and intrinsically an act of the intellect – for to be wise is to know. Men are called wise who understand and judge correctly."[85]

St Thomas says that the gift of wisdom has its "cause in the will, which cause is charity, but it has its essence in the intellect, whose act is to judge aright."[86] Two things are involved when the gift of wisdom is operating. An illumination that happens in the intellect enables a person to judge rightly of God and Divine things; and an experience happens in the will that can be described as a kind of *taste*. When the gift of wisdom is operating, along with this loving union and taste, there must always be an illumination which comes from the Holy Spirit so that the person can know and judge rightly of Divine things.[87] The Holy Spirit "enlightens the intellect and enkindles the affections and will."[88] St Thomas speaks of this "based both on the special inspiration of the Holy Ghost and on the connaturalness with divine things."[89] When a person receives this love and knowledge, it is because the Holy Spirit has given a special prompting; in other words, an operating grace is given, and the gifts of the Holy Spirit render a person docile to receive this prompting.[90] Thus, the gifts are "made ready for

---

[85] John of St Thomas, *The Gifts of the Holy Ghost*, 54.
[86] *ST* II-II, q. 45, a. 2.
[87] Cf. St Thomas Aquinas, *In Sent.*, III, d. 35, q. 2, a. 1, qc. III, ad 1.
[88] St Thomas Aquinas, *Super I Ep. ad Cor.*, cap. 2, lec. 3, n. 117: "Spiritu Dei et illuminatur secundum intellectum, et inflammatur secundum affectum et voluntatem."
[89] Garrigou-Lagrange, *Three Ages of the Interior Life*, vol. II, 333.
[90] Garrigou-Lagrange, *Three Ages of the Interior Life*, vol. II, 332-333. Royo and Aumann say that it is a characteristic of each of the seven

action by a special impulse of the Holy Ghost."[91] This love and knowledge cannot be produced when a person desires; rather it is a special grace given by the Lord. The intensity of this illumination and taste, which is made possible through the gift of wisdom, can always increase in this life, "just as charity can."[92]

The Gift of Wisdom is Only Present in those who are in the State of Grace

St Thomas says that the gifts of the Holy Spirit can only be possessed by those who are in a state of grace and that the gifts are "connected together in charity."[93] The seven gifts including the gift of wisdom can never be present when a person is in the state of mortal sin. This is because the gifts have charity as their "life giving principle."[94] The seven different names of the gifts of the Holy Spirit obviously stand for "seven differences;" however, the gifts are all related to each other.[95] The gifts strengthen one another and are connected in the theological virtue of charity; when a person has the virtue of charity, he or she will possess

---

gifts of the Holy Spirit that there is a special "movement of the Holy Ghost" (*Theology of Christian Perfection*, 420).

[91] John of St Thomas, *The Gifts of the Holy Ghost*, 49.
[92] Garrigou-Lagrange, *Christian Perfection and Contemplation*, 316.
[93] *ST* I-II, q. 68, a. 5.
[94] Brennan, *The Seven Horns of the Lamb,* 75. Garrigou-Lagrange points out: "These gifts, as habitual dispositions rendering us docile to the [promptings] of the Holy Ghost, grow, as do the infused virtues, with charity, which in this life ought always to develop" (*Christian Perfection and Contemplation*, 350).
[95] Vonier, *The Spirit and the Bride*, 186-187.

The Gift of Wisdom

all seven gifts of the Holy Spirit.[96] It is specifically through acts of charity that the seven gifts develop, because "they are deeply rooted in charity."[97]

In order to experience the connatural knowing which has been explained above, a person must be in a state of grace. There are many people who know that God exists either through natural knowledge or by the theological virtue of faith, but their faith is not informed by charity; in other words they have uninformed faith (because they have forfeited grace and charity through mortal sin), and therefore the Spirit of God does not dwell in their soul.[98] They are not in a state of grace and therefore even though they have some knowledge of God, that knowledge is limited and they do not have a supernatural love for God, because they are not united to God through grace and charity.

A person must be united to God in some way in order that the mind can be moved by God, and in order that the operation of the gifts can take place. Take the example of an artist. In order for him to paint a picture he needs to have an instrument so that he can produce the end product. He cannot do this unless he has some type of contact with the instrument. There must be a union between a person and God for the mind to be moved through the operation of the gifts of the Holy Spirit. This union between the soul and

---

[96] *ST* I-II, q. 68, a. 5.
[97] Michael D. Griffin, *Welcome to Carmel* (Hubertus, WI: Teresian Charism Press, 2006), 210-211.
[98] St Thomas Aquinas, *Super I Ep. ad Cor.*, cap. 3, lec. 3, n. 173: "Inde est quod multi cognoscunt Deum, vel per naturalem cognitionem, vel per fidem informem, quos tamen non inhabitat Spiritus Dei."

God happens through the theological virtues, the highest one being charity. Hence, as St Thomas says, the theological virtues are "presupposed to the gifts, as being their roots."[99] Once charity is gone, then a connatural type of knowing cannot take place because this connatural knowing is a knowing that comes from loving and is based on charity and the effect of charity. Therefore a person must always be in the state of grace in order to have the gift of wisdom, which enables one "to judge aright of Divine things or of other things according to Divine rules."[100] Hence, charity is essential to the gift of wisdom, just as it is essential to all the seven gifts of the Holy Spirit, and therefore, the person who is without sanctifying grace is also without the gift of wisdom.[101]

Charity is Perfected by the Gift of Wisdom; Nevertheless, Charity is Higher than this Gift

The seven gifts of the Holy Spirit are given to help the virtues;[102] it is the gift of wisdom which corresponds to the theological virtue of charity.[103] The reason that St Thomas places the gift of wisdom as corresponding with the virtue of charity seems to be twofold. Firstly, the name wisdom (*sapientia*) comes from the word

---

[99] *ST* I-II, q. 68, a. 4, ad 3.
[100] *ST* II-II, q. 45, a. 4.
[101] *ST* I-II, q. 68, a. 5.
[102] St Thomas Aquinas, *Super Is.*, cap. 11: St Thomas expresses this using the words *dona dantur in adjutorium virtutum*.
[103] Cf. *ST* II-II, q. 9, 2, ad. 1.

sapere which means to *taste* and tasting is something that pertains especially to the theological virtue of charity. The second reason is that among all the virtues charity is the highest virtue; similarly the highest gift among the seven gifts of the Holy Spirit is the gift of wisdom.[104] Furthermore, since the gift of wisdom is about judging and ordering things according to Divine rules, it seems likely that St Thomas saw the relationship between the gift of wisdom and charity in the Scripture passage which says, "he set in order charity in me."[105] (Sg 2:4) When a person is

---

[104] Ramirez, *De Donis Spiritus Sancti deque Vita Mystica*, 315: "Consequenter considerandum est de dono sapientiae. Circa quod occurrit dubium cur a S. Thoma ponatur ut correspondens virtuti caritatis et non potius ut correspondens fidei. *Ratio* huius attributionis crederim quod est duplex. 1a, ex *nomine*, quod venit a sapere et sapiendo vel gustando, ut dicitur postea; gustus autem et saporatio experimentalis divinorum maxime pertinet caritatem, utpote quae est amor et amicitia hominis ad Deum; 2a, *ex re* per nomen significata, nam inter omnes virtutes altior et perfectior est caritas; similiter inter omnia dona Spiritus Sancti, maius et altius et perfectius est donum sapientiae: iustum erat ergo quod supremum donum supremae virtuti attribuatur." O'Connor explains that Labourdette in *Cours de Théologie morale, la Charité*, "has argued persuasively that it is because charity is the greatest of all the virtues and Wisdom the greatest of all the Gifts, that the two are associated; 'as the theological life is fully developed in charity, so the regime of inspiration, in which the theological life is made divine in its very mode, is fully developed in the Gift of Wisdom" ("The Gifts of the Holy Spirit," appendix 4 to *Summa Theologiae*, vol. 24, 126).

[105] Cf. Daria E. Spezzano, "The Grace of the Holy Spirit, the Virtue of Charity and the Gift of Wisdom: Deification in Thomas Aquinas' Summa Theologiae" (Ph.D. diss., University of Notre Dame, 2011), 404: "The view that wisdom perfects charity by ordering its objects seems to be corroborated by the placement of

advanced in the spiritual life, as a result of wisdom's effect on charity, this virtue has become "so well ordered that the soul forgets itself and loves God as is required 'with all one's heart and with all one's strength....and one's neighbour as oneself.' "[106] As a result of the operation of the gift of wisdom one knows "the true order of things to beloved."[107]

All the virtues need the aid of the gifts of the Holy Spirit. Even though a person has the theological and moral virtues present within the soul, there is still need of the gifts of the Holy Spirit to help bring the virtues to perfection. Matters that are subject to human reason can be worked out through the judgment of reason and directed to their end. But in

---

q. 45. This question on wisdom immediately follows one on the precepts of charity, which examines the scriptural commands to love God and neighbor—what is at stake throughout q. 44, in effect, is the question of how charity should be ordered."

[106] Ven. Arintero, *The Mystical Phenomena. The Mystical Life of Saint Thérèse of the Child Jesus,* translated from the Original Spanish text by Jose L. Morales, (Spanish original published in Salamanca: Spain Editorial Fides, 1926. English translation: 1973), 38. St Bernard of Clairvaux, in Sermon 50 commenting on *Song of Songs* 2:4, explains that through wisdom one tastes the sweetness of the Lord, and this helps to inflame one's love for God and orders one's charity. He writes: "O Wisdom, reaching mightily from end to end in establishing and controlling things, and arranging all things sweetly by enriching the affections and setting them in order! Guide our actions as your eternal truth requires, that each of us may confidently boast in you and say, 'he set love in order in me.' For you are the strength of God and the Wisdom of God, Christ the Church's bridegroom, our Lord and God who is blessed forever. Amen." St Bernard of Clairvaux, *Sermons on the Song of Songs,* Sermon 50.

[107] Spezzano, "The Grace of the Holy Spirit, the Virtue of Charity and the Gift of Wisdom: Deification in Thomas Aquinas' Summa Theologiae," 406.

The Gift of Wisdom

matters that are directed to the supernatural end, to which our reason moves us, "according as it is, in a manner, and imperfectly, informed by the theological virtues, the motion of reason does not suffice, unless it receive in addition the prompting or motion of the Holy Ghost."[108] If one compares the seven gifts of the Holy Spirit to the theological virtues, it is the theological virtues which are the most perfect because they have "God Himself as their immediate object."[109] The gifts are not as perfect because they "refer only to docility in following the inspirations."[110] But even though the gifts are not higher than the theological virtues, they serve the virtues in order that they "can be practised perfectly."[111] Both the theological and moral virtues need to be perfected by the gifts of the Holy Spirit. St Thomas says: "By the theological and moral virtues, man is not so perfected in respect of his last end, as not to stand in continual need of being moved by the yet higher promptings of the Holy Ghost."[112] The theological virtues unite the soul to God, its ultimate end, while the gifts of the Holy Spirit

---

[108] *ST* I-II, q. 68, a. 2.

[109] Royo & Aumann, *Theology of Christian Perfection*, 100. St Thomas says that even though the gifts are given to help the virtues and are more perfect than the "moral and intellectual virtues ... they are not more perfect than the theological virtues." (*ST* II-II, q. 9, a. 1, ad 3; I-II, q. 68, a. 8). He also says: "Charity is a theological virtue; and such we grant to be more perfect than the gifts" (*ST* I-II, q. 68, a. 8, ad 1).

[110] Royo & Aumann, *Theology of Christian Perfection*, 100.

[111] Yves Congar, *I Believe in the Holy Spirit*, vol. II, translated by David Smith (New York: The Seabury Press, 1983), 136.

[112] *ST* I-II, q. 68, a. 2, ad 2.

help to move us to our final end.[113] We need the help of the gifts in order to help the theological virtues because we possess them imperfectly. St Thomas explains:

> Now man's reason is perfected by God in two ways: first, with its natural perfection ... the natural light of reason; secondly, with a supernatural perfection ... the theological virtues ... And, though this latter perfection is greater than the former, yet the former is possessed by man in a more perfect manner than the latter: because man has the former in his full possession, whereas he possesses the latter imperfectly, since we love and know God imperfectly.[114]

Now if anything has a nature, virtue, or form perfectly, then of itself it can "work according to them."[115] This does not exclude God's operation, "Who works inwardly in every nature and in every will."[116] However, when something has a nature, virtue, or form imperfectly, then it cannot work by itself, unless it is moved by another. For example, the sun has a perfect possession of light and therefore shines by itself; whereas "the moon which has the nature of light imperfectly, sheds only borrowed light."[117] This analogy helps us to understand the theological virtues. The theological virtues are infused by God into the soul and are of the supernatural order, but they are possessed by us in an imperfect way, this

---

[113] John of St Thomas, *The Gifts of the Holy Ghost*, 67.
[114] *ST* I-II, q. 68, a. 2.
[115] *ST* I-II, q. 68, a. 2.
[116] *ST* I-II, q. 68, a. 2.
[117] *ST* I-II, q. 68, a. 2.

means we are unable to reach our ultimate and final goal without the aid of the gifts of the Holy Spirit which are perfections, whereby we are "disposed so as to be amenable to the promptings of God."[118]

We possess the virtues imperfectly because of "the *human modality* that inevitably attaches to them."[119] When the virtues are infused into the soul, they take on the "human atmosphere." Therefore, the human soul possesses these supernatural virtues in an imperfect way, and it is not until they receive the help

---

[118] *ST* I-II, q. 68, a. 2.
[119] Antonio Royo Marín, OP, *The Great Unknown: The Holy Ghost and His Gifts* (Carmel, N.Y.: Western Hemisphere Cultural Society, 1991), 73. St Thomas explains: "Concerning the first, it is to be known that, as Gregory says, the gifts are given to assist the virtues, by which the powers of the soul are perfected for acts that are proportionate according to a human manner, as faith, which makes us to see in a glass and obscurity. Now there is a twofold defect of virtue: one accidental, from the indisposition of the one who has the habit, from which the virtue remains imperfect in the subject, and this defect is removed through the increase of the virtue; the other defect is essential on the part of the habit itself, as faith is continually imperfect according to its disposition, because it is obscure, and this defect is removed through a higher habit, which is called a gift, for as it exceeds the manner of human operation, it is given by God: as the gift of understanding, which in some manner makes things of faith to be seen clearly and distinctly. An operation, however, proceeding from a virtue perfected by a gift is called a beatitude, which is nothing other than operation according to perfect virtue, as the Philosopher says, as is said in Matthew 5:8: *blessed are the clean of heart: they shall see God*. But delight necessarily follows such operation, for delight is the unhindered operation of a proper habit, as the Philosopher says; and according to this, it is called a fruit; hence Ambrose on *the fruits of the Spirit* (Gal 5:22), says that they are called fruits in as much as they renew minds with sincere delight" (*Super Is.*, cap. 11).

of the gifts of the Holy Spirit that the virtues can be practised more perfectly. The gifts have a Divine mode of operation and not a human mode; therefore "they bestow on the infused virtues, and especially the theological virtues, that *divine atmosphere* they need in order to develop all their supernatural virtuality."[120] Without the help of the gifts the theological virtues would remain limited by a human mode of operation. But when the gifts are operating, they "elevate the subject to the divine plane which is proper to the theological virtues and thus give us a full and perfect possession of them. They eliminate the human mode of operation and bestow a divine mode."[121]

One of the main reasons why the virtues need the help of the seven gifts of the Holy Spirit is because of "the great disproportion between the infused virtues and the subject wherein they reside: the human soul."[122] Hence, in order for the theological virtues to be perfected they need a corresponding gift "because their inherent supernatural perfection demands a divine modality which only the gifts can bestow."[123] Thus, the gifts give to the virtues the Divine modality which is proper to them.[124] They assist the virtues and accomplish what the virtues are unable to accomplish.[125] It is the gift of wisdom that assists the

---

[120] Royo Marín, *The Great Unknown*, 73.
[121] Royo & Aumann, *Theology of Christian Perfection*, 94.
[122] Royo Marín, *The Great Unknown*, 72.
[123] Royo & Aumann, *Theology of Christian Perfection*, 94-95.
[124] Royo Marín, *The Great Unknown*, 70.
[125] *ST* I- II, q. 68, a. 8.

theological virtue of charity, even though charity (queen of all virtues)[126] is higher than the gift.[127]

---

[126] Congar, *I Believe in the Holy Spirit*, vol. II, 137. St Thomas explains the difference between the gift of knowledge and the gift of wisdom and why the gift of wisdom corresponds more to charity: "Although matters of faith are Divine and eternal, yet faith itself is something temporal in the mind of the believer. Hence to know what one ought to believe, belongs to the gift of knowledge, but to know in themselves the very things we believe, by a kind of union with them, belongs to the gift of wisdom. Therefore the gift of wisdom corresponds more to charity which unites man's mind to God" (*ST* II-II, q. 9, 2, ad 1).

[127] O'Connor points out that St Thomas "does not say expressly that the Gift of Wisdom in any way aids or perfects the virtue of charity. And he makes it very clear that charity, along with faith and hope, is greater than Wisdom, is the root from which Wisdom derives, and is the cause of it. But since this is true of all three theological virtues, in relationship to all seven Gifts, it does not explain the special connection between charity and Wisdom. Nevertheless, in every other case, the Gift is associated with the virtue which it assists; and in the one case in which Thomas argues *ex professo* for the connection of the Gift with the virtue, namely that of Counsel with prudence, it is on the grounds of the aid rendered by the former to the latter. Hence it seems probable that he saw Wisdom as perfecting charity, at least in the sense of freeing it from some of the imperfections inherent in the human mode of its exercise" ("The Gifts of the Holy Spirit," appendix 4 to *Summa Theologiae*, vol. 24, 125-126). Aumann says of St Thomas, "In the treatise *De Caritate*, written towards the end of his life (1270-1272) ... after asserting that the gifts perfect the virtues by raising them to a superhuman mode of operation, he says that as regards the love of God, there is no imperfection in it that must be perfected by a gift; therefore charity is not given as the name of a gift but it is more excellent than all the gifts." One might ask how we can say that St Thomas relates the gift of wisdom to the theological virtue of charity if he says that there is no imperfection in regard to charity. Aumann says, "[T]he virtue of charity does not have any *essential* imperfection; that is, no imperfection

The gift of wisdom perfects charity "by giving it the divine modality it lacks as long as charity is subject to human reason, even illumined by faith."[128] It is precisely this gift which enables charity to develop and grow rapidly and carry the soul to the heights of perfection. Without the aid of this gift, charity would remain under the rule of human reason and, in a sense, would have to "compromise in accordance with prudence, due to its weak condition."[129] However, when the gift of wisdom is operating, a person will not have to act laboriously, but will act intuitively under the influence of this gift "by a special instinct which proceeds from the Holy Ghost,"[130] and the light of the gift of wisdom will set "the heart on fire with love."[131] The gift of wisdom, the highest gift of the Holy Spirit, is the gift which is "most suited to lighting and reviving the flame of love, charity."[132] It is through the theological virtue of charity that the soul loves "God in Himself; through the gift of wisdom we know His

---

precisely as an operative habit ... [T]he gift of wisdom perfects charity by disposing the soul for experiencing divine things connaturally and intuitively. In this way the gift of wisdom corrects the distance or remoteness from its object, which is the imperfection of charity in this life. And it is in this respect that the virtue of charity needs the gift of wisdom for its full perfection *in via*. To have charity at all means to love God appreciatively above all things, but to experience the benevolent and mutual love that is friendship, this requires the operation of the gift of wisdom" (Aumann "Mystical Experience, the Infused Virtues and the Gifts," 47- 48).

[128] Royo & Aumann, *Theology of Christian Perfection*, 418.
[129] Royo & Aumann, *Theology of Christian Perfection*, 421.
[130] Royo & Aumann, *Theology of Christian Perfection*, 420.
[131] Martinez, *Sanctifier*, 189.
[132] Àngel de les Gavarres, *Thérèse: The Little Child of God's Mercy* (Washington, D.C.: ICS Publications, 1999), 353.

infinite goodness because we taste and experience it."[133] Thus:

> In relating wisdom to the virtue of charity, St. Thomas is referring not simply to a lofty speculative knowledge of divine things, but a loving knowledge wherein the knowledge stimulates a more intense love, and the intensified love produces a more intuitive and connatural knowledge. It is a contemplative knowledge, a loving awareness of God.[134]

This gift perfects the virtue of charity, and charity "extends the divine influence to all the other virtues, because charity is the form of all the other virtues."[135] Therefore the gift of wisdom helps a person to soar in the spiritual life because through its workings a person grows in charity and consequently all of the other virtues increase, and the more this gift operates in a person's life the more he or she will have an immense love for God and neighbour.

Towards a Deeper Understanding of Judgment through the Gift of Wisdom

St Thomas says, "The spiritual man judges all things, namely, because a man with an intellect enlightened by the Holy Spirit and set in good order by Him has a

---

[133] Martinez, *Sanctifier*, 188.
[134] Jordan Aumann, "Mystical Experience, the Infused Virtues and the Gifts,"48.
[135] Royo & Aumann, *Theology of Christian Perfection*, 425.

sound judgment about the particulars which pertain to salvation."[136] There are four intellectual gifts of the Holy Spirit, all of which are "ordained to supernatural knowledge, which, in us, takes its foundation from faith."[137] In other words, a characteristic common to these four gifts is that all four of them are related to the theological virtue of faith.[138] By faith a person believes all that God has revealed through His Son Jesus Christ and His Church. Faith guides us and through it we know all the truths that are necessary for salvation.[139]

In order to understand the gift of wisdom better, it can be helpful to look briefly at the other intellectual gifts. Each of the seven gifts of the Holy Spirit has its own particular function,[140] and each of the four intellectual gifts has something that is specific to its own operation and purpose. The four intellectual gifts of the Holy Spirit are wisdom, understanding, knowledge, and counsel.[141] As mentioned above, the intellectual gifts are all "ordained to supernatural knowledge, which, in us, takes its foundation from

---

[136] St Thomas Aquinas, *Super I Ep. ad Cor.*, cap. 2, lec. 3, n. 118: "Et secundum hunc modum Apostolus hic dicit quod *spiritualis iudicat omnia*, quia scilicet homo habens intellectum illustratum et affectum ordinatum per Spiritum Sanctum, de singulis quae pertinent ad salutem, rectum iudicium habet."
[137] *ST* II-II, q. 8, a. 6.
[138] Martinez, *Sanctifier*, 151.
[139] Martinez, *Sanctifier*, 151-152.
[140] John of St Thomas, *The Gifts of the Holy Ghost*, 243.
[141] See *ST* II-II, q. 45, a. 1 (Wisdom); *ST* II-II, q. 8, a. 1. (Understanding); *ST* II-II, q. 9, a. 1 (Knowledge); *ST* II-II, q. 52, a. 1 (Counsel).

faith."[142] St Thomas says that when things are proposed for our belief, they must be

> penetrated or grasped by the intellect, and this belongs to the gift of understanding. Secondly, it is necessary that man should judge these things aright, that he should esteem that he ought to adhere to these things, and to withdraw from their opposites: and this judgment, with regard to Divine things belongs to the gift of wisdom, but with regard to created things, belongs to the gift of knowledge, and as to its application to individual actions, belongs to the gift of counsel.[143]

The Gift of Understanding

The gift of understanding helps us to penetrate and understand Divine things.[144] It is particular to the gift of understanding to penetrate the revealed truths of the faith and even natural truths "so far as they are related to a supernatural end."[145] The gift of wisdom differs from the gift of understanding in that the latter "enables us to know the divine truths in themselves and in their mutual relations, but not in their ultimate

---

[142] *ST* II-II, q. 8, a. 6. In this article, St Thomas says that faith comes through hearing and that faith "first and principally, is about the First Truth, secondarily, about certain considerations concerning creatures, and furthermore extends to the direction of human actions, in so far as it works through charity."
[143] *ST* II-II, q. 8, a. 6.
[144] *ST* II-II, q. 8, a. 3.
[145] Royo & Aumann, *Theology of Christian Perfection*, 370.

causes and does not make us relish them directly,"[146] as does the gift of wisdom.

The Gift of Knowledge

Regarding the gift of knowledge, St Thomas quoting St Augustine says: "The knowledge of Divine things may be properly called wisdom, and the knowledge of human affairs may properly receive the name of knowledge."[147] The gift of knowledge judges concerning created things or human things; through this gift a judgment is "formed through second causes."[148] It does not make a judgment about all created things, but only "those which pertain to the building up of faith."[149] As a result of the operation of

---

[146] Adolphe Tanquerey, SS, DD, *The Spiritual Life*, translated by Herman Branderis SS, AM (New York: Desclee and Co., 1930), 629.
[147] *ST* II-II, q. 9, a. 2: "Accordingly, since the word knowledge implies certitude of judgment ... if this certitude of the judgment is derived from the highest cause, the knowledge has a special name, which is wisdom: for a wise man in any branch of knowledge is one who knows the highest cause of that kind of knowledge, and is able to judge of all matters by that cause: and a wise man absolutely, is one who knows the cause which is absolutely highest, namely God. Hence the knowledge of Divine things is called wisdom, while the knowledge of human things is called knowledge, this being the common name denoting certitude of judgment, and appropriated to the judgment which is formed through second causes. Accordingly, if we take knowledge in this way, it is a distinct gift from the gift of wisdom, so that the gift of knowledge is only about human or created things."
[148] *ST* II-II, q. 9, a. 2.
[149] St Thomas Aquinas, *Super I Ep. ad Cor.*, cap. 14, lec. 2, n. 825: "Vel est de terrenis, et non de quibuscumque, sed de illis tantum,

the gift of knowledge, we know what we "ought to hold by faith,"[150] whether something is in accord with the truths of the faith, and what we ought to believe; but through the gift of wisdom, we "know in themselves the very things we believe, by a kind of union with them."[151] Through the operation of the gift of knowledge, we judge whether something is in conformity with the teaching of the Church and if something should be believed; whereas through the operation of the gift of wisdom, we know the very things which we believe by having a sort of union with them. We have an experiential knowledge of them, by which we taste them.

The Gift of Counsel

Finally, the gift of counsel "is about what has to be done for the sake of the end."[152] Through the operation of the gift of counsel one judges concerning the application of practical concrete acts.[153] This gift helps us to judge concerning certain acts or events, which ought to be done in view of their supernatural end.[154] The gifts of wisdom and counsel are distinct in that the gift of counsel is concerned with governing actions, whereas the gift of wisdom is concerned with

---

quae sunt ad aedificationem fidei, et hoc pertinet ad donum scientiae."
[150] *ST* II-II, q. 9, a. 3.
[151] *ST* II-II, q. 9, a. 2, ad 1.
[152] *ST* II-II, 52, a. 2.
[153] Royo & Aumann, *Theology of Christian Perfection*, 418-19.
[154] Royo & Aumann, *Theology of Christian Perfection*, 433.

"the contemplation of divine things through their ultimate causes."[155]

The Gift of Wisdom

Through the four intellectual gifts of the Holy Spirit, a person can have a profound penetration of the truths of the faith and can judge either according to ultimate causes or according to secondary causes, and also judge in regard to practical actions.[156] In differentiating the gift of wisdom from the other intellectual gifts, it can be seen that wisdom is unique.[157] Whereas it belongs to the other gifts to judge or perceive things "distinct from God, the gift of wisdom is primarily concerned with God Himself."[158] Thus, wisdom judges all other things through their highest reasons, Divine reason, and judges everything so far as it pertains to God.[159] Through the gift of wisdom a person is "moved to uncover the cause or reason of whatever it tends to know through wisdom."[160] This type of wisdom gives a knowledge "which imparts certitude of great and marvellous things unknown to others."[161] It guarantees correct judgment "concerning the contemplation or examination of divine realities."[162] Through the operation of this gift we judge

---

[155] John of St Thomas, *The Gifts of the Holy Ghost*, 134.
[156] John of St Thomas, *The Gifts of the Holy Ghost*, 47-48.
[157] John of St Thomas, *The Gifts of the Holy Ghost*, 125.
[158] Royo & Aumann, *Theology of Christian Perfection*, 419.
[159] Royo & Aumann, *Theology of Christian Perfection*, 419.
[160] John of St Thomas, *The Gifts of the Holy Ghost*, 125.
[161] John of St Thomas, *The Gifts of the Holy Ghost*, 125-126.
[162] Congar, *I Believe in the Holy Spirit*, vol. II, 137.

and discern spiritual truths[163] and we are able to judge all things from God's point of view and see all things, in a sense, through the eyes of God.

The Gift of Wisdom and Infused Contemplation

Through the theological virtue of charity there is a friendship established between the soul and God; this provides the foundation for the life of prayer to flourish and grow.[164] But even when we are united to God through charity, we also need the extra help of the gifts of the Holy Spirit. The gifts perfect the virtues by helping them attain to things that otherwise they would not be able to accomplish without the aid of the gifts; so also in regard to prayer, we need the assistance of the gifts of the Holy Spirit. The theological virtue of faith is left in a kind of obscurity without the help of the gifts.[165] If someone is praying by way of meditation, with faith but without the adornment of the gifts, then that person will often grow tired.

---

[163] John of St Thomas, *The Gifts of the Holy Ghost*, 125.
[164] Giardini, "The Growth Process of Christian Prayer Life," 400-401. In *ST* II-II, q. 27, a. 2, St Thomas says that love "denotes a certain union of affections between the lover and the beloved, in as much as the lover deems the beloved as somewhat united to him, or belonging to him, and so tends towards him."
[165] Cf. St Thomas Aquinas *Super Is.*, cap. 11: "Sicut fides secundum dispositionem est continue imperfecta, quia aenigmatica. Et iste defectus tollitur per altiorem habitum, qui vocatur donum, quia quasi excedit modum humanae operationis, a Deo datum."

Heavenly things may seem closed to the understanding and remain veiled by the "shroud of faith."[166] Faith cannot reach the type of prayer which is called infused contemplation without the aid of charity and the gifts because this type of contemplation depends upon charity and the operation of the gifts.[167]

Through the aid of the gifts of the Holy Spirit and a heart that loves, things are seen in a better light, and made more clearer and more luminous.[168] This happens especially through the operation of the gift of wisdom; thus, the gift of wisdom has a particular role to play in prayer. St Thomas explains that it is particular to the gift of wisdom that this gift "proceeds according to a deiform contemplation and sort of explanation of the articles which faith holds enveloped according to a human manner (of knowing)."[169] The result is that through infused contemplation what before had been an "object of a faith in some way detached from us, and to this extent obscure, becomes the object of an experience."[170] This experience may be intense or it may be so subtle that one is hardly aware it is happening; for it is a gentle and peaceful loving inflow of light and love from

---

[166] John of St Thomas, *The Gifts of the Holy Ghost*, 32.

[167] Jacques Maritain, *The Range of Reason*, 214. Garrigou-Lagrange explains that this type of prayer is quite different; here prayer has become passive, God is infusing His love and light into the soul and hence there is an "inspiration and special illumination of the Holy Ghost" (*Christian Perfection and Contemplation*, 316).

[168] John of St Thomas, *The Gifts of the Holy Ghost*, 34-35.

[169] St Thomas Aquinas, *In Sent.*, III, d. 35, q. 2, a. 1, ad 1, as quoted in John of Saint Thomas, *The Gifts of the Holy Ghost*, 133.

[170] Louis Bouyer, Cong. Orat., *Introduction to Spirituality*, translated by Mary Perkins Ryan (Collegeville, MN: Liturgical Press, 1961), 80.

The Gift of Wisdom

God. When a person is blessed with the prayer of infused contemplation, the Holy Spirit accomplishes this through the gift of wisdom, and also the gifts of understanding and knowledge.[171] However, while the gifts of understanding and knowledge do have a part to play in infused contemplation, it pertains particularly to the gift of wisdom. In other words, infused contemplation is a result of the operation of the gifts of the Holy Spirit and in particular the gift of wisdom.

One must be careful when using the term *contemplation*. For St Thomas the word *contemplation* (*contemplatio*) is "interchangeable with the term *speculatio* and does not necessarily refer to any supernatural or even religious activity."[172] In other words, for St Thomas the term contemplation does not necessarily have to be a religious act or have anything to do with prayer; it can be a simple gaze upon truth. *Infused contemplation* is always religious and supernatural and can be found only in those who are in a state of grace. We do not find the term *infused contemplation* in the works of St Thomas; nevertheless, the principles for understanding this kind of prayer

---

[171] John of St Thomas, *The Gifts of the Holy Ghost*, 33.

[172] Giertych, "Why are there so few Thomist Saints?", 996: "The term *contemplatio* as it appears in Aquinas is interchangeable with the term *speculatio*, and does not necessarily refer to any supernatural or even religious activity. It refers to a function of the mind that is the intellect, as it experiences a direct intuition of truth – *simplex intuitus veritatis*. That simple intuition of the mind that reaches out to the end, to the truth, is extremely important in life, not only in the intellectual life."

can be found. In order to grasp St Thomas' understanding of this infused prayer, one can look at his questions concerning faith, charity, grace, the gifts of wisdom, understanding and knowledge, and the indwelling of the Most Holy Trinity.[173] In II-II, q. 45, St Thomas explains that it belongs to the gift of wisdom, first of all, to contemplate,[174] and that this gift "denotes a certain rectitude of judgment in the contemplation … of Divine things."[175] He says that this contemplative wisdom, which is a gift of the Holy Spirit is infused into the soul; it is a wisdom which is received.[176] In other words, it is infused into the soul by the Holy Spirit. Wisdom is the

---

[173] Cf. Giertych, "Why are there so few Thomist Saints?", 996. Giertych explains that "contemplative prayer in the Carmelite understanding consists essentially in the perseverant attachment to God through faith and love. It is not an intellectual exercise of great minds engaged in speculative metaphysics. It is always supernatural, a fruit of grace" (995). So when the Carmelites use the word contemplation, they are referring to a contemplation which is infused. In other words, it is an "encounter with the divine Person in faith and love. The decisive moment is not the action of the intellect alone, but the intellect and the will, moved from within by grace in faith and charity" (997).
[174] *ST* II-II, q. 45, a. 3, ad 3.
[175] *ST* II-II, q. 45, a. 5. Jacques Maritain says, "of the three wisdoms recognized by Saint Thomas, metaphysical wisdom, theological wisdom and the wisdom of contemplation, this last, which operates in the superhuman way of the Gift of Wisdom is rooted in the living faith, pre-eminently deserves the name of wisdom" (The Range of Reason, 214).
[176] *ST* II-II, q. 45, a. 5. Here, St Thomas uses the Latin word *sortiuntur* which means *received*. Boyer explains how "Under various expressions, Macarius, Evagrius and Dionysius, Augustine and Gregory, all emphasize as clearly as possible the fact that contemplation, however they understand it, is supremely the gift of God: the especially privileged experience that we can have of His grace, of His very presence in us taking possession of us,

highest of the gifts, and it is the gift which is most responsible for infused contemplation. In fact, Garrigou-Lagrange says:

> According to St Thomas and St John of the Cross, the full normal actualisation of the gift of wisdom deserves the name of infused contemplation, properly so called and ... without this contemplation the full normal actualisation of this gift does not yet exist.[177]

When a person begins to receive infused contemplation, the gift of wisdom begins to permeate one's whole prayer life. The more a person receives infused contemplation, "the more the soul increases in understanding, and the wider is the aperture in the heavens for the soul to behold the glory of God... it now explores and contemplates the magnitude of God."[178] Hence, the gift of wisdom is very significant when it

---

and to that extent restoring us to the primal design of our creation to His image and likeness. It is in this sense that contemplation can be called 'passive.' Not that grace is not just as active in us from the beginning of our meditation on the Word of God by which He is revealed to us, and not that in contemplation we become inert under His action. Far from that, we are then acting far more truly, far more effectively perhaps, than at any of those moments in which we seem, at first sight, left to ourselves and our own efforts. But now we experience to the degree that is possible here below that, as the Apostle says, it is in fact God Who created in us both the willing and the doing. More profoundly, we here attain what St Paul again calls 'the knowledge I have of the mystery,' the mystery that he further defines as 'Christ in us, the hope of glory'" (*Introduction to Spirituality*, 79).

[177] Garrigou-Lagrange *Three Ages of the Interior Life*, vol. II, 339.
[178] John of St Thomas, *The Gifts of the Holy Ghost*, 33. St John of the Cross says this contemplation can be "very delightful because it is

comes to understanding infused contemplation. This gift plays a very important role in a person's life of prayer. It is precisely the operation of this gift (more than the other gifts) which is responsible for infused contemplation.

The Gift of Wisdom is Both Speculative and Practical

St Thomas says the gift of wisdom is not only speculative; it is practical also, directing us "not only to contemplation but also to action."[179] Thus, he says

---

a knowledge through love" (*Spiritual Canticle, stanza* 27, 5, 518). St Teresa of Avila says the "delights which often accompany this type of prayer, are spiritual delights which "begin in God, but human nature feels and enjoys them'" (*Interior Castle*, IV Mansions, ch. 1, 4, 318). St Teresa also says that through "perfect contemplation," a person enjoys "without understanding how they are enjoying. The soul is being enkindled in love, and it doesn't understand how it loves. It knows that it enjoys what it loves, but it doesn't know how. It clearly understands that this joy is not a joy the intellect obtains merely through desire. The will is enkindled without understanding how. But as soon as it can understand something, it sees that this good cannot be merited or gained through all the trials one can suffer on earth. This good is a gift from the Lord of earth and heaven, who, in sum, gives according to who He is" (*Way of Perfection*, ch. 25, 2, 131).

[179] *ST* II-II, q. 45, a. 3. O'Connor observes some developments in the thought of St Thomas regarding the intellectual gifts of the Holy Spirit. In his *Commentary on the Sentences*, St Thomas had said that the gift of knowledge and counsel are both concerned with the "practical direction of man's active life." St Thomas also maintains this in the I-II of the *Summa Theologiae*; in the II-II, however, he declares that the "Gift of Knowledge has to do with all truths of faith, speculative as well as practical." The gifts of

The Gift of Wisdom

it "belongs to wisdom, as a gift, not only to contemplate Divine things, but also to regulate human acts."[180] This gift operates not only when a person is at prayer, but also in the midst of daily work and actions. Through the operation of the gift of wisdom, there is a consideration and contemplation of Divine and heavenly things; and from this consultation a person is able to judge human affairs and then direct and regulate his or her acts "according to Divine rules."[181] As with the other gifts of the Holy Spirit, wisdom operates in the everyday life of the person and can often work in a hidden manner, so that the action cannot always be distinguished from the operation of the virtues; or it can work in a manner that is more experiential and its operation much more evident.[182]

When a soul reaches the state of the perfect, the highest of the three stages of the spiritual life, there is usually a gift which predominates; often it is the gift

---

wisdom and understanding are also "reinterpreted as being both speculative and practical, while Counsel becomes fully and solely responsible for the functions it previously shared with Knowledge" ("The Gifts of the Holy Spirit," appendix 4 to *Summa Theologiae*, vol. 24, 125).

[180] *ST* II-II, q. 45, a. 6, ad 3.

[181] *ST* II-II, q. 45, a. 3. St Thomas says that the virtue of wisdom extends to many things. Now, when one virtue is considered higher than another then it necessarily follows that it extends to a greater number of things. Therefore, from the fact that the gift of wisdom is more excellent than the virtue of wisdom, because it "attains to God more intimately by a kind of union of the soul with Him, it is able to direct us not only in contemplation but also in action" (*ST* II-II, q. 45, a. 3, ad 1).

[182] Aumann, *Spiritual Theology*, 272-273.

of wisdom. In some this gift is very striking while in others it is diffuse. Where the operation of the gift of wisdom is not so evident, the gift of counsel, fortitude, or one of the other gifts may be more discernible. However, these gifts are all directed by the light and spirit of wisdom.[183] In some souls who have reached an advanced stage in the spiritual life, the intellectual gifts of the Holy Spirit, even the gift of wisdom, do not necessarily take the form of a brilliant striking light, as they do with some very contemplative souls; rather the light is diffused. Nevertheless, this diffused light is extremely precious because it illumines everything from above, especially one's conduct and the good that should be done to one's neighbour.[184] Even when someone's life appears to be very active, it does not mean that he or she is not under the influence of the intellectual gifts of the Holy Spirit. Rather, these gifts, including the gift of wisdom, could be highly operative. This has been the case with many of the Saints down through the centuries; these gifts have been manifested principally "under a practical form."[185]

---

[183] Garrigou-Lagrange, *Christian Perfection and Contemplation*, 327-328.

[184] Garrigou-Lagrange, *Three Ages of the Interior Life*, vol. II, 338.

[185] Garrigou-Lagrange, *Three Ages of the Interior Life*, vol. II, 319, footnote 39. Garrigou-Lagrange gives the example of St Vincent de Paul, "whereas in others these same intellectual gifts are manifested under a clearly contemplative form, as in St John of the Cross" (*Three Ages of the Interior Life*, vol. I, 319). Likewise, Aumann remarks, "Aquinas shows that the active life may have an ascetical value as a preparation for contemplation, but it may have a mystical value of its own as when the apostolate flows from the perfection of charity and a deep interior life" (*Christian Spirituality in the Catholic Tradition*, 132).

Contemplation which proceeds from the gift of wisdom can continue during external work and occupations, during intellectual work, and even during conversation.[186] Even if the Holy Spirit is working frequently through the gift of wisdom, a person is able to do all kinds of work, including work which involves intense concentration; and, in the centre of the soul, tranquillity and peace remain. It is also possible for that person to experience the indwelling of the Most Holy Trinity whilst in the midst of various other occupations, other than at times of prayer.[187]

Three Stages in the Spiritual Life

The gift of wisdom has a huge role in bringing a person to the heights of sanctity. St Thomas says that there are three stages in the spiritual life which are distinguished by the degree of charity the person in a state of grace possesses. These three stages are referred to as the stages of the beginner, the proficient, and the perfect.[188] St Thomas explains that the beginner is chiefly occupied with "avoiding sin and resisting concupiscence, which moves him in opposition to charity."[189] The proficient is one who has reached a higher stage in the spiritual life and

---

[186] Garrigou-Lagrange, *Three Conversions of the Spiritual Life* (Rockford, IL: Tan Books and Publishers, Inc., 2002), 94-95.
[187] Aumann, *Spiritual Theology*, 272-273.
[188] *ST* II-II, q. 24, a. 9. The stages of the spiritual life *beginner*, *proficient*, and *perfect* are also referred to in Catholic tradition as the *purgative way*, the *illuminative way*, and the *unitive way*.
[189] *ST* II-II, q. 24, a. 9.

whose "chief pursuit is to aim at progress in good" and to strengthen charity.[190] The person who has reached the highest stage in the spiritual life aims "chiefly at union with and enjoyment of God: this belongs to the perfect who 'desire to be dissolved and to be with Christ.'"[191] St Thomas says that a person should always try to advance in the spiritual life and ought to have a desire to "be made perfect."[192] In the state of the perfect, all pride is gone and all self-seeking has departed; charity has reached its heights and has been highly perfected by the gift of wisdom.[193]

A person who advances through the particular stages in the spiritual life and remains open to the working of the Holy Spirit can finally reach the state of the perfect, which is also called the unitive stage in some spiritual writings.[194] At this stage the soul has been purified from all pride and selfishness, and charity has reached great heights through the

---

[190] *ST* II-II, q. 24, a. 9.

[191] *ST* II-II, q. 24, a. 9.

[192] St Thomas Aquinas, *Super Ep. ad Phil.*, cap. 1, lec. 2. n. 16: "Primo quantum ad iterioris caritatis augmentum. Affectus enim interior perficitur per caritatem, et ideo non habenti caritatem optandum est ut habeat; habenti vero, ut perficiatur." St Thomas says that it "is essential to the charity of a wayfarer that it can increase, for if it could not, all further advance along the way would cease" (*ST* II-II q. 24, a. 4).

[193] Brennan, *The Seven Horns of the Lamb*, 89. Cf. Garrigou Lagrange, *Christian Perfection and Contemplation*, 308.

[194] Garrigou-Lagrange says that the "distinction of the three ways owes its origin to the doctrine of Christian contemplation as formulated by St Augustine and Dionysius" (*Christian Perfection and Contemplation*, 171).

operation of the gift of wisdom.[195] In order for a person to grow in the spiritual life and ultimately reach the state of the perfect, St Thomas says, that person needs to be purified from "whatever hinders the mind's affections from tending wholly to God."[196] If a person has reached this stage, he or she has gone through the dark night[197] and has been purged from many imperfections. This purification is primarily due to infused contemplation,[198] which begins in the

---

[195] Brennan, *The Seven Horns of the Lamb*, 89.

[196] *ST* II-II, q. 184, a. 2. In this article St Thomas explains, "Charity is possible apart from this perfection, for instance in those who are beginners and in those who are proficient." In other words, a person is still united to God in charity before having gone through the purification to remove these obstacles.

[197] St John of the Cross says, "This dark night is an inflow of God into the soul, which purges it of its habitual ignorances and imperfections, natural and spiritual, and which the contemplatives call infused contemplation or mystical theology. Through this contemplation, God teaches the soul secretly and instructs it in the perfection of love without its doing anything nor understanding how this happens. Insofar as infused contemplation is loving wisdom of God, it produces two principal effects in the soul: it prepares the soul for the union with God through love by both purging and illumining it ... Yet a doubt arises: Why, if it is a divine light (for it illumines and purges a person of his ignorances), does the soul call it a dark night? In answer to this, there are two reasons why this divine wisdom is not only night and darkness for the soul, but also affliction and torment. First, because of the height of the divine wisdom which exceeds the capacity of the soul. Second, because of the soul's baseness and impurity, and on this account it is painful, afflictive, and also dark for the soul" (*Dark Night*, bk II, ch. 5, 1-2, 335).

[198] The soul has been purified particularly through the gift of understanding. St Thomas says that "being cleansed by the gift of understanding, we can, so to speak, 'see God'" (*ST* I-II, q. 69, a. 2, ad 3).

passive night of the senses and continues in the night of the spirit. St John of the Cross explains, "This dark night is an inflow of God into the soul, which purges it of its habitual ignorances and imperfections, natural and spiritual."[199] A person must go through this purification in order to grow in the spiritual life and be at peace with oneself and with God; this peace comes as a consequence of becoming more ordered within. St Thomas explains:

> There are three things which have to be put in order within us: the intellect, the will and sense appetency. The will should be directed by the mind or reason, and sense appetency should be directed by the intellect and will. Accordingly, Augustine, in his *The Words of our Lord*, describes the peace of the saints by saying: "Peace is a calmness of mind, a tranquillity of soul, a simplicity of heart, a bond of love and a fellowship of charity." Calmness of mind refers to our reason, which should be free, not

---

[199] St John of the Cross, *Dark Night*, bk II, ch. 5, 1, 335. According to Garrigou-Lagrange, the cognitive gifts of the Holy Spirit working through infused contemplation cause the night of the spirit and the senses. The passive purification begins in the night of the senses and then continues with the night of the spirit. The cause of these nights is infused contemplation. In the night of the senses the gift of knowledge predominates and in the night of the spirit the gift of understanding. Garrigou-Lagrange explains: "In the aridity of the night of the senses, the gift of knowledge dominates by acquainting us especially with the vanity of created things; (II-II, q. 9, a. 4) in the night of the soul, the gift of understanding (II-II, q. 8, a. 7) shows us not so much the goodness of God as His Infinite majesty, and by contrast our wretchedness. Between the two nights and especially after the second, the superhuman mode of the gift of wisdom is not only latent, but becomes more and more manifest to an experienced spiritual director" (*Christian Perfection and Contemplation*, 327).

tied down, nor absorbed by disordered affections; tranquillity of soul refers to our sense appetency, which should not be harassed by our emotional states; simplicity of heart refers to our will, which should be entirely set toward God, its object; the bond of love refers to our neighbor; and the fellowship of charity to God.[200]

The writings of St John of the Cross are focused on how the soul becomes more ordered – in other words, how the soul progresses through the various stages in the spiritual life, from the beginning stages right up to the transforming union. He shows the role of infused contemplation in helping both to purify the soul and to bring it to the heights of perfection. St John of the Cross was faithful to the Thomistic training which he had received at Salamanca; he had a great respect for

---

[200] St Thomas Aquinas, *Super Ioan.*, cap. 14, lec. 7, n. 1962: "Sed notandum, quod in nobis tria ordinari debent: scilicet intellectus, voluntas et appetitus sensitivus: ut videlicet voluntas dirigatur secundum mentem, seu rationem; appetitus vero sensitivus secundum intellectum et voluntatem. Et ideo Augustinus in Lib. de verbis domini, pacem sanctorum definiens dicit: pax est serenitas mentis, tranquillitas animae, simplicitas cordis, amoris vinculum, consortium caritatis: ut serenitas mentis referatur ad rationem, quae debet esse libera, non ligata, nec absorpta aliqua inordinata affectione; tranquillitas animi referatur ad sensitivam, quae debet a molestatione passionum quiescere; simplicitas cordis referatur ad voluntatem, quae debet in Deum obiectum suum totaliter ferri: amoris vinculum referatur ad proximum; consortium caritatis ad Deum." St John of the Cross describing a person that has reached the transforming union explains how this soul is now filled with tranquillity and peace. The appetites have been quieted and the person has been cleansed from "all its imperfections," so far as it is "possible in this life" (*Spiritual Canticle*, stanza 20 and 21, 4, 489).

the works of St Thomas Aquinas, and he followed his theology with great care, especially his teaching on sanctifying grace, actual grace, the infused theological and moral virtues, and the seven gifts of the Holy Spirit.[201] In fact, in *The Ascent of Mount Carmel*, St John of the Cross relies on St Thomas Aquinas' moral theology from the *Summa Theologiae*,[202] and in *The Dark Night*, a work which is also based on solid Thomistic principles, St John of the Cross describes infused contemplation as "a science of love, which…is an infused loving knowledge, that both illumines and enamors the soul, elevating it step by step unto God, its Creator."[203] The intensity of this infused contemplation continues to develop as a soul grows in the spiritual life until it reaches the way of the perfect.[204] Even when a person has reached this stage, there is

---

[201] Garrigou-Lagrange, *The Love of God and The Cross of Jesus*, 5-7.
[202] Aumann, "*Spiritual Theology in the Thomistic Tradition*," Angelicum 51 (1974): 585-586.
[203] St John of the Cross, *Dark Night*, bk II, ch. 18, 5, 372. St Teresa of Avila explains that when God begins to bless a soul with infused contemplation, and it is faithful to God, He continually blesses it until it reaches a high degree of sanctity (*Way of Perfection*, ch. 16, 9, 96- 97).
[204] Aumann, "Mystical Experience, the Infused Virtues and the Gifts," 33-34. Aumann notes that John Baptist Scaramelli, seems to have had the most influence in promoting the erroneous teaching that the mystical state and infused contemplation are not the normal development of Christian life, but rather an "extraordinary grace, similar to a grace *gratis data*, and therefore it is not to be proposed as the goal of the Christian life" (Aumann, "Mystical Experience, the Infused Virtues and the Gifts," 33). Aumann explains that Scaramelli believed most Christians can only hope to reach an "ascetical perfection" and those who reach perfection through the mystical state are very few. Eventually the theory of Scaramelli's which indicated that there are two different

still room for growth, which means that infused contemplation can also go on increasing in intensity even in the stage of the perfect.

At various stages of the spiritual journey, one or more of the seven gifts of the Holy Spirit will predominate. The gift of knowledge predominates during the night of the senses; the gift of understanding predominates in the night of the spirit, and the gift of wisdom predominates between the two nights. When a person has reached the stage of the perfect, the gift of wisdom is highly operative.[205] Describing these three gifts, St Thomas explains that it is through the operation of the gift of knowledge that we are weaned from inordinate love for created things;[206] this is what happens during the night of the senses. Concerning the gift of understanding,[207] he says that our mind is purified; this happens particularly during the night of the spirit. Finally, it is through the operation of the gift of wisdom that we have a connatural knowledge of Divine things.[208] This helps us to advance in the spiritual life and to grow in

---

paths which lead to perfection became known as the two-way theory. Fr John G. Arintero and Fr Reginald Garrigou-Lagrange dedicated much time and effort in attempting to show by theological reasoning that the two-way theory is not tenable. Further, they demonstrated that infused contemplation and the mystical state are the normal consequence of a life lived out in charity and cooperation to God's grace. In other words, infused contemplation and the mystical life are the normal development of our baptismal grace (33-34).

[205] Garrigou-Lagrange, *Christian Perfection and Contemplation*, 327.
[206] *ST* II-II, q. 9, a. 4.
[207] *ST* II-II, q. 8, a. 7.
[208] *ST* II-II, q. 45, a. 2.

charity. It is primarily wisdom's influence on the theological virtue of charity, and subsequently all of the virtues, which helps the soul to reach the stage of the perfect, and as indicated above, in the state of the perfect the gift of wisdom is highly operative.

Wisdom is in all who have Sanctifying Grace, though it is Present in Different Degrees

According to St Thomas, all those who possess sanctifying grace have the gift of wisdom and are able to direct their affairs according to Divine rules through this gift. Therefore, everyone who remains in a state of sanctifying grace will possess this gift and will have a sufficient measure of wisdom to reach salvation. St Thomas says that nature never fails in what is necessary; therefore, "much less does grace fail."[209] Some will receive the gift of wisdom so that they not only direct their own affairs, but they are also able to impart to others knowledge of the Divine mysteries and to direct others "according to Divine rules."[210] St Thomas says that this latter "degree of wisdom is not common to all that have sanctifying grace, but belongs rather to the gratuitous graces, which the Holy Ghost dispenses as He will."[211]

St Thomas points out that in 1 Corinthians, wisdom is called the "utterance of wisdom" and not just

---

[209] *ST* II-II, q. 45, a. 5.
[210] *ST* II-II, q. 45, a. 5.
[211] *ST* II-II, q. 45, a. 5.

"wisdom;" this is in order to show that what St Paul is referring to is a charism, as distinct from wisdom which is one of the seven gifts of the Holy Spirit.[212] Charisms, or gratuitous graces, are given in order to help lead others to God, for the building up of the body of Christ.[213] Hence the utterance (or word) of wisdom is counted among the graces *gratis data* and is

---

[212] St Thomas Aquinas, *Super I Ep. ad Cor.*, cap. 12, lec. 2, n. 727: "Est tamen notandum quod sapientia et scientia inter septem dona Spiritus Sancti computantur, sicut habetur Is. XI, 2. Unde Apostolus signanter inter gratias gratis datas non ponit sapientiam et scientiam, sed sermonem sapientiae et scientiae, quae pertinent ad hoc ut homo aliis persuadere valeat per sermonem, ea quae sunt sapientiae et scientiae." Here, St Thomas explains that the utterance of wisdom is given so that a person can persuade others in things that pertain to the "knowledge of divine things" and another person will be given the utterance of knowledge so that they "might manifest things of God through creatures." In the *Summa Theologiae*, St Thomas explains that knowledge is also one of the seven gifts of the Holy Spirit and considered as a gratuitous grace. St Thomas says "Wisdom and knowledge can be considered in one way as gratuitous graces, in so far ... as man so far abounds in the knowledge of things Divine and human, that he is able both to instruct the believer and confound the unbeliever. It is in this sense that the Apostle speaks, in this passage, about wisdom and knowledge: hence he mentions pointedly the word of wisdom and the word of knowledge. They may be taken in another way for the gifts of the Holy Ghost: and thus wisdom and knowledge are nothing else but perfections of the human mind, rendering it amenable to the promptings of the Holy Ghost in the knowledge of things Divine and human. Consequently it is clear that these gifts are in all who are possessed of charity" (*ST* I-II, q. 68, a. 5, ad 1).
[213] *ST* I-II, q. 111, a. 1. *Gratia gratis data* means *graces freely given* often referred to as *gratuitous graces*, or *charismatic graces*.

"directed to the profit of others."[214]

Wisdom which is one of the seven gifts of the Holy Spirit is given to all who are in a state of grace. *Sermo Sapientias*, the charism of wisdom, which is a grace *gratis data* can be given not only to the person who is in a state of grace but may also be given to those who are without sanctifying grace. When it is given to a person who is in a state of grace, then it is joined to the gift of wisdom; however when it is given to those who are not in a state of grace, it is separated from the gift.[215] St Thomas says that it is not possible that wisdom as a gift (wisdom as numbered among one of the seven gifts of the Holy Spirit) can be possessed without charity. On the other hand, wisdom as it pertains to one of the charismatic gifts can be received without charity.[216]

Juan Arintero, in his work *Stages in Prayer*, explains that when the charism of wisdom and the gift of wisdom are joined together, it can happen that a person has such a superabundance of the gift of wisdom, that what is actually happening is not due to

---

[214] *ST* II-II, q. 177, a. 1, ad 4. According to St Thomas, wisdom is numbered as a gratuitous grace when there is such an abundance of wisdom that a person can "instruct others and overpower adversaries" (*ST* I-II, q. 111, a. 4, ad 4).

[215] Ramirez, *De Donis Spiritus Sancti deque Vita Mystica*, 337, 338.

[216] St Thomas Aquinas, *Super I Ep. ad Cor.*, cap. 13, lec. 1, n. 767: "Est autem notandum quod apostolus hic loquitur de sapientia et scientia, secundum quod pertinent ad dona gratiae gratis datae, quae sine caritate esse possunt. Nam secundum quod computantur inter septem dona spiritus sancti, numquam sine caritate habentur. Unde et Sap. I, 4 dicitur: *in malevolam animam non intrabit sapientia.*"

"a grace properly to be called *gratis data*."[217] This is because the *gift* of wisdom is so abundant that there is an overflowing of this gift which then redounds "to the great profit of one's neighbours."[218] St Thomas explains:

> Some, however, receive a higher degree of the gift of wisdom, both as to the contemplation of Divine things (by both knowing more exalted mysteries and being able to impart this knowledge to others) and as to the direction of human affairs according to Divine rules (by being able to direct not only themselves but also others according to those rules).[219]

When a person has a high degree of wisdom it is first and foremost for the sanctification of that person's own soul. However, because the person so abounds in this wisdom to the point that he or she can also instruct others, it can be referred to as a gratuitous grace, since it is also for the benefit of others. In other words, a person contemplates the lofty mysteries of God through this high degree of wisdom, and then this wisdom overflows to benefit one's neighbours in order that they can be helped and guided according to Divine rules. Hence, this wisdom participates "somewhat in the condition of the *gratis data*."[220]

---

[217] Ven. Juan G. Arintero, OP, *Stages in Prayer*, translated by Kathleen Pond (London: Blackfriars, 1957), 78.

[218] Arintero, *Stages in Prayer*, 78.

[219] *ST* II-II, q. 45, a. 5.

[220] Ven. Arintero, *Stages in Prayer*, 78-79: "If these favours are, in addition, ordained to the good of other souls, this also can be the work, not of a grace properly to be called *gratis data*, but one of the

The gift of wisdom operates at different levels in each person's life, and it becomes more operative as a person advances in the spiritual life. Therefore, when someone has reached a very high degree of perfection, the goodness of the gift of wisdom will often overflow for the spiritual benefit of others.[221] When this happens, a person has reached a very high degree of sanctity. That person tastes the goodness of the Lord in abundance and is then able to direct others because of the abundance of wisdom he or she has received. One tastes the goodness of God to such an extent that one can communicate to others the wisdom one has received through the operation of this gift.[222]

The Seventh Beatitude Corresponds to the Gift of Wisdom

There are eight beatitudes as laid down by Our Lord in the Gospel of St Mathew.[223] Of the seventh

---

gifts of the Holy Spirit, always primarily ordained to the soul's own sanctification and which, in an eminent degree, redound to the great profit of one's neighbour ... Although in this they participate somewhat in the condition of the graces *gratis data*, yet it is always to the great profit of their own soul, true complement as it is of their own virtue and sanctity, that there is communicated to it in this way a very special light."

[221] Brennan, *The Seven Horns of the Lamb*, 83.
[222] Arintero, *Stages in Prayer*, 78-79.
[223] Mathew 5:9. St Thomas says that the "eighth beatitude is a confirmation and declaration of all those that precede. Because from the very fact that a man is confirmed in poverty of spirit, meekness, and the rest, it follows that no persecution will induce him to renounce them. Hence the eighth beatitude corresponds, in a way, to all the preceding seven" (*ST* I-II, q. 69, a. 3 ad 5).

beatitude – "Blessed are the peacemakers, for they shall be called sons of God," (Mt 5:9) – St Thomas, following St Augustine writes: "The seventh beatitude is fittingly ascribed to the gift of wisdom."[224] God, Who is so good, has given us the blessing of the beatitudes which Jesus preached.[225] The rewards that are contained in the beatitudes refer to two stages: the beginning of perfect happiness in this life, which can be found in a person who has reached perfection, and the fullness of perfection which can only be found in the next life.[226] The rewards of the beatitudes will be "fully consummated in the life to come: but meanwhile they are, in a manner, begun, even in this life."[227] Through the operation of the gift of wisdom, the soul begins to experience a wonderful peace, even in this life, a peace which can also be experienced in the midst of suffering. St Thomas says: "The worldly, who are not united to God by love, have troubles without peace; while the saints, who have God in their hearts by love, have peace in Christ even if they have troubles from the world."[228]

The beatitudes are not habits like the virtues and the gifts. Rather, they are acts which come forth from

---

[224] *ST* II-II, q. 45, a. 6.
[225] Martinez, *Sanctifier*, 261-262.
[226] *ST* I-II, q. 69, a. 2.
[227] *ST* I-II, q. 69, a. 2, ad 3.
[228] St Thomas Aquinas, *Super Ioan.*, cap. 16, lec. 8, n. 2174: "Et inde est quod homines mundani, qui Deo per amorem non sunt coniuncti, habent tribulationes absque pace; sed sancti qui Deum per amorem habent in corde, etsi ex mundo habeant tribulationes, in Christo habent pacem."

habits;[229] they "have the virtues and the gifts as their origin."[230] Whereas the fruits of the Spirit (Gal 5) are acts which proceed from the infused virtues, the beatitudes can be "distinguished from the fruits in that they are even better acts."[231] So, an act proceeding from a virtue perfected by a gift is called a beatitude, which is nothing other than an act according to a perfect virtue.[232] Hence, St Thomas assigns the beatitudes to the seven gifts of the Holy Spirit instead of the virtues – due to their perfection.[233] The beatitude *"blessed are the peacemakers for they shall be called sons of God"* corresponds to wisdom's action on the theological virtue of charity.[234] In other words, the beatitude of the peacemakers is attributed to the gift of wisdom rather than solely to the virtue of charity.

St Thomas says that "the seventh beatitude is fittingly ascribed to the gift of wisdom, both as to the merit and as to the reward. The merit is denoted in the

---

[229] *ST* I-II, q. 69, a. 1.

[230] Torrell, *Saint Thomas Aquinas*, vol. 2, *Spiritual Master*, 217.

[231] Torrell, *Saint Thomas Aquinas*, vol. 2, *Spiritual Master*, 217.

[232] St Thomas Aquinas, *Super Is.*, cap. 11: "Operatio autem procedens a virtute perfecta dono dicitur beatitudo; quae nihil aliud est quam operatio secundum virtutem perfectam." Also, in his commentary of St Matthew, St Thomas says: "Ergo ista merita vel sunt actus donorum, vel actus virtutum secundum quod perficiuntur a donis," (*Super Matt.*, cap. 5, lec. 2, n. 410).

[233] *ST* I-II, q. 70, a. 2: "More is required for a beatitude than for a fruit. Because it is sufficient for a fruit to be something ultimate and delightful; whereas for a beatitude, it must be something perfect and excellent. Hence all the beatitudes may be called fruits, but not vice versa. For the fruits are any virtuous deeds in which one delights: whereas the beatitudes are none but perfect works, and which, by reason of their perfection, are assigned to the gifts rather than to the virtues."

[234] Brennan, *The Seven Horns of the Lamb*, 85.

words, "Blessed are the peacemakers." For a peacemaker is someone who "makes peace", either in himself/herself or "in others."[235] St Thomas explains that "peace is nothing else than the tranquillity arising from order, for things are said to have peace when their order remains undisturbed."[236] He says that wisdom is something which "sets things in order;" and therefore wisdom gives peace, peace which is nothing else than "tranquillity of order."[237] Therefore the beatitude of the peacemakers fittingly corresponds to the gift of wisdom, "blessed are the peacemakers," and their reward, "they shall be called children of God."[238]

---

[235] *ST* II-II, q. 45, a. 6.
[236] St Thomas Aquinas, *Super Ioan.*, cap. 14, lec. 7, n. 1962: "Sciendum est, quod pax nihil aliud est quam tranquillitas ordinis: tunc enim aliqua dicuntur pacem habere quando eorum ordo inturbatus manet."
[237] *ST* II-II, q. 45, a. 6.
[238] *ST* II-II, q. 45, a. 6. Augustine explains: *'Blessed are the peacemakers, for they shall be called the children of God.'* Where there is no contention, there is perfect peace. And, because nothing can contend against God, the children of God are peacemakers; for of course, children ought to have a likeness to their father. And those who calm their passions and subject them to reason, that is, subject them to mind and spirit, and who keep their carnal lusts under control-those engender peace within themselves and become a kingdom of God. [They become a kingdom] in which all things are so well ordered that everything in man which is common to us and to the beasts is spontaneously governed by that which is chief and pre-eminent in man, namely, mind and reason; and that this same pre-eminent faculty of man is itself subject to a still higher power, which is Truth Itself, the only begotten Son of God. Man is unable to rule over the lower things unless he in turn submits to the rule of a higher being. And this peace which is promised 'on earth to men of good will.' This is the life of a man of consummate

The perfect type of peace which can be attained in this life is not reached in an instant; rather, it is a peace which grows as one advances in the spiritual life. The gift of wisdom helps us to do this; in other words, the gift of wisdom helps us to grow in holiness. As explained above, it belongs to the gift of wisdom "not only to contemplate Divine things, but also to regulate human acts."[239] James 3:17 states:

> Wisdom, that is from above, first indeed is chaste, then peaceable, modest, easy to be persuaded, consenting to the good, full of mercy and good fruits, judging without dissimulation.

St Thomas interprets this Scripture passage saying that wisdom, which is the gift of the Holy Spirit, is first of all chaste because it avoids sin, and is then peaceable for peace is the ultimate effect of the gift of wisdom. He goes on to explain that the following order contained in this Scripture passage is the "means whereby wisdom leads to peace."[240] The first

---

and perfect wisdom." St Augustine, *Commentary on the Lord's Sermon on the Mount*, translated by Denis J. Kavanagh, OSA (Washington D.C.: The Catholic University of America Press in association with Consortium Books, 1951), bk I, ch. 2, 9, 23-24. O'Connor says, "Augustine's most important text, at least from the point of view of its historical influence ... [is the] commentary on the Sermon on the Mount, composed while he was still a very young priest ... he ingeniously correlated the seven *operationes* of the Holy Spirit with the Beatitudes. To do this he first has to reduce the Beatitudes to seven, by treating the eighth (which partly reiterates the first) as merely a confirmation of the others" ("The Gifts of the Holy Spirit," appendix 2 to *Summa Theologiae*, vol. 24, 90-91).

[239] *ST* II-II, q. 45, a. 6, ad 3.
[240] *ST* II-II, q. 45, a. 6, ad 3.

thing we must do in order to avoid the "corruption of sin… [is] to be moderate in all things," hence wisdom is first "said to be modest."[241] When there are matters in which we need the advice and guidance of others, advice is sought, and hence, wisdom is said to be easily persuaded. These first two conditions, modesty and persuadable counsel, are the conditions that are needed in order for us to be at peace within ourselves. However, in order for us to be at peace, not just within ourselves but also with others, we must consent to the good of the other. We ought to be full of mercy, compassion, and a willingness to act. Thirdly, we must "strive in all charity to correct the sins of others… [hence] judging without dissimulation."[242] Therefore in referring to the seventh beatitude we can say, "Blessed is the man that findeth wisdom,"[243] because in finding this wisdom it follows that a person finds peace.

"Wisdom is becoming to the peacemakers, in whom there is no movement of rebellion, but only obedience

---

[241] *ST* II-II, q. 45, a. 6, ad 3: "Now the first thing, to be effected in this direction of human acts is the removal of evils opposed to wisdom: wherefore fear is said to be the beginning of wisdom, because it makes us shun evil, while the last thing is like an end, whereby all things are reduced to their right order; and it is this that constitutes peace. Hence James said with reason that 'the wisdom that is from above' (and this is the gift of the Holy Ghost) 'first indeed is chaste,' because it avoids the corruption of sin, and 'then peaceable,' wherein lies the ultimate effect of wisdom."

[242] *ST* II-II, q. 45, a. 6, ad 3.

[243] *ST* I-II, q. 69, a. 3, ad 4. St Thomas says "when we read, Blessed is the man that findeth wisdom, this must be referred to the reward of the seventh beatitude. The same applies to all others that can be adduced" (*ST* I-II, q. 69, a. 3, ad 4).

to reason."[244] When we have true interior peace our faculties are stilled; we also have "peace with God" and we are "entirely conformed to his direction."[245] The holier we become, the less we are disturbed by unruly movements of the passions. Only God can "deliver the heart from all disturbance; [therefore] it is necessary that it come from Him."[246] Hence, the peace that is a result of the operation of the gift of wisdom is very different from the peace of the world. Worldly peace is "imperfect since it is not concerned with the interior tranquillity of a person but only with externals."[247] On the other hand, the saintly person has

---

[244] *ST* II-II, q. 45, a. 6. In his *Commentary on the Gospel of John*, St Thomas says: "Accordingly, Augustine, in his *The Words of our Lord*, describes the peace of the saints by saying: 'Peace is a calmness of mind, a tranquillity of soul, a simplicity of heart, a bond of love and a fellowship of charity.' Calmness of mind refers to our reason, which should be free, not tied down, nor absorbed by disordered affections; tranquillity of soul refers to our sense appetency, which should not be harassed by our emotional states; simplicity of heart refers to our will, which should be entirely set toward God, its object; the bond of love refers to our neighbor; and the fellowship of charity to God. The saints have this peace now, and will have it in the future. But here it is imperfect because we cannot have an undisturbed peace either with ourselves, or with God, or with our neighbor. We will enjoy it perfectly in the future, when we reign without an enemy and there can never be conflicts" (*Super Ioan.*, cap. 14, lec. 7, n. 1962).

[245] St Thomas Aquinas, *Super Ioan.*, cap. 14, lec. 7, n. 1962: "Quaedam intrinseca secundum quam pacificatur sibi ipsi, absque perturbatione virium."

[246] St Thomas Aquinas, *Super Ep. ad Phil.*, cap 4, lec. 1, n. 159: "Quia vero cor nostrum ab omni perturbatione non potest esse alienum nisi per Deum, oportet quod per ipsum fiat."

[247] St Thomas Aquinas, *Super Ioan.*, cap. 14, lec. 7, n. 1964: "Tertio quantum ad perfectionem: quia pax mundi est imperfecta, cum sit tantum quantum ad quietem exterioris hominis et non interioris."

"well-ordered affections of the soul."[248]

As a result of the gift of wisdom's influence on charity, a person continues to grow in peace; as St Thomas says, "charity, according to its very nature, causes peace. For love is a unitive force and peace is the union of the appetite's inclinations."[249] When a person has the peace which only God can give, truly it can be said, "Blessed are the peacemakers." They are peacemakers of their own movements, they approach to the likeness of God, and they are called "the children of God."[250] They are "promised the glory of the Divine sonship, consisting in perfect union with God through consummate wisdom."[251]

Of all the seven gifts of the Holy Spirit, it is by way of the operation of the gift of wisdom that we are most conformed to Christ. St Thomas explains that people

> are called the children of God in so far as they participate in the likeness of the only-begotten and natural Son of God, according to Romans 8:29, "Whom He foreknew . . . to be made conformable to the image of His Son," Who is Wisdom Begotten. Hence by participating in the gift of wisdom, man attains to the sonship of God.[252]

"To be like God by being adoptive 'children of God,' corresponds to the gift of wisdom."[253] Through the

---

[248] *ST* I-II, q. 69, a. 2, ad 3.
[249] *ST* II-II, q. 29, a. 3, ad 3.
[250] *ST* I-II, q. 69, a. 2, ad 3.
[251] *ST* I-II, q. 69, a. 4.
[252] *ST* II-II, q. 45, a. 6.
[253] *ST* I-II, q. 69, a. 3, ad 1.

operation of the gift of wisdom we are most conformed to Christ, and for this reason, St Thomas says that "the seventh beatitude is fittingly ascribed to the gift of wisdom, both as to the merit and as to the reward."[254] God is their reward, for He has said, "Blessed are the peacemakers for they shall be called the children of God."[255]

> [Those] who possess the gift of wisdom in its perfection are the peaceful ones; they are the children of God. They have the perfect adoption, the perfect filiation, because wisdom has engraved on their souls the most perfect image that one can have on earth, the image of the Son of God.[256]

The Effects of the Gift of Wisdom

With the gift of wisdom having been examined in detail, the effects that accompany this gift can now be explained. This will in turn facilitate identifying the gift of wisdom in the life of St Thérèse of Lisieux, in order that the gift of wisdom may be understood, not only as described by St Thomas, but also in the practical circumstances of the life of a Saint and Doctor of the Church.

---

[254] *ST* II-II, q. 45, a. 6.
[255] Gardeil, *The Gifts of the Holy Ghost*, 109.
[256] Martinez, *Sanctifier*, 216.

Connaturality with Divine Things

Wisdom is "not merely speculative but affective knowledge, that is knowledge which leads to love."[257] In other words it is an "affective and savorous knowledge ... [a] knowledge that is joined to love and *sapor*."[258] The operation of the gift of wisdom brings a spiritual taste of Divine things; it is a connatural knowing, which can be described as an intimate kind of experience.[259] This experiential knowledge is based on an inspiration of the Holy Spirit and a connatural spiritual taste of Divine things which flows from charity, and happens by way of the operation of the gift of wisdom. It is a quasi-experiential knowledge by which the soul has a "simple and loving knowledge of God and His works, which is the fruit not of human activity aided by grace but a special inspiration of the Holy Ghost."[260] This connatural knowing, which is an effect of the operation of the gift of wisdom, gives us a spiritual taste of Divine things. It is through the gift of wisdom that we *taste and see that the Lord is sweet* (Ps 33:9). After having tasted the sweetness and goodness of the Lord, nothing can compare.[261] This is the gift which makes saints "live the mysteries of faith in an entirely divine manner."[262]

---

[257] Dedek, "Quasi Experimentalis Cognitio," 380.
[258] Dedek, "Quasi Experimentalis Cognitio," 383.
[259] Ven. Arintero, *The Mystical Phenomena*, 25.
[260] Garrigou-Lagrange, *Three Ages of the Interior Life*, vol. II, 310.
[261] Tanquerey, *Spiritual Life*, 630.
[262] Royo & Aumann, *Theology of Christian Perfection*, 423.

The Gift of Wisdom Judges and Orders All Things According to Divine Rules

As a result of the operation of this gift, a person is able to judge and order all things with accuracy.[263] Furthermore, as St John Paul II once stated: this "sapiential awareness ... gives us a special ability to judge human things according to God's standard, and in God's light."[264] The gift of wisdom gives a "Divine sense" by which we judge all things; the saints who possess a very high degree of the gift of wisdom see all things from "God's point of view."[265] In all events of life, both big and small, they see God's hand. For example, if they are insulted, they immediately realize that God either wants or permits this event so that they can grow in virtue. In fact, as a result of growth in wisdom there are some who remain unconcerned when they are insulted or injured. St Thomas says that to "be unconcerned when one is injured is sometimes due to the fact that one has no taste for worldly things, but only for heavenly things. Hence this belongs not to worldly but to Divine wisdom."[266] A person who

---

[263] Ven. Arintero, *The Mystical Phenomena*, 25.
[264] St John Paul II, "Regina Coeli," 2, Pentecost, 9 April 1989.
[265] Royo & Aumann, *Theology of Christian Perfection*, 422. Garrigou-Lagrange points out that "every good thing comes from Him, and evil occurs only when it is permitted in view of a greater good. The gift of wisdom thus reveals the admirable order of the providential plan" (*Christian Perfection and Contemplation*, 333-334).
[266] *ST* II-II, q. 46, a. 1, ad 4. St Thomas points out that there are some people who remain unconcerned when injured by others, but this is because they have not discerned what can injure them, and that this is due to folly (*ST* II-II, q. 46, a. 1, ad 4). He says, on the other

judges according to Divine rules does not consider worldly things as attractive; this person sees very clearly that the only true treasure is God Himself. Of course, this does mean that we cannot appreciate the beautiful things of creation; rather, in appreciating created things, we understand that they are not ends in themselves.[267]

The Gift of Wisdom Gives the Soul Certitude

When the gift of wisdom is operating, a soul judges everything with the greatest of certitude.[268] St Thomas states that through the operation of the gift of wisdom "one may even have in himself a certitude about great and wonderful things which are unknown to others."[269] Through this gift, we judge of Divine things with a certitude which is higher than one can have through the theological virtue of faith.[270] Hence,

---

hand "a person who loves God patiently endures any adversity for love of Him" (*Super I Ep. ad Cor.*, cap. 13, lec. 2, n. 772).
[267] Royo & Aumann, *Theology of Christian Perfection*, 422. Garrigou-Lagrange explains how the gift of wisdom "illuminates the whole interior of the spiritual edifice and makes us see all things as coming from God, supreme Cause and last End, from His love or at least by His permission for a greater good which we shall someday see and which from time to time becomes visible here on earth" (*Three Ages of the Interior Life*, vol. II, 74).
[268] John of St Thomas, *Gifts of the Holy Ghost*, 125-126. Cf. *In Sent.*, III, d. 35, q. 2, a. 1.
[269] St Thomas Aquinas, *In Sent.*, III, d. 35, q. 2, a. 1, qc. 1.
[270] John of St Thomas, *Gifts of the Holy Ghost*, 129.

through the gift of wisdom, we receive a "certitude which fills the soul with ineffable consolation."[271]

Through the Effect of the Gift of Wisdom, a Person can Reach a Heroic Degree of Charity

The theological virtue of charity is an infinite treasure which leads us to contemplation:

> Introduced by charity into the intimacy of the divine Persons and the very heart of the Trinity, the divinised soul, under the impulse of the Spirit of love, contemplates all things from this center.[272]

Through this simple contemplation which proceeds from the gift of wisdom, we experience a profound love for God and neighbour. The effect of the gift of wisdom can be so strong that we think constantly of God and how we can serve Him better. Through this precious gift, charity continues to grow and can lead us to the heights of union with God.

As a result of the operation of the gift of wisdom, charity is perfected; and as a consequence, all the other virtues become more perfect. This gift helps us reach tremendous heights in the spiritual life. Often, when a soul has been led to the heights of holiness, it does not quite understand how this could have happened; nevertheless, there is a strong awareness that it could not have attained this degree of virtue by its own efforts. There is a clear sense that this degree of

---

[271] Garrigou-Lagrange, *Theology of Christian Perfection and Contemplation*, 307.
[272] Royo and Aumann, *Theology of Christian Perfection*, 423.

perfection is a gift from the Lord and not something that has been acquired.[273]

There is no limit to the increase in charity that we can have in this life.[274] The spiritual life is never static, but always dynamic; and increase in charity is without limit precisely because it is from God, Who Himself is Infinite Love, Mercy, and Goodness. When the gift of wisdom is operating, love is not limited to (or restricted by) the rule of reason; and therefore, charity can grow in leaps and bounds in a soul that remains open to the Holy Spirit. As a result of the operation of the gift of wisdom, charity is refined, purified, and perfected; this gift helps charity to grow and gives love an extra divine push along the road to sanctity.

By purifying and refining our love, the gift of wisdom can raise us to a heroic degree of charity. One of the effects of this gift is that it helps us to become totally selfless. The soul that has reached these heights loves God without any self-interest or human motive; its love has become so pure that it loves the Lord solely for His infinite goodness. Love for one's neighbour has also reached sublime heights because of the gift of wisdom. Through this gift, a person always sees God in his or her neighbour and loves the neighbour with a tenderness that is supernatural. In fact, one of the effects of this gift is that we see Christ in everyone – in those who suffer, in the poor, in all

---

[273] St Teresa of Avila, *Life*, ch. 17, 3, 153.
[274] *ST* II-II q. 24, a. 7. According to St Thomas, to grow in charity is not just a matter of counsel, but it "falls under the first precept as the end to which all must tend, each one according to his condition" (*ST* II-II, q. 184, a. 3).

our brothers and sisters – and we run with love to help them.[275]

The Gift of Wisdom Gives the Soul a Desire to Suffer in Conformity to Christ; It Makes the Bitter Sweet and the Labour Rest

St Thomas says that when the gift of wisdom directs a person to acts, there is no "bitterness or toil...on the contrary the result of wisdom is to make the bitter sweet, and labor rest."[276] Wisdom's effect on charity gives a person a tremendous love of God and neighbour, and also a deep love of the Cross.[277] One of the powerful effects of the gift of wisdom is that it makes the soul understand that suffering is truly a treasure; it can even give the soul a great desire for suffering.[278] Wisdom's effect on charity helps one to understand why St Augustine says that "love makes all hard and repulsive tasks easy and next to nothing,"[279] and why St John of the Cross says that when a person has reached a high degree of perfection, everything that is suffered is suffered "with the delight of love."[280] When charity has reached a high degree of perfection, the soul can perform works of charity with great ease and delight; the soul

---

[275] Royo & Aumann, *Theology of Christian Perfection*, 424-425.
[276] *ST* II-II, q. 45, a. 3, ad 3.
[277] Cf. Garrigou-Lagrange, *Three Ages of the Interior Life*, vol. II, 467-468.
[278] Martinez, *Sanctifier*, 193.
[279] St Augustine, *De Verbis Domini*, Sermone 70, as quoted in *ST* I-II, q. 114, a. 4, ad 2.
[280] St John of the Cross, *Spiritual Canticle*, stanza 28, 8, 522.

that has a great love for God can do all things for Him, even the most difficult. It sees that even the torments and sufferings of the martyrs were not as difficult as they might appear because with so much help from the Lord, suffering is made much lighter and is easier to bear.

The gift of wisdom can also give us a burning desire "for the salvation of souls, a thirst for souls, which recalls Christ's words on the Cross: 'I thirst.'"[281] Those with a high degree of charity are often willing to suffer any trial which God allows, in order that souls may be saved. The gift of wisdom gives a profound understanding of the immense value of suffering. Whether the soul suffers for its own purification or for the Mystical Body of Christ, it is able to bear all sufferings by offering them to Christ out of love. Through the operation of the gift of wisdom, the soul not only bears these trials; the sufferings can become for the soul something sweet. When a person firmly decides to carry his or her cross and to endure all trials and sufferings for God, that person "will discover in all of them great relief and sweetness."[282] In fact, someone who has reached a high degree of sanctity may even, as St Teresa of Avila says, "complain to His Majesty when no opportunity for suffering presents itself."[283]

---

[281] Martinez, *Sanctifier*, 468-469.
[282] St John of the Cross, *Ascent of Mount Carmel*, bk. II, ch. 7, 7, 123.
[283] St Teresa of Avila, *Interior Castle*, VI Mansions, ch. 4, 15, 384.

Peace

As explained above, according to St Thomas, peace is the ultimate effect of the gift of wisdom.[284] One of the signs of the beatitude of the peacemakers is that a person is at peace even in extremely difficult moments, and can also bring peace to others, even those who are greatly troubled.[285] Through the operation of the gift of wisdom, a person is given to consider and judge the causes of all the troubles and strifes of life, and can help others to have "order, tranquillity, and peace."[286] Through a high degree of the operation of the gift of wisdom, souls understand that peace comes not as a result of all the difficulties of life being taken away. Rather, peace can be found in the midst of the difficult circumstances of life; it is a peace which only God can give. Through the operation of the gift of wisdom, souls can be constantly at peace amongst all the ups and downs of life. They have a very pure love of God, and they are nearly always thinking of Him.[287] As a result of the operation of the gift of wisdom, we can know the goodness of God,

---

[284] *ST* II-II, q. 45, a. 6.

[285] Garrigou-Lagrange, *Three Ages of the Interior Life*, vol. II, 469. Garrigou explains that one of the signs of the unitive life is that we can see the effects of the gift of wisdom, in that a person remains at peace in very difficult circumstances and is also able to bring peace and encouragement to those who are otherwise discouraged. They are able to do this because they are able to see everything from "God's point of view" (*Three Ages of the Interior Life*, vol. II, 232- 233).

[286] Gardeil, *The Gifts of the Holy Ghost in the Dominican Saints*, 108-109: Peace can only be obtained when one is able to "see the detail in the whole."

[287] Garrigou-Lagrange, *Three Conversions of the Spiritual Life*, 94-95.

have profound peace, judge of Divine things, and know the mercy of God, the power of God, and the wisdom of God: "how Good is his goodness, how powerful his power, how wise his wisdom."[288]

Through the Gift of Wisdom, Man Attains to the Sonship of God and is Conformed to His Image

As explained above, the reward of the beatitude which corresponds to the gift of wisdom is "they shall be called children of God." Through the gift of wisdom, we are made "conformable to the image of (God's Son) Who is Wisdom Begotten."[289] Through the operation of the gift of wisdom, we taste the sweetness and goodness of the Lord, and this in turn gives us the desire to conform ourselves more and more to the Beloved.[290] At the moment of Baptism, we become adopted sons and daughters of the Father. Jesus, the natural Son of God, gives us a share in the "likeness of sonship by adoption."[291] As we advance in the spiritual life as a result of the operation of the gift of wisdom, we "take on the likeness of the only begotten Word of the Father."[292] We become more and more conformed to the image of Christ as we grow in His likeness. In other words, this precious gift "produces

---

[288] Heath, "Gift of Wisdom" appendix 4 to *Summa Theologiae*, vol. 35, 201.
[289] *ST* II-II, q. 45, a. 6.
[290] Tanquerey, *Spiritual Life*, 630.
[291] *ST* III, q. 3, a. 8.
[292] Brennan, *The Seven Horns of the Lamb*, 86.

in us the most faithful resemblance to Jesus Christ."[293] People who have reached a high degree of perfection possess the seven gifts of the Holy Spirit "most perfectly; but, in a singular manner, they possess the gift of wisdom."[294] We can witness a person's high degree of charity when we see that they are totally conformed to the will of Christ, even during the greatest of trials.[295] When "wisdom has reached its perfect development in the soul, then the soul has the image of Jesus, it has the reflection of infinite Wisdom."[296] It has received the "full communication of the Spirit of adoption,...[and] sees that it is now deified with God."[297] This soul's exclusive desire is to be conformed to the Beloved, Whose only desire is to do the will of His Father. Thus, the adopted sonship, which was received in the moment of Baptism, reaches its full potential through the operation of the gift of wisdom; we become totally conformed to Christ.

---

[293] Martinez, *Sanctifier*, 191.

[294] Martinez, *Sanctifier*, 191.

[295] Garrigou-Lagrange, *Three Ages of the Interior Life*, vol. II, 468.

[296] Martinez, *Sanctifier*, 191-192.

[297] Ven. Juan Arintero, OP, *The Mystical Evolution in the Development and Vitality of the Church*, vol. II, translated by Jordan Aumann, OP (St Louis, MO: B. Herder Book Co., 1951) 204. St Thomas says that God deifies the soul by "bestowing a partaking of the Divine Nature by a participated likeness" (*ST* I-II, q. 112, a. 1).

Experience of the Indwelling of the Trinity

In his tract on the Trinity, in question 43 of the *Summa Theologiae* (I), concerning the Indwelling of the Most Holy Trinity, St Thomas describes an "experimental knowledge" which "is properly called wisdom."[298] In other words, it is a knowledge which is experiential because this knowledge is accompanied by a kind of spiritual taste.[299] It is a connatural knowing by which the Holy Trinity "occasionally makes itself felt in us especially by the gift of wisdom."[300] The gift of wisdom is the "principle of a quasi-experiential knowledge of the presence of God in us."[301] It has been testified by certain mystics and Saints that they experience, in the centre of their souls, the presence of the Most Holy Trinity; this experience of many mystics verifies the lofty heavenly teaching of mystical theology.[302] This experience is the summit of the spiritual life, which has been reached through an increase of grace in one's soul, the theological virtues, and the gifts of the Holy Spirit; it is truly the "mystical life", and a prelude to heavenly glory. [303]

---

[298] *ST* I, q. 43, a. 5 ad 2. Here St Thomas is quoting St Augustine (*De Trinitate* iv, 20).
[299] Dedek, "Quasi Experimentalis Cognitio," 380.
[300] Garrigou-Lagrange, *Christian Perfection and Contemplation*, 126.
[301] Garrigou-Lagrange, *Three Ages of the Interior Life,* vol. II, 332-333.
[302] Royo & Aumann, *Theology of Christian Perfection*, 51.
[303] Garrigou-Lagrange, *Three Ages of the Interior Life,* vol. II, 467-468.

The Gift of Wisdom – A Truly Ineffable Gift

The mysteries of God are so numerous that no matter how much the Saints and Doctors of the Church have uncovered or discovered over the years, there is no end to the mysteries that are yet to be understood. Christ has many treasures and no matter how much we learn, we will never know or understand everything; there are always more riches to be discovered. "On this account St. Paul said of Christ: *In Christ dwell hidden all treasures and wisdom.* (Col. 2:3)."[304] *Lumen Gentium* encourages the laity to ask God for an increase in this gift: "Let the laity ... earnestly beg of God the gift of wisdom."[305] Through this gift, we can come to know God in a much deeper way than we could ever know Him by our own efforts. Who would not desire such a beautiful gift? The gift of wisdom is truly a gift for which we should all pray; it is one of God's most precious treasures.

---

[304] St John of the Cross, *Spiritual Canticle*, stanza 37, 4, 551.
[305] *Lumen Gentium*, IV, 35.

3

THE CHILDHOOD YEARS AND THE LIFE OF ST THÉRÈSE

In order to recognize clearly the effects of the gift of wisdom in the life of St Thérèse, it is important to have a picture of her whole life. By presenting the stages of her early life, the development of her life in Christ and her growth in holiness can be better appreciated. Thérèse understood that everything is grace. This primacy of grace is manifested most beautifully throughout her life, even starting from a very early age.

"The Lord nurtured and taught her; he guarded her as the apple of his eye. As the eagle spreads its wings to carry its young, he bore her on his shoulders."[1] Marie Françoise Thérèse Martin was born on the 2 January 1873 to Louis Martin and Zélie Martin.[2] Louis and Zélie had prayed that the Lord would bless them with many children and that the Lord would take these children for Himself. The Lord answered their prayers and Zélie gave birth to nine children, four of whom God took to Himself at an early age and the

---

[1] Antiphon for Canticle 1 (Dt. 32:3-7, 10-12), Feast of St Thérèse of the Child Jesus, Virgin, October 1, *Carmelite Proper of the Liturgy of the Hours* (Rome: Institutum Carmelitanum, 1993), 404.

[2] St Thérèse of Lisieux, *Story of a Soul*, 3rd ed., translated from the Original Manuscripts by John Clarke, OCD (Washington, D.C.: ICS Publications, 1996), 7.

remaining five, all girls, Jesus took as His Spouse.³ Thérèse was the youngest of all the girls. The two oldest sisters, Pauline and Marie, were the first to enter Carmel; the third daughter, Leonie, went to the Visitation convent and despite the fact that Thérèse was the youngest of the Martin sisters she entered Carmel before her older sister Céline.⁴

Thérèse's parents, Louis and Zélie Martin, whom Thérèse described as being "more worthy of heaven than of earth,"⁵ had both desired to enter religious life;⁶ however, God had different plans for them, and Louis Martin and Zélie Guérin married. Zélie was determined to serve God in some way and hoped that she could do this by having many children. Zélie's prayers were eventually answered; however, this took some time because on the night of her wedding, Louis Martin announced to Zélie that he intended that they

---

³ St Thérèse of Lisieux, *General Correspondence,* vol. II, translated from the original manuscripts by John Clarke, OCD, (Washington D.C.: ICS Publications, 1988), LT 261, 1165. Henceforth cited as *GC* II. Thérèse had two brothers and two sisters who died before she was born. Peter T. Rohrbach, "Thérèse de Lisieux, St," *New Catholic Encyclopedia,* second edition, vol. 13 (Washington D.C.: Thomson, Gale, in association with The Catholic University of America, 2003), 938.
⁴ *GC* II, LT 261, 1165. Céline was four years older than Thérèse.
⁵ *GC* II, LT 261, 1165.
⁶ Vita Sackville-West, *The Eagle and the Dove* (London: Michael Joseph Ltd, 1943), 101: In September 1843 at the age of twenty Louis presented himself at a Cistercian monastery. However, he was not accepted because his credentials were very few, and more was needed in order to be a Cistercian monk. However, he was told if he went away and studied hard, then he would be accepted. Zélie was an extremely religious woman and she desired to enter the Order of St. Vincent de Paul. However, she was told by the Superior that it was "not God's will."

live as brother and sister. Zélie was submissive to his wishes and for some months they lived together as brother and sister, and both worked each day – Louis as a jeweller and watch maker, and Zélie as a lace-maker.[7] Eventually, Zélie and Louis Martin had children; they knew that each child was a gift from God, a gift that He had given for some time to form in faith and virtue.[8] Louis and Zélie were very devout and gave the five girls – Pauline, Leonie, Marie, Céline and Thérèse – the love, nurturing, and Christian environment that enabled them to grow in their love for God and neighbour from a very early age.

Thérèse's Character

Thérèse was quite a little character; she was very stubborn and strong willed, and this was apparent from a very young age. A confessor once told Thérèse that with her character she could be either a saint or a devil. Thanks to the grace of God and Thérèse's cooperation, she became a great Saint. One of Zélie's letters shows that Thérèse must have struggled to overcome all of her natural imperfections. Zélie writes in a letter to Pauline:

> My little Céline is drawn to the practice of virtue; it's part of her nature; she is candid and has a horror of evil. As for the little imp, one doesn't

---

[7] Vita Sackville-West, *The Eagle and the Dove*, 101-102.
[8] Mary Ann Budnik, "Heroic Parents – Models for Our Times," in Franciscan Friars of the Immaculate, *Saint Thérèse: Doctor of the Little Way* (New Bedford, MA: The Academy of the Immaculate, 1997), 38.

know how things will go, she is so small, so thoughtless! Her intelligence is superior to Céline's, but she's less gentle and has a stubborn streak in her that is almost invincible; when she says *"no"* nothing can make her give in, and one could put her in the cellar a whole day and she'd sleep there rather than say "yes". But she still has a heart of gold; she is very lovable and frank.[9]

In another letter to Pauline from Mme Martin (Zélie) one can also see the stubborn and strong will of Thérèse the Saint to be:

> Céline is playing blocks with the little one, and they argue every once in a while. Céline gives in to gain a pearl for her crown. I am obliged to correct this poor little baby who gets into frightful tantrums; when things don't go just right and according to her way of thinking, she rolls on the floor in desperation like one without any hope. There are times when it gets too much for her and she literally chokes. She's a nervous little child, but she is very good, very intelligent, and remembers everything.[10]

Even though Thérèse had a very strong stubborn streak, she liked to confess to her parents (from a very young age) whenever she had done something wrong. Trusting in her loving mother and father, she believed that she would be pardoned, and like a child who runs to her heavenly Father for absolution, Thérèse runs to her parents to seek forgiveness. Writing about Thérèse, Zélie Martin says:

---

[9] Ms A 7r, 22.
[10] Ms A 8r, 23; see also GC II, extracts, 5 December 1875, 1219.

> She is a child who becomes easily overexcited. As soon as she had done some wrong, everybody must know it. Yesterday, without willing to do so, she knocked off a little corner of wallpaper, and she was in a state to be pitied, and her father must be told very quickly. He came home four hours later, we were no longer thinking of it, but she went quickly to Marie to say: "Tell Papa quickly that I tore the paper." She is there like a criminal awaiting condemnation, but she has in her little mind that we will pardon her more easily if she accuses herself.[11]

The environment in which Thérèse grew up was full of love and compassion and Thérèse never hesitated to seek it out. Again, realising she had done something wrong Thérèse ran to her mother to make her confession. Zélie says:

> Her little face was bathed in tears: "Mamma," she said, throwing herself at my knees, "Mamma, I was naughty, pardon me!" Pardon was quickly granted. I took my cherub in my arms, pressing her to my heart and covering her with kisses.[12]

Zélie also describes an event where Thérèse runs after her "making her confession: "Mamma, I pushed Céline once, I hit her once, but I won't do it again." She says, "It's like this for everything she does."[13]

Thérèse had to overcome many weaknesses; even by the young age of four, before her mother died, she said that virtue was charming to her, and that she had

---

[11] *GC* II, extracts, 21 May 1876, 1224-1225.
[12] *GC* II, extracts, 13 February 1877, 1231.
[13] Ms A 7r, 22.

a firm control over her actions.[14] In one of the testimonies given for the Beatification of St Thérèse, Geneviève of St Teresa, OCD, (Céline Martin) said:

> A temperament such as hers, had it not been restrained, could have exposed her to eternal damnation, as she said herself, but her love of what was right, together with extraordinary will-power, sufficed to preserve her from evil. Even at that tender age, I saw her practise acts of heroic virtue. She knew how to master herself perfectly, and had already acquired absolute control over all her actions.[15]

Thérèse was already thinking of heaven at this young age. Zélie Martin writes in a letter to Pauline, "[S]he was telling me this morning that she wanted to go to heaven and that, for this, she was going to be a nice little angel."[16] In another letter to Pauline, Zélie writes:

> Little Thérèse asked me the other day if she would go to heaven? I told her "yes" if she were very good; She answered: "Yes, but if I were not good, I would go to hell… but I know what I would do. I would fly to you who would be in heaven. What would God do to take me? You would hold me tightly in your arms." I saw in her eyes that she

---

[14] Ms A 11r-11v, 29.
[15] Christopher O'Mahony, *St Thérèse of Lisieux by those who knew her* (Dublin, Ireland: Veritas Publications, 1975), 111.
[16] *GC* II, extracts, 12 March 1876, 1222.

positively believed that God could do nothing to her if she were in the arms of her mother.[17]

In later years Thérèse would also have this kind of confidence in her heavenly Mother, the Blessed Mother. Thérèse had a great love of prayer; she loved to go to the Holy Sacrifice of the Mass and to Vespers.[18] Describing how Thérèse never wanted to miss prayer, Zélie writes:

> When I went to bed, she told me she had not said her prayers. I answered: "Sleep you will say them tomorrow." Yes, but she did not give up her ideas. To end it, her father made her say them. But he did not know how to say all she was accustomed to reciting, and, then, he had "to ask the grace of …" He did not understand what she meant by this. Finally, he said something quite close to it in order to satisfy her, and she fell asleep until the next morning.[19]

Sickness and Struggles in Her Early Years

Thérèse suffered from various illnesses and many struggles throughout her short life. She had to be separated from her mother at a very early age because she was very sick and would not take any milk; she therefore had to live with a wet nurse for one year. If Zélie Martin had not taken Thérèse to this wet nurse Thérèse would not have survived. At first there did

---

[17] GC II, extracts, 29 October 1876, 1226.
[18] GC II, extracts, 14 March 1875, 1213.
[19] GC II, extracts, 7 November 1875, 1218.

not seem to be any hope for Thérèse because they could not get her to take milk from the wet nurse. Zélie however, who had already lost four children, hurried to the statue of St Joseph and threw herself at his feet imploring him to cure Thérèse. When Zélie went back downstairs she was delighted to see that Thérèse was wholeheartedly taking milk from the wet nurse. She explains that after Thérèse had drunk the milk she

> threw up a few mouthfuls and fell back on the wet-nurse as though she were dead. We were five around her, all were struck, there was a worker who was weeping, and I felt my blood turn to ice. The little one was apparently not breathing; we bent over her in vain trying to find some signs of life and we saw none. However, she was so calm, so peaceful, that I thanked God for having had her die so easily. Finally, after fifteen minutes passed by, my little Thérèse opened her eyes and began to smile. From that moment on she was totally cured; her healthy appearance returned and her gaiety as well. Since then all goes better.[20]

For the first four years of Thérèse's life she had lived in Alençon; now she was entering a new period of her life and she was to move to Lisieux – the place where she would spend the rest of her life and eventually enter Carmel. This move was due to the fact that Zélie Martin died – she died of breast cancer at a very young age, leaving behind five young girls. Thérèse was only four and a half years old at the time and this event changed her whole life. St Thérèse describes her life

---

[20] *GC* II, extracts, 16 March 1873, 1203-1204.

in terms of three periods – and it is this event, the death of her mother, which launches her into the second period. Even though Thérèse received so much love from the whole family, the period after Zélie Martin's death was extremely difficult for her. This second period of Thérèse's life she describes as "the most painful of the three."[21] This period lasted from the young age of four and a half up to the age of fourteen. When her mother died Thérèse went from being a child with a very happy disposition, and someone who was very lively, to a child that was timid and excessively sensitive. She could very easily burst into tears and did not want to be around anyone except within the familiarity and intimacy of her own family.[22] It was after the death of Zélie that the family moved to Lisieux, where Thérèse was sent to a Benedictine school. She was a good student, bright and retentive; however she was very shy and sensitive, and therefore found her school life somewhat unpleasant.[23] Nevertheless, God was with Thérèse through each step of her young life, forming and instructing His *Little flower* so that she would eventually reach the heights of sanctity. Thérèse said:

> Ah! If God had not showered His beneficent *rays* upon his little flower, she could never have accustomed herself to earth, for she was too weak to stand up against the rains and the storms. She needed warmth, a gentle dew, and the springtime

---

[21] Ms A 13r, 34.
[22] Ms A 13r, 34-35.
[23] Peter T. Rohrbach, *New Catholic Encyclopedia*, 938.

breezes. Never were these lacking. Jesus had her find them beneath the snow of trial![24]

God had a new little mother for Thérèse after she had lost Zélie – this was one of her older sisters, Pauline. Thérèse had a great love for all her sisters, but Pauline was particularly special to her.[25] Pauline loved Thérèse very much; she was always tender and compassionate with her; she helped her in her spiritual life and helped her in all her struggles.[26] It was to Pauline that Thérèse would confide everything, and it was Pauline who would clear up all of Thérèse's doubts.[27] Thérèse often heard people say that Pauline would one day become a religious, and so at the age of two, without really knowing much about what this meant, she said, *"I too will be a religious."* This was one of Thérèse's first childhood memories and from then on, she did not change her resolution.[28] It was not only Pauline who showered Thérèse with so much love when she was young; the whole family loved Thérèse with a special tenderness. Louis Martin loved Thérèse; they had a very special love for each other. Louis used to call Thérèse his "little queen," and Thérèse called her father her "dear King."[29]

Soon Thérèse was to lose her second mother, Pauline, who had decided to enter the Carmel of Lisieux. It was another very painful experience for

---

[24] Ms A 13r-13v, 35.
[25] Ms A 6r, 20.
[26] Ms A 19r, 44.
[27] Ms A 19r, 44.
[28] Ms A 6r, 20.
[29] Ms A 14v, 37.

Thérèse and caused her a lot of heartache. Pauline tried to console Thérèse with as much tender love and care as she could. She explained the life of a Carmelite to Thérèse at this time, and the life seemed very beautiful to her. As Thérèse thought about everything Pauline had told her about Carmel she felt very strongly that this was the *"desert* where God wanted [her] to go and hide."[30] She said, "I felt this with so much force that there wasn't the least doubt in my heart; it was not the dream of a child led astray but the *certitude* of a divine call; I wanted to go to Carmel not for *Pauline's sake* but for *Jesus alone."*[31] Pauline entered Carmel on 2 October 1882 – this was a day of many tears, but also a day of many blessings.[32]

Not long after Pauline entered Carmel, Thérèse suffered from a strange sickness. She began to have constant headaches until finally one night, around Easter time, she began to shake uncontrollably and had to take to her bed. This strange illness lasted a number of months. The doctor said that her illness was serious and one which he had never seen attack such a young person.[33] Thérèse describes this incident saying, "I appeared to be almost always delirious, saying things that had no meaning. And still I am *sure* that I *was not deprived of the use of my reason for one single instant."*[34] A miracle was needed to cure little Thérèse who continued to show no signs of improvement. Finally on Pentecost Sunday, during a Novena of

---

[30] Ms A 26r, 58.
[31] Ms A 26r, 58.
[32] Ms A 26v, 59.
[33] Ms A 27v, 60-61.
[34] Ms A 28v, 62.

Masses which Therese's father had requested to be offered at Our Lady of Victories in Paris, Thérèse was completely cured. Marie, Céline and Leonie had knelt to pray in front of a statue of the Blessed Mother and Thérèse had also prayed to the Blessed Mother and asked with all her heart that she would have "pity on her."[35] Thérèse says:

> All of a sudden the Blessed Virgin appeared *beautiful* to me, so *beautiful* that never had I seen anything so attractive; her face was suffused with an ineffable benevolence and tenderness, but what penetrated to the very depths of my soul was the *"ravishing smile of the Blessed Virgin."* At that instant all my pain disappeared.[36]

After Pauline had entered Carmel Thérèse turned to one of her other sisters, Marie. However, soon Thérèse was to have yet another separation – her "dear Marie, the only support of [her] soul," was now also leaving the family home.[37] Marie also had plans to go to Carmel and now Thérèse was to be separated not only from her dear Pauline, but also Marie. She says, "As soon as I learned of Marie's determination, I resolved to take no pleasure out of earth's attractions."[38] On 15 October 1886, Marie entered Carmel and now there were only three members of the family left at the Martin home – Thérèse, Céline, and their father Louis.[39]

At this stage of Thérèse's life she was still extremely

---

[35] Ms A 30r, 65.
[36] Ms A 30r, 65-66.
[37] Ms A 41r, 88.
[38] Ms A 42v, 90.
[39] Ms A 43v, 92.

sensitive – she became upset very easily. Thérèse says:

> I was really unbearable because of my extreme touchiness if I happened to cause anyone I loved some little trouble, even unwittingly, instead of forgetting about it and not crying, which made matters worse, I cried like a Magdalene and then when I began to cheer up, I'd begin to cry again for having cried... I really don't know how I could entertain the thought of entering Carmel when I was still in the swaddling clothes of a child![40]

However, it would not be too long until Thérèse would be the next girl to fly away from the nest of the Martin household and enter Carmel. Thérèse said that God was going to have to perform a "little miracle."[41] This miracle happened after midnight Mass, Christmas 1886 – Thérèse says:

> On that night when He made Himself subject to weakness and suffering for love of me, He made me strong and courageous, arming me with His weapons. Since that night I have never been defeated in any combat, but rather walked from victory to victory, beginning, so to speak, "to run as a giant"! The source of my tears was dried up and has since re-opened rarely and with great difficulty.[42]

Thérèse called this the grace of her "complete conversion."[43] It was on this night that the "third period" of Thérèse's life began. This third period, she said,

---

[40] Ms A 44v, 97.
[41] Ms A 44v, 97.
[42] Ms A 44v-45r, 97.
[43] Ms A 45r, 98.

was the "most beautiful and most filled with graces from heaven."[44] Thérèse had been changed. "Jesus had changed her heart! ... Thérèse had discovered once again the strength of soul which she had lost at the age of four and a half, and she was to preserve it forever!"[45] In an instant Jesus did what Thérèse was not able to do in ten years.[46] She says:

> The night of Christmas 1886, was, it is true, decisive for my vocation, but to name it more clearly I must call it: the night of my conversion. On that blessed night, about which it is written that it sheds light even on the delights of God Himself, Jesus, who saw fit to make himself a child out of love for me, saw fit to have me come forth from the swaddling clothes and imperfections of childhood. He transformed me in such a way that I no longer recognised myself. Without this change I would have had to remain for years in the world. Saint Teresa, who said to her daughters: "I want you to be women in nothing, but that in everything you may equal strong men," would not have wanted to acknowledge me as her child if the Lord had not clothed me in His divine strength, if He had not Himself armed me for war.[47]

Pauline and Marie, Thérèse's two older sisters, were both in the Carmelite convent which Thérèse was going to enter. Thérèse felt that Jesus was inspiring her to enter the same Carmelite convent, and she

---

[44] Ms A 45v, 98.
[45] Ms A 45r, 98.
[46] Ms A 45v, 98.
[47] GC II, LT 201, 1016-1017.

could not "resist the grace" He was giving her.[48] She tried to enter Carmel at the age of fourteen. The sisters of the convent were willing to accept Thérèse at this tender age of fourteen; however, the ecclesiastical superior of the Carmel convent did not approve and felt that it would be best if Thérèse waited until she was twenty-one to enter. Of course, Thérèse was not at all happy with this reply and so she went to visit the bishop to ask for permission to enter Carmel early. Whilst the bishop was considering her request, Thérèse, along with her father and her sister Céline, went on pilgrimage to the eternal city, Rome. There, they went to a general audience with the Pope. Despite the fact that it was not permitted to speak to the Pope during a general audience, when it was Thérèse's turn to kneel before the Pope – (at this time each pilgrim was allowed to kneel before the Pope and get his blessing) – she asked if she could enter Carmel at the young age of fifteen. The Pope at this time was Pope Leo XIII, and he assured Thérèse that "she would enter if it were God's will."[49]

Entrance into Carmel

At the age of fifteen, after many struggles, Thérèse was the next one of the Martin girls to fly away to Carmel. It was on 9 April 1888 that she finally entered.

---

[48] St Thérèse of Lisieux, *General Correspondence,* vol. I, translated from the original manuscripts by John Clarke, O.C.D, (Washington D.C.: ICS Publications, 1982) LT 38A, 380. Henceforth cited as *GC* I.
[49] Peter T. Rohrbach, *New Catholic Encyclopedia,* 938.

She said – when the doors of Carmel closed behind her and her desires were finally accomplished – "My soul experienced a PEACE so sweet, so deep, it would be impossible to express it. For seven years and a half that inner peace has remained my lot, and has not abandoned me in the midst of the greatest trials."[50]

Thérèse's father had now brought three of his children to Carmel. Thérèse says: "It was with a heroic courage that my father, like a new Abraham, climbed *three times* the mountain of Carmel to immolate to God what was most dear to him.[51] When the time came for Thérèse to take the habit, her father, who had previously suffered from a stroke, was able to be there. He escorted her into the chapel and as he had desired, she was dressed in "white velvet." [52]

---

[50] Ms A, 69r-69v, 148. This peace, even in the midst of the greatest of trials, is an effect of the operation of the gift of wisdom and is beautifully articulated in the seventh beatitude (as has been stated in the first part of this dissertation). This will be further unpacked in subsequent chapters.

[51] GC II, LT 261, 1165.

[52] Vita Sackville-West, *The Eagle and the Dove*, 125. In the years that St Thérèse was in the Carmelite convent the new novices were escorted into the chapel of the convent by a procession of nuns who chanted the *Magnificat*, wore white-habits, and held candles which were all alight. The new novice would kneel in front of the grille and a Cross was held in front of her; she would kiss the Cross and then listen to a priest speak to her from behind the grille. He would then emphasise the new life that she was now to embrace. This would include the renunciation of pleasures, a life of silence, privations, and working hard from then until she left this world. After this the novice would be led to a place where she was given a very short haircut and then given a brown tunic, sandals and a white veil. She was also given a black belt which symbolises servitude, a scapular which symbolises the yoke of Christ; and finally, she was given a white cloak which is a symbol of candour

Thérèse spent the next nine years of her life hidden in the Lisieux Carmel, until her death at the young age of twenty-four. In the last four years of her life, she was appointed as novice mistress.[53] She experienced many trials throughout her short time in Carmel; however, Jesus was always leading and guiding her, and peace always remained in the depth of her soul. As Thérèse grew in years she also grew in virtue, and God poured out His graces upon His *little flower* so that she blossomed into the Saint that He had destined her to be. One of Thérèse's older sisters, Céline, many years after the death of Thérèse, said:

> Our Thérèse had to reach a high level of perfection quickly; and she led us, me above all, her Céline, by the path she followed… God allowed her apparent strictness not to discourage me but to incite me to perfection. It was in his designs that my virtues and graces would be "slow" in coming. With Thérèse, the "bomb" of graces exploded on the spot![54]

When Thérèse became sick because she had contracted tuberculosis, she still continued her observances at the convent up to a year after the first signs of her illness.[55] Then in the month of June 1897, she was finally moved into the infirmary. Here she completed her autobiography, and it was here she died on 30 September. Her autobiography was then published and very quickly became one of the most

---

and purity of heart.

[53] Peter T. Rohrbach, *New Catholic Encyclopedia*, 939.

[54] Stephane-Joseph Piat OFM, *Céline*, translated by the Carmelite Sisters of the Eucharist of Colchester (San Francisco: Ignatius Press, 1997), 143.

[55] Peter T. Rohrbach, *New Catholic Encyclopedia*, 939.

widely read books of the time.⁵⁶ After Thérèse's death, a form of her autobiography was privately published and sent to some of the other convents of Carmel. Immediately, there was a great demand for further copies, and there was an official printing ordered.⁵⁷ Over the next fifteen years, there was a demand for *Story of a Soul* in many different countries; and so it was translated into many different languages, and over a million copies were printed.⁵⁸ Today, this most well-known work of St Thérèse continues to be read and "disseminated throughout the world." ⁵⁹

Before Thérèse died she had said "I'm a little seed; no one knows yet what will develop."⁶⁰ This seed certainly did develop; for only one century after her death Thérèse was given various titles in the Church and became known and loved in many countries. Pope Pius XI beatified Thérèse in 1923, then two years later in the year 1925 he proclaimed Thérèse a Saint, and in 1927 he made Thérèse co-patroness of missions along with St Francis Xavier.⁶¹ Interestingly Louis and Zélie Martin had earnestly prayed for a missionary son. God did not give them a missionary son; however, Thérèse as co-patroness of missions has guided

---

[56] Jordan Aumann, *Christian Spirituality in the Catholic Tradition*, 262.
[57] Peter T. Rohrbach, *New Catholic Encyclopedia*, 939.
[58] Peter T. Rohrbach, *New Catholic Encyclopedia*, 939.
[59] Benedict XVI, General Audience, St. Peter's Square, 6 April 2011, "St. Thérèse of Lisieux."
[60] St Thérèse of Lisieux, *Her Last Conversations*, translated from the original manuscripts by John Clarke, O.C.D. (Washington D.C.: ICS Publications, 1977), 103. Henceforth cited as LC.
[61] Franciscan Friars of the Immaculate, *St. Thérèse Doctor of the Little Way*, (New Bedford, MA: The Academy of the Immaculate, 1997), 157.

numerous sons and daughters in the mission field. She is co-patroness of missions and today she goes throughout the entire world helping missionaries and people everywhere.[62]

In the year 1944, Thérèse was declared by Pius XII – together with the heroic St Joan of Arc – co-patroness of France. Then on 16 October 1997, Pope John Paul II declared St Thérèse of Lisieux a Doctor of the Universal Church.

---

[62] St Thérèse believed that this prayer was fulfilled in a missionary that she was praying for, she says, "If, as I believe, my father and mother are in heaven, they must be looking at and blessing the brother whom Jesus has given me. They had so much wanted a missionary son! ... I have been told that before my birth my parents were hoping their prayer was finally going to be realized. Had they been able to pierce the veil of the future, they would have seen it was indeed through me their desire was fulfilled; since a missionary has become my brother, he is also their son, and in their prayers they cannot separate the brother from his unworthy sister" (GC II, LT 226, 1094).

4

THE GIFT OF WISDOM IN THE LIFE OF ST THÉRÈSE – ACCORDING TO CERTAIN EFFECTS OF THIS GIFT

Introduction

The remaining chapters of Part II will focus on the prominent effects of the operation of the gift of wisdom in the life of St Thérèse. The various divisions of this fourth chapter will be drawn from the list of the effects of the gift of wisdom expounded in Part I. The goal is not to give an exhaustive account, but to highlight some very definite manifestations of the gift of wisdom, and to show the clear correspondence between the teaching of St Thomas on the gift of wisdom and how this gift is operating in the life of St Thérèse. When reading Thérèse's works one cannot help but notice the depth of spiritual insight that is contained in her writing; in this chapter, it will be shown that this deep spiritual insight is a consequence of "the lights of the gift of wisdom."[1] It is evident that Thérèse's understanding of the spiritual life is a gift from God. *Story of a Soul*, her letters and poems, and

---

[1] Garrigou-Lagrange uses this expression – "the lights of the gift of wisdom" – to describe the insight received as a consequence of infused contemplation (*Three Ages of the Interior Life*, II, 324).

her other writings contain an abundance of evidence that clearly points to the quasi-experiential connatural knowledge which is a consequence of the operation of the gift of wisdom.

Connaturality with Divine Things

St Thomas says that through the operation of the gift of wisdom a person judges of Divine things "on account of connaturality with them."[2] This knowledge through connaturality is not easily expressed in human language.[3] However, Thérèse has a wonderful way of expressing what she is experiencing by way of this connatural knowing. She often experiences this type of connatural knowing through the operation of the gift of wisdom, in which she is given to *taste the goodness of the Lord*. François Jamart in his work *Complete Spiritual Doctrine of St Thérèse* gives an excellent description of how the gift of wisdom is operating in the life of St Thérèse. He points out that Thérèse often uses the expression *to feel* in order to explain that she has received some light during her times of prayer and also during times when she is going about her daily work. It is important to note that this term *to feel,* in the context that St Thérèse is using it, is not a "sensible impression"[4] or a "sen-

---

[2] *ST* II-II, q. 45, a. 2.
[3] Jacques Maritain, *The Range of Reason*, 23.
[4] François Jamart, *Complete Spiritual Doctrine of St. Thérèse of Lisieux*, translated by Walter Van de Putte (New York: St. Paul Publications, 1961), 244.

"timental savour,"[5] but rather, a "knowledge that springs from love."[6] It is not something experienced with the senses; rather it is analogous to sense, and something which Thérèse often experiences.[7] Jamart remarks that it seems this was Thérèse's "habitual way of knowing supernatural things."[8] Likewise, Arintero says that Thérèse was

> endowed with a profound feeling for the things of God and with an ability to penetrate the mysteries of the supernatural life ... So at every step we hear her saying "I feel, I see, I understand" or "I am given to understand that this ought to be like this or that God wishes such and such a thing of me."[9]

Both of these authors point out that Thérèse uses the expression *to feel* in order to describe a certain knowledge through love. These types of lights or feelings are the fruit of love; they are something "perceived by the way of the heart."[10] When a soul has given itself entirely to God, "the Holy Spirit makes

---

[5] Claude Sarrasin, "La contemplation de Sainte Thérèse de l'Enfant-Jésus," in *Thérèse au Milieu des Docteurs Colloque avec Thérèse de l'Enfant-Jésus:19-22 Septembre 1997 à Notre Dame de Vie*, 44. Claude Sarrasin, in his work "La contemplation de Sainte Thérèse de l'Enfant-Jésus," also says that the experience received through the gift of wisdom is not a sentimental savour: "Cette saveur n'est pas une saveur sentimentale" ("La contemplation de Sainte Thérèse de l'Enfant-Jésus,"44).
[6] Jamart, *Complete Spiritual Doctrine of St. Thérèse of Lisieux*, 244.
[7] Forward, from translator José L. Morales, in Juan G. Arintero, *The Mystical Phenomena. The Mystical Life of Saint Thérèse of the Child Jesus*, xiii.
[8] Jamart, *Spiritual Doctrine of St. Thérèse*, 244.
[9] Ven. Arintero, *Mystical Phenomena*, 35-36.
[10] Jamart, *Spiritual Doctrine of St. Thérèse*, 246.

Himself known and the soul relishes Him through the gift of wisdom."[11] Through the operation of this gift the soul receives a quasi-experiential knowledge of God. This way of knowing is precisely what St Thomas is describing when he explains that through the gift of wisdom one has a connatural knowing of Divine things. This experience is not something outside the ordinary path of the spiritual life, because it happens as a result of the operation of this gift. This connatural way of knowing and judging is Thérèse's common way of knowing things. The words *to feel* (or *I feel*) is the expression she always uses when trying to explain what she knows connaturally through the operation of the gift of wisdom.

All Christians receive the sevenfold gift of the Holy Spirit at Baptism, and these gifts are operative in the lives of all those who are in a state of grace. God often wants one of the gifts of the Holy Spirit to shine in a person's life in a particular way.[12] The gift of wisdom shone brightly in the life of St Thérèse, and "as though by *divine instinct*, she knew and felt and judged spiritual things with complete accuracy."[13] The following examples are selected texts from St Thérèse's writing where she uses the words *I feel* or *I felt*; these texts indicate that she knows things connaturally. This way of knowing is truly an infused science of love, brought about by the operation of the gift of wisdom.

Thérèse is constantly speaking of this kind of

---

[11] Jamart, *Spiritual Doctrine of St. Thérèse*, 246.

[12] Mary Ann Fatula, OP, *Thomas Aquinas, Preacher and Friend* (Collegeville, Minnesota: The Liturgical Press, 1993), 232.

[13] Ven. Arintero, *Mystical Phenomena*, 39.

knowing; she experiences this knowledge, which springs from love, from a very early age. She always *felt* that she was destined for great things – she says:

> When I was beginning to learn the history of France, the account of Joan of Arc's exploits delighted me; I *felt* in my heart the desire and the courage to imitate her. It seemed the Lord destined me, too, for great things. I was not mistaken, but instead of voices from heaven inviting me to combat, I heard in the depths of my soul a gentler and stronger voice, that of the Spouse of Virgins, who was calling me to other exploits, to more glorious conquests, and into Carmel's solitude. I understood my mission was not to have a mortal king crowned but to make the King of heaven loved, to submit to Him the kingdom of hearts.[14]

Here one can see that Thérèse begins with the expression *I felt*, and very quickly moves on to using language which explicitly indicates certitude about the knowledge Jesus has given her (in the depths of her soul) concerning His will for her life. This was not a prophetic knowledge – in other words the charism of prophecy – but rather a connatural knowledge and certitude which comes from the operation of the gift of wisdom. Thérèse describes how

> God made [her] *feel* that true glory is that which will last eternally, and to reach it, it isn't necessary to perform striking works but to hide oneself and

---

[14] *GC* II, LT 224, 1085 (emphasis added). Note: Unless otherwise indicated, all emphasis in the St Thérèse quotes remain as in the original text.

practice virtue in such a way that the left hand knows not what the right is doing.[15]

Thérèse says that God had inspired these sentiments and that she felt within her heart a "burning zeal," a "heavenly inspiration."[16] She describes one of the greatest graces which she received, and she has no doubt this knowledge is from God:

> I received a grace which I have always looked upon as one of the greatest in my life because ...I wasn't receiving the *lights* I'm now receiving when I am flooded with them. I considered that I was born for *glory* and when I searched out the means of attaining it... He made me understand my own *glory* would not be evident to the eyes of mortals, that it would consist in becoming a great *saint*![17]

Thérèse is often thought of as a Saint who was in darkness and aridity. She did indeed have times of great aridity; nevertheless, she also had times when she received great lights. Thérèse's own recognition of these lights bears witness to this fact: Comparing a previous period of her life, to the present, Thérèse' remarks, "I wasn't receiving the *lights* I'm now receiving when I am flooded with them."[18] The Lord guided her very clearly and spoke to her in the depth of her heart; she never spoke to anyone about her "interior sentiments." She says: "The way I was

---

[15] Ms A 31v-32r, 72 (emphasis added).
[16] Ms A 32r, 72.
[17] Ms A 32r, 72.
[18] Ms A 32r, 72.

walking was so straight, so clear, I needed no other guide but Jesus."[19]

Thérèse has periods when she already tastes the delights of heaven. In one of her poems, she speaks passionately about what she *feels* and *tastes*:

> My cheeks are coloured with his precious blood.
> Already I *feel* I am *tasting* the delights of Heaven,
> For I can gather both milk and honey
> From his sacred lips.[20]

Thérèse experiences connaturally the tenderness of Jesus' infinite love. She describes how she felt on the day of her First Communion: "Ah! how sweet was that first kiss of Jesus! It was a kiss of *love*; I *felt* that *I was loved*, and I said, 'I love You, and I give myself to You forever!'"[21]

It is evident that Thérèse often feels that the Lord communicates certain truths to her connaturally. This connatural type of knowing is accompanied by an unshakable certainty: "God shows me truth; *I feel* so much that everything comes from Him."[22] On one occasion when Thérèse feels God showing her these truths, she remarks, "Lord, I believe it, but above all *I feel* that Your words are the truth, for they bring *peace*,

---

[19] Ms A 48v, 104-105.
[20] St Thérèse of Lisieux, *The Poetry of Saint Thérèse of Lisieux*. Translated by Donald Kinney, OCD. Washington, D.C.: ICS Publications, 1996, 26, 8, 138 (emphasis added). Henceforth cited as PN.
[21] Ms A 35r, 77.
[22] *LC*, August 4th, 3, 132 (emphasis added).

[and] joy to my *little* heart."[23]

A person can be so united to God in love that he or she *tastes the sweetness of the Lord*. This experience is felt in the depths of the soul and often cannot be expressed; a person must "remain mute, must adore in silence, and not profane this gift with human language."[24] Writing to her sister Céline, Thérèse says:

> Céline, life is very mysterious; we know nothing ... we see nothing ... and yet Jesus has already revealed to our souls what the eye of man has not seen! ... Yes, our heart has a presentiment of what the heart would be unable to understand since at times we are without any thoughts to express something ineffable which we *feel* in our soul![25]

Jamart highlights Thérèse's words to Mother Agnes: "How very much I would tell you if I could find the words to express to you what I think, or what I don't think, but *feel*."[26] Thérèse even experiences things connaturally when she is in times of great trial. On one occasion when she is trying to point out how spiritually poor she is, she says to her Mother superior: "Ah! Mother, intuitions! If you only knew how spiritually poor I really am. I know nothing that you yourself don't know! I know only what I see and *feel*!"[27] Remarkably Thérèse also experiences charity

---

[23] *GC* II, LT 190, 961.
[24] Ven. Arintero, *The Mystical Evolution and Vitality of the Church*, vol. I, 257.
[25] *GC* II, LT 124, 713 (emphasis added). Cf. Jamart, *Spiritual Doctrine of St. Thérèse*, 244.
[26] Jamart, *Spiritual Doctrine of St. Thérèse*, 244.
[27] *LC*, Sept 24, 10, 199 (emphasis added). Cf. Jamart, *Spiritual Doctrine of St. Thérèse*, 244.

entering her soul and that Jesus is acting through her: "I felt *charity* enter into my soul, and the need to forget myself and to please others."[28] She understands and experiences that it is Jesus Who loves through her: "Yes, *I feel it,* when I am charitable, it is Jesus alone who is acting in me, and the more united I am to Him, the more also do I love my Sisters."[29] And in moments when Thérèse is not so inclined to perform acts of virtue, she nevertheless tries to perform small acts of charity. She says that she experiences Jesus keeping the fire of love burning in her heart. In a letter to Céline, Thérèse writes, "Jesus …throws on the fire a lot of wood. We do not see it, but we do *feel the strength of love's warmth*. I have experienced it."[30]

It is evident from Thérèse's own words that she has an acute awareness that Jesus is acting in and through her – that it is He who is acting in her when she loves. Thérèse has absolute confidence that all these experiences of the quasi-experiential science of love are from Jesus; she tastes the mysteries and truths of God with great clarity. This is due to a *knowledge of love*, a connaturality which she experiences by way of the operation of the gift of wisdom. Bl. Marie-Eugène of the Child Jesus remarks, "Knowledge of God was to constitute the foundation of the spirituality of St Thérèse. Everything would flow from it."[31]

---

[28] Ms A 45v, 99.
[29] Ms C 12v, 221 (emphasis added).
[30] *GC* II, LT 143, 801 (emphasis added).
[31] Bl. Marie-Eugène of the Child Jesus, *Under the Torrent of His Love*, 36.

Confidence and Certitude in God's Mercy

When the gift of wisdom is operating, a soul judges with the greatest of certitude.[32] St Thomas says that through the operation of the gift of wisdom "one may even have in himself a certitude about great and wonderful things which are unknown to others."[33] The connatural knowledge that is experienced through the operation of the gift of wisdom is accompanied with immense certitude. Even though it is experienced with the obscurity of faith, it still surpasses all "particular knowledge, and produces practical certitude."[34] This certitude fills the "soul with ineffable consolation,"[35] and can impart "experimental knowledge of the things of God that is so positive and so secure that these things are impressed on it with the evidence of a tangible fact."[36] When Thérèse experiences this connatural knowing she is filled with certitude and a bold confidence due to the operation of the gift of wisdom. She experiences this certitude particularly in regard to the attribute of God's mercy and she always knows deep within her soul that God is all powerful, loving, and merciful. She knows that God is waiting at each moment to shower us with His infinite love and mercy and that He wants us to trust in Him. Writing

---

[32] St Thomas Aquinas, *In Sent.*, III, d. 35, q. 2, a. 1. As quoted in John of St Thomas, *Gifts of the Holy Ghost,* 125-126.
[33] St Thomas Aquinas, *In Sent.*, III, d. 35, q. 2, a. 1, qc. 1.
[34] Jamart, *Spiritual Doctrine of St. Thérèse,* 246.
[35] Garrigou-Lagrange, *Christian Perfection and Contemplation,* 307.
[36] Ven. Arintero, *The Mystical Evolution and Vitality of the Church,* vol. I, 257.

to Sister Marie of the Sacred Heart, Thérèse explains what it is that pleases God: "*Ah! I really feel...* what pleases Him is that He sees me loving my littleness and my poverty, the blind hope that I have in His mercy."[37] She says:

> *I always feel...* the same bold confidence of becoming a great saint because I don't count on my merits since I have none, but I trust in Him who is virtue and Holiness. God alone, content with my weak efforts, will raise me to Himself and make me a saint, clothing me in His infinite merits.[38]

Thérèse wishes that she could explain what she is experiencing:

> I know that "he to whom less is forgiven, loves less", but I know that Jesus has forgiven me more than St. Mary Magdalene since He forgave me in advance by preventing me from falling. *Ah! I wish I could explain what I feel.*[39]

Thérèse understands that it is because of the abundant grace which God has given her that she has been prevented from falling into sin: "*Ah! I feel it!* Jesus knew I was too feeble to be exposed to temptation; perhaps I would have allowed myself to be burned entirely by the misleading light had I seen it shining in my eyes."[40] Again, in the following text, Thérèse uses the word *feel* in regard to the bold

---

[37] *GC* II, LT 197, 999 (emphasis added).
[38] Ms A 32r, 72 (emphasis added).
[39] Ms A 38v, 83 (emphasis added).
[40] Ms A 38v, 83 (emphasis added).

confidence she has in God's mercy. This confidence is not due to the fact that she has been preserved from serious sin, but because she is certain that God is all merciful. She says:

> Yes, *I feel it*; even though I had on my conscience all the sins that can be committed, I would go, my heart broken with sorrow, and throw myself into Jesus' arms, for I know how much He loves the prodigal child who returns to Him. It is not because God, in His anticipating Mercy, has preserved my soul from mortal sin that I go to Him with confidence and love.... [41]

Thérèse's confidence is such that she has absolutely no doubt that Jesus is all merciful, and she runs to Him with her arms wide open, trusting in His grace, love, and mercy. In a letter to Sister Marie of the Sacred Heart, Thérèse expresses this connatural knowing which is due to the operation of the gift of wisdom:

> Oh! how I would like to be able to make you understand what I *feel!* ... It is confidence and nothing but confidence that must lead us to Love ... Since we see the *way*, let us run together. Yes, I *feel* it, Jesus wills to give us the same graces, He wills to give us His heaven gratuitously.[42]

St Thérèse always maintains this confidence even when things are very difficult. On one occasion when

---

[41] Ms C 36v, 259 (emphasis added). Cf. Jamart, *Spiritual Doctrine of St. Thérèse*, 245.
[42] GC II, LT 197, 1000 (emphasis added). Cf. Jamart, *Spiritual Doctrine of St. Thérèse*, 245.

she is experiencing a great trial, she says to her sister, "Oh! Pauline, if you could have read my heart, you would have seen there a great confidence."[43] Thérèse is also certain that God will grant her desires because she *feels* He has placed these desires within her heart:

> I am certain then, that you will grant my desires: I *feel* it, O my God, the more you want to give, the more you make us desire. I *feel* within my heart immense desires and it is with confidence I ask you to come and take possession of my soul.[44]

St Thérèse does not hide this certitude which the gift of wisdom provides for her.[45] Her confidence and certitude are extremely apparent to others. Agnes of Jesus (Pauline) gives testimony to Thérèse's confidence in the process for her beatification: Thérèse's "loving confidence in Our Lord made her extraordinarily daring in the things she asked Him for. When she thought of His all-powerful love, she had no doubts about anything."[46] Needless to say, this confidence is the foundation of Thérèse's prayers: "Let us not grow tired of prayer; confidence works miracles."[47] She always knows that everything is a gift from God, that all things come to her from His grace

---

[43] *GC* I, LT 36, 353.
[44] St Thérèse of Lisieux, *The Prayers of Saint Thérèse*, translated by Aletheia Kane, OCD. (Washington, D.C.: ICS Publications, 1997) 6, 58 (emphasis added). Henceforth cited as *Prayers*.
[45] Sarrasin, "La contemplation de Sainte Thérèse de l'Enfant-Jésus,"44: "Et Thérèse n'a pas caché les certitudes que ce don de sagesse lui a fournies."
[46] Christopher O'Mahony, *St. Thérèse of Lisieux by those who knew her*, 46.
[47] *GC* II, LT 129, 729.

and from His Divine Hand. She knows that without God she can do nothing: "*I feel* sustained by the divine grace of my Loving King."[48] Thérèse is also sure that God wants to shower others with grace and mercy, that He is ready to shower all little souls that approach Him with a sincere heart and confidence. She exclaims, "Ah! If all weak and imperfect souls felt what the least of souls *feels*, that is, the soul of your little Thérèse, not one would despair of reaching the summit of the mount of love. Jesus does not demand great actions from us, only surrender and gratitude."[49]

One can see that Thérèse has a trust and confidence that is supernatural and certain. Her absolute confidence bears witness to the experiential mode by which she knows – this knowledge of love – this connatural knowing, which is due to the operation of the gift of wisdom. Thérèse is certain about the way that God has been leading her. This trust and confidence are not limited to a few areas of Thérèse's life; rather, it permeates every part of it. As her life unfolds, this becomes more and more evident. Enlightened by this quasi- experiential knowledge, this science of love which is an effect of the operation of the gift of wisdom, Thérèse continues to advance in her union with God. The Holy Spirit has filled her with this light and love from a very young age, and He will continue to give her this knowledge through love throughout her life, until her death – her martyrdom of love – at the age of twenty-four.[50]

---

[48] PN 26, 7, 138 (emphasis added).
[49] Ms B 1v, 188 (emphasis added).
[50] Jamart, *Spiritual Doctrine of St. Thérèse*, 246.

Infused Contemplation

St Thomas explains that it belongs to the *gift of wisdom* first of all to contemplate,[51] and that this contemplative wisdom, which is a gift of the Holy Spirit, is infused into the soul; it is a wisdom which is received.[52] Furthermore, he says that it is particular to the gift of wisdom that this gift "proceeds according to a deiform contemplation and sort of explanation of the articles which faith holds enveloped according to a human manner."[53]

The gift of wisdom plays a major role in our life of prayer. As we advance in the spiritual life, the Holy Spirit begins to do a lot of the work when we are at prayer. In other words, we begin to receive the prayer of infused contemplation; we are moved into a more passive (receptive) form of prayer. At this stage we also begin to experience a tremendous growth in all of the virtues and an increase in the operation of the gifts of the Holy Spirit.

When a person receives the gift of infused contemplation, it is not received with any kind of image; however, the soul understands and tastes this delicate wisdom. It can be likened to a soul that beholds a certain object that it has never seen before, nor has

---

[51] *ST* II-II, q. 45, a. 3, ad 3.
[52] *ST* II-II, q. 45, a. 5.
[53] St Thomas Aquinas, *In Sent.*, III, d. 35, q. 2, a. 1, ad 1, as quoted in John of St Thomas, *Gifts of the Holy Ghost,* 133. This text from St Thomas' Commentary on the Sentences can also be rendered as: The gift of wisdom "proceeds to a certain deiform contemplation, and to a contemplation in a certain way explicit of the articles which faith holds according to a human manner under a certain wrapped up mode."

it experienced anything that remotely resembles the object. St John of the Cross explains that it is difficult to find language to describe this simple wisdom which has not entered "through the senses,"[54] particularly when it has become "so simple" that a person is "hardly aware of it. All that they can manage to say is that they are satisfied, quiet, and content, and aware of God, and that in their opinion all goes well."[55] By means of this simple contemplation a soul passes from "radiance to brighter radiance until it images Christ."[56]

Thérèse's prayer, her simple gaze, is the prayer of infused contemplation which is the result of the operation of the gifts of the Holy Spirit. This contemplation gives her a connatural knowledge of God, the type of knowledge which St Thomas says is given to the soul as a consequence of being united to the Lord through charity.[57] It is a loving peaceful gaze upon the Lord, which St John of the Cross says "is nothing else than a secret and peaceful and loving inflow of God, which, if not hampered, fires the soul in the spirit of love."[58] It is a "science of love, which is an infused loving knowledge that both illumines and enamors the soul, elevating it step by step to God, its Creator."[59]

The first quote of the *Catechism of the Catholic Church* in the section on prayer is taken from the writing of St Thérèse. In this quote, Thérèse describes very simply

---

[54] St John of the Cross, *Dark Night*, bk II, 17, 3, 369.
[55] St John of the Cross, *Dark Night*, bk II, 17, 5, 369-370.
[56] Bl. Marie-Eugène, *Under the Torrent of His Love*, 121.
[57] *ST* II-II, q. 45, a. 2.
[58] St John of the Cross, *Dark Night*, bk I, ch. 10, 6, 318.
[59] St John of the Cross, *Dark Night*, bk II, ch. 18, 5, 372.

what prayer means: "prayer is a surge of the heart; it is a simple look turned toward heaven, it is a cry of recognition and of love, embracing both trial and joy."[60] However, there is more to Thérèse's description of prayer. In *Story of a Soul,* she states: "finally, it is something great, supernatural, which expands my soul and unites me to Jesus."[61] Thérèse's prayer is a loving prayer of the heart which can be identified with infused contemplation because it is a simple loving contemplative gaze. Marie-Eugène of the Child Jesus explains:

> Thérèse herself tells us that it is love that holds her gaze. It is certainly love which has brought her to this simplicity. It is remarkable to note that the gaze as she describes coincides completely with the definition of contemplation given by St Thomas and completed by his commentators at Salamanca: Simplex intuitus veritatis sub inflexu amoris: "A simple gaze upon the truth under the impulse of love."[62]

---

[60] CCC 2558. St Teresa of Avila also speaks very simply of the way to pray explaining that we do not have to make long reflections; all we have to do is look at the Lord (*Way of Perfection,* ch. 26, 3 134).

[61] Ms C 25r-25v, 242.

[62] Bl. Marie-Eugène, *Under the Torrent of His Love,* 127. Marie-Eugène explains: "This infused contemplation is fully supernatural. Its object is the divine Truth itself. It is realized by faith, an infused supernatural virtue; and it is perfected by direct intervention of God through the gifts of the Holy Spirit.

The supernatural organism of infused contemplation is brought into action by love: *sub influx amoris,* say the *Salmanticenses.* Love is essential to it. Love is at the beginning of the movement of faith towards divine Truth. It is through love that God intervenes to hold faith to its divine object; and it is through the

Marie-Eugène describes the contemplation of Thérèse as a "child's gaze" which is a "gaze of high contemplation."[63] Thérèse's prayer is the prayer of infused contemplation. There are many ways in which one can see clearly that Thérèse is receiving infused contemplation. We shall examine various texts which demonstrate this fact as we progress through this chapter. One of the reasons we know that a person is receiving infused contemplation is that they are no longer able to meditate. Thérèse is unable to fix her mind upon the meditations of the rosary, even though she loves the Blessed Mother very much and faithfully prays the rosary with her community: "the recitation of the rosary is more difficult for me than the wearing of an instrument of penance, I feel I have said this so poorly! I force myself in vain to meditate on the mysteries of the rosary; I don't succeed in fixing my mind on them."[64] Thérèse is also unable to meditate when she reads a book: "If I open a book composed by a spiritual author (even the beautiful, the most

---

gifts of the Holy Spirit, those 'capacities engendered in the soul by the love of charity,' that the divine interventions take place. Again, it is in a touch with the Divinity, a union of love, that the act of faith and the divine rapture of the soul terminate. Finally, it is from contact of love that contemplative knowledge proceeds" (*I Want to See God*, 464).

[63] Bl. Marie-Eugène, *Under the Torrent of His Love*, 128.

[64] Ms C 25v, 242. Thérèse loved the Blessed Mother and was concerned about having a *lack* of devotion: "For a long time I was desolated about this lack of devotion that astonished me, for *I love* the Blessed Virgin so much that it should be easy for me to recite in her honor prayers which are so pleasing to her. Now I am less desolate; I think that the Queen of heaven, since she is *my MOTHER*, must see my good will and she is satisfied with it" (Ms C 25v, 242-243).

touching book), I feel my heart contract immediately and I read without understanding, so to speak. Or if I do understand, my mind comes to a standstill without the capacity of meditating."[65]

As the Lord gives the soul this prayer of infused contemplation, the soul's experience of prayer becomes more and more passive and receptive. Hence, active meditation becomes virtually impossible.

Mystical State

The mystical state is constituted by "the predominance of the gifts and their effects."[66] If a person is sincerely following the gospel message and seeking God faithfully and diligently then "sooner or later through the operation of the gifts they will be living in the mystical state."[67] In the present work, whenever

---

[65] Ms A 83r, 179. Cf. Ida Friederike Görres, *The Hidden Face*, translated by Richard and Clara Winston (London: Burns and Oates, 1959), 251. St John of the Cross explains that when a person enters into the night of the senses that person is "no longer bound to discursive meditation ... The soul readily finds in its spirit, without the work of meditation, a very serene, loving contemplation and spiritual delight" (*Dark Night*, bk II, ch. 1, 1, 330).

[66] Ven. Arintero, *Mystical Evolution and Vitality of the Church*, vol. II, 425.

[67] Ven. Arintero, *Mystical Evolution and Vitality of the Church*, vol. II, 297. Garrigou explains that the soul who is faithful and generous to God "will come more and more under the immediate direction of the Holy Ghost ... a condition which characterizes the mystical life" (*Christian Perfection and Contemplation*, 350). He also states: "The mystical state in general must not be confounded with

the expression *mystical graces* is used, it means either the operation of one of the seven gifts of the Holy Spirit, the grace of infused contemplation, or any concomitant phenomena which may accompany infused contemplation. Hence, we are not referring to the works of the infused virtues, which are supernatural in essence, but nevertheless have a human mode of operation; nor are we referring to extraordinary graces (*gratis datae*), the charisms which St Paul enumerates in 1 Cor. 12.

In the prayer of infused contemplation, through the operation of the gifts, the Holy Spirit infuses His light and love into the soul in order to help us grow in the spiritual life.[68] A person must be united to God in faith and charity in order for infused contemplation to take place. This kind of prayer has many degrees, beginning with the initial stages of infused contemplation and increasing in intensity up to the stage of the transforming union, the highest stage in the spiritual life. St Thérèse never explicitly uses the words *infused contemplation* when she describes her life of prayer. And, unlike St Teresa of Avila and St John of the Cross, she does not speak explicitly about the various stages of the spiritual life. This, however, does not indicate that there is an absence of a high degree of infused contemplation

---

its consoling phases, or with its complete flowering; it often exists under the form of arid quiet" (*Three Ages of the Interior Life*, vol. II, 319).

[68] Garrigou-Lagrange, *Christian Perfection and Contemplation*, 243-244. Garrigou-Lagrange, insists that everyone "may legitimately desire infused contemplation." Infused contemplation helps the soul to grow in the virtues, love of neighbour, and love of God, and therefore it is not wrong to desire it. Indeed, it is of great benefit to the soul (*Three Ages of the Interior Life*, vol. II, 323).

in her life of prayer. In fact, Arintero asserts that Thérèse does not speak so much about contemplation or focus a lot on the graces she has received due to her humility, and also misunderstandings of the times in which she lived:

> If she never spoke of infused contemplation or of mystical graces, though she knew them so well through her own experience, such omission was perhaps quite deliberate and because of the misunderstanding of these terms by those who wrongly believe that it is an act of pride to aspire to such graces. The fact is that without these graces it is impossible to reach true humility, complete perfection and sanctity – to which we are all called...[69]

When Arintero refers to *mystical graces* in this quotation, he is speaking of the operation of the gifts of the Holy Spirit, infused contemplation, and any kind of concomitant phenomena which might accompany infused contemplation, such as divine touches or flights of the spirit. When one enters the mystical state, one is receiving infused contemplation and the seven gifts of the Holy Spirit are operating much more frequently than they do in the ascetical state.

It is clear that St Thérèse reached the full blossoming of the mystical state. We can see this from the evidence of her heroic virtues, which have been made perfect through the operation of the gifts of the

---

[69] Ven. Arintero, *Mystical Phenomena*, 50.

Holy Spirit.[70] "We see her wholly possessed by the Divine Spirit, instructed by the heavenly Master, moved and directed by a higher instinct which bears her in security, although sometimes in darkness."[71] Thérèse was not an "ascetic soul" as some consider her; rather her life was mystical, in the fullest possible sense.[72] All of Thérèse's acts "even those that seem the most ascetic, have a certain mystical hue."[73] God enriches Thérèse with His gifts and she receives numerous lights. She prefers these experiences of love, which deepen her relationship with God, to any type of revelation or extraordinary experience.[74] She is constantly receiving a connatural knowledge of

---

[70] Ven. Arintero, *Mystical Phenomena*, 38.

[71] Ven. Arintero, *Mystical Phenomena*, 33.

[72] Ven. Arintero, *Mystical Phenomena*, 33. Hans Urs Von Balthasar, in his book, *Thérèse of Lisieux* (New York: Sheed and Ward, 1954) "stated categorically that this saint never 'crossed the threshold into what is known as mystical phenomena.'" See James A. Wiseman, "Mysticism." In *The New Dictionary of Catholic Spirituality*, edited by Michael Downey (Collegeville, MN: The Liturgical Press,1993), 682. Thérèse did indeed, enter the mystical state and experienced mystical phenomena.

[73] Ven. Arintero, *Mystical Phenomena*, 33.

[74] Bl. Marie-Eugène, *Under the Torrent of His Love*, 140-141. Thérèse did experience some extraordinary phenomena in her short life; however, they were very few. She saw the smile of the Blessed Mother when she was very sick, and at "that instant, all [her] pain disappeared" (Ms A 30r, 65-66). She also had a vision, which she says happened at the age of six or seven. The vision was of a man who covered his face and which Thérèse believed to be her father. Later she discovered that the vision was indeed a vision of her father; she realised that it represented the illness her father would experience in later years (Ms A 20v, 46-47). On another occasion she had a dream in which Venerable Anne of Jesus, Foundress of Carmel in France, told Thérèse that she would soon go to heaven (Ms B 2r, 190-191).

Divine things through the operation of the gift of wisdom: "Instead of voices from heaven... I heard in the depths of my soul a gentler and stronger voice."[75] Thérèse was always receiving God's gifts of grace, and even though these mystical graces would not have attracted attention, they are greatly sanctifying to the soul. These ordinary graces can be received by each baptized soul, if the soul allows itself to be moved by the Holy Spirit.[76] These graces do not constitute something extraordinary; rather, they belong to the normal development of grace in the life of a soul that seeks greater union with God.[77] These mystical graces are something that everyone can experience. Hence, they do not take away from Thérèse's ordinary way.

It is important to note that Thérèse had a particular mission in the Church. When we speak of the ordinary way of Thérèse "'ordinary' does not here mean *'common'* or 'usual' but rather what is *normal* in sanctity."[7] These graces are characterized as "normal" because the operation of the gifts of the Holy Spirit and infused contemplation are within the normal development of grace in the life of a soul; they help a person increase in love and grace and advance

---

[75] *GC* II, LT 224, 1085.

[76] Ven. Arintero, *Mystical Phenomena*, 38. The action of God working in our lives is often overlooked. There is a common misunderstanding that the gifts of the Holy Spirit are something extraordinary, that they are connected with visions, prophecies, and other phenomena, and are only given to a chosen few; on the contrary, the operation of the gifts of the Holy Spirit is part of the ordinary path to holiness.

[77] Aumann, "Mystical Experience, the Infused Virtues and the Gifts," 34.

[78] Ven. Arintero, *Mystical Phenomena*, 50.

toward union with God. Therefore, they are nothing outside of the ordinary way of sanctification, but rather the full flowering of the operation of the seven gifts of the Holy Spirit, which are received at baptism.

The life of Thérèse is constantly guided by the Holy Spirit, and His sevenfold gift permeates her whole life. The gift of wisdom is highly operative in Thérèse's life; according to Arintero, most of Thérèse's mystical graces – even when she is a young girl – can be attributed to the gift of wisdom and to the gift of piety.[79] St Thérèse experiences the very heights of infused contemplation because she is imbued with the gift of wisdom. Marie-Eugène says that Thérèse is "before all else a soul possessed by God, a contemplative."[80] This is truly the summit of the mystical life and the normal unfolding of grace; charity and the gift of wisdom have reached an eminent degree.[81] In fact, Marie-Eugène asserts that Thérèse's whole mission is based primarily on her contemplation:

> St Thérèse of the Child Jesus has a mission which extends beyond the Carmel to the entire Church, and this mission is based primarily on her contemplation .... with her everything flows from her knowledge of God.[82]

---

[79] Foreword, from translator José L. Morales, in *Mystical Phenomena*, xiii.
[80] Bl. Marie-Eugène, *Under the Torrent of His Love*, 100.
[81] Garrigou-Lagrange, *Three Ages of the Interior Life*, vol. II, 467-468.
[82] Bl. Marie-Eugène, *Under the Torrent of His Love*, 35.

Marie-Eugène also says that St Thérèse can help us more fully understand the gift of wisdom according to St Thomas' teaching:

> I assure you that I have studied her in depth for forty years and her greatness has often overwhelmed me. She has renewed our understanding of the gifts of the Holy Spirit, as we see them operating in her contemplation. It harmonises with the teaching of St Thomas. It is not a matter of sentimentality or of novelties. It is a rediscovery, an illustration of the traditional doctrine. I believe this is one of the greatest graces of our times.[83]

Hence, in the life of Thérèse one can see "the full normal actualization of the gift of wisdom."[84] This, in accord with the teaching of St Thomas and St John of the Cross, "deserves the name of infused contemplation, properly so called, and … without this contemplation the full normal actualization of this gift does not yet exist."[85]

Experiences of Infused Contemplation

Whenever a person receives infused contemplation, it is due to the operation of the gifts of wisdom, understanding, and knowledge.[86] As infused contemplation

---

[83] Bl. Marie-Eugène, *Under the Torrent of His Love*, 31.
[84] Garrigou-Lagrange, *Three Ages of the Interior Life*, vol. II, 339.
[85] Garrigou-Lagrange, *Three Ages of the Interior Life*, vol. II, 339.
[86] Garrigou-Lagrange explains: "in the passive night of the senses the gift of knowledge predominates, showing the vanity of created

increases in intensity and a person continues to advance in the spiritual life, there can also be various phenomena which can accompany infused contemplation. It is evident that St Thérèse had various experiences which indicate she was indeed receiving infused contemplation; some of these are mentioned explicitly in her works. Thérèse explains one such experience which can be identified with a Divine favour that St Teresa of Avila says the Lord sometimes grants in the prayer of quiet.[87]

> It was as though a veil had been cast over all the things of this earth for me ... I was entirely hidden under the Blessed Virgin's veil. At this time, I was placed in charge of the refectory, and I recall doing things as though not doing them; it was as if someone had lent me a body. I remained that way for one whole week.[88]

This Divine favour can last for a few minutes or even a number of days, though the latter is more uncommon. In the prayer of quiet, the will is captivated by the Lord, but the intellect, memory, and imagination remain free, and therefore one can engage in various occupations. *St Teresa of Avila* explains:

---

things; in the night of the spirit the soul experiences chiefly the deep penetration of the gift of understanding, but without experiencing the sweetness of the gift of wisdom. This gift appears in its full development and its greatest influence in the transforming union" (*Three Ages of the Interior Life,* vol. I, 319).

[87] St Teresa of Avila, *Way,* 31, 4, 154.

[88] *LC,* July 11, 2, 88. Royo and Aumann recognise this experience as the prayer of quiet. See *Theology of Christian Perfection,* 173.

When this quiet is great and lasts for a long while, it seems to me that the will wouldn't be able to remain so long in that peace if it weren't bound to something. For it may happen that we will go about with this satisfaction for a day or two and will not understand ourselves – I mean those who experience it – and they definitely see that they are not wholly in what they are doing, but that the best part is lacking, that is the will. The will, in my opinion, is then united with its God, and leaves the other faculties free to be occupied in what is for His service – and they then have much more ability for this. But in worldly matters, these faculties are dull and at times as though in a stupor. This is a great favour for those to whom the Lord grants it; the active and the contemplative lives are joined. The faculties all serve the Lord together: the will is occupied in its work and contemplation without knowing how; the other two faculties serve in the work of Martha. Thus Martha and Mary walk together. [89]

---

[89] St Teresa of Avila, *Way of Perfection*, ch. 31, 4 -5, 154-155. In *The Way of Perfection* St Teresa says this experience is the prayer of quiet. In the *Book of Her Life* (an earlier work), she describes this type of prayer as something higher than the prayer of quiet: "...while the will is united, the soul sees clearly and understands that the will is held fast and is rejoicing. I say "it sees clearly," and that the will alone is in deep quiet; and the intellect and the memory, on the other hand, are so free that they can tend to business affairs and engage in works of charity. Although this prayer seems entirely the same as the prayer of quiet I mentioned, it is different –partly because in the prayer of quiet the soul didn't desire to move or stir, rejoicing in that holy idleness of Mary, and in this prayer it can also be Martha in such a way that it is as though engaged in both the active and contemplative life together" (*Life*, 17, 4, 153-154).

A person can be experiencing the prayer of quiet whilst being in the midst of his or her daily occupations. This kind of prayer can happen at any time – in the chapel, on a walk, at the beach, at work, etc. It is given and received; hence, it is not something which we can make happen. It will last only as long as the Lord wills; we can never produce this prayer or hold on to it. An intense degree of the prayer of quiet can be seen quite clearly in the writings of St Thérèse.

In addition, it is worth mentioning another of Thérèse's experiences:

> I should be desolate for having slept (for seven years) during my hours of prayer and my *thanksgivings* after Holy Communion; well, I am not desolate. I remember that *little children* are as pleasing to their parents when they are asleep as well as when they are wide awake; I remember, too that when they perform operations, doctors put their patients to sleep. Finally, I remember that: *"The Lord knows our weakness, that he is mindful that we are but dust and ashes."*[90]

Arintero describes the way a person can feel whilst experiencing infused contemplation:

> ... although these souls were fearful of losing time and of having actually been asleep, they soon realize from the effects of this sleep that actually they were never more vigilant or more active. They have come forth from that sleep reanimated,

---

[90] Ms A 75v-76r, 165.

possessing greater valor for the fulfillment of the divine will in all things.[91]

In the Carmelite tradition, the word "sleep" is used to refer to a supernatural sleep. Interestingly, St Thomas in his Commentary on the Gospel of St John describes how in Sacred Scripture the word sleep is used to refer to a number of things, one of which is "the repose of contemplation: 'I slept, but my heart was awake (Song 5:2).'"[92] Sometimes, the soul experiencing infused contemplation feels as if asleep. Describing what can happen in this kind of prayer which St Teresa calls the prayer of union, she says that it

---

[91] Ven. Arintero, *Mystical Evolution and Vitality of the Church*, vol. II, 103-104.

[92] St Thomas Aquinas, *Super Ioan.*, cap. 11, lec. 3, n. 1495: "Quandoque pro quiete contemplationis; Cant. V, 2: ego dormio, et cor meum vigilat." Describing ways in which the word sleep can be understood in Scripture, St Thomas says: "We should note that the word 'sleep' can be understood in several ways. Sometimes it refers to a natural sleep: 'So Samuel went and lay down [slept] in his place' (1 Sam 3:9); and 'You shall sleep securely' [Job 11:18]. Sometimes it indicates the sleep of death: 'We would not have you ignorant, brethren, concerning those who are asleep, that you may not grieve as others do who have no hope' (1 Thess 4:13). Sometimes it is understood as some kind of negligence: 'Behold, he who keeps Israel will neither slumber nor sleep' (Ps 121:4). And sometimes it means the sleep of sin: 'Awake, O sleeper, and arise from the dead' (Eph 5:14). Again, it can mean the repose of contemplation: 'I slept, but my heart was awake' (Song 5:2). It can also signify the rest of future glory: 'In peace I will both lie down and sleep' (Ps 4:8). Death is called a sleep because of the hope we have of a resurrection; so death has come to be called a sleep from the time that Christ died and arose: 'I lie down and sleep' (Ps 3:6)" (emphasis added).

seems that the soul is asleep; for neither does it really think it is asleep nor does it feel awake ... all the faculties are asleep in this state – and truly asleep – to the things of the world and to ourselves. As a matter of fact, during the time that the union lasts the soul is left as though without its senses, for it has no power to think even if it wants to.... In sum, it is like one who in every respect has died to the world so as to live more completely in God.[93]

It seems likely that Thérèse was actually experiencing a deep contemplation when she describes that she was *sleeping*. But it is important to be faithful to the text of St Thérèse, and therefore it cannot be assumed that when she says that she was "sleeping after communion" that she was always experiencing infused contemplation. Nevertheless, it is probable that God was infusing His Light and Love into her soul at these moments of prayer, and that this *sleep* was nothing other than a result of a deepening of charity and an intense operation of the gift of wisdom – in other words, it was infused contemplation.

Concomitant Phenomena

On other occasions, Thérèse experiences certain spiritual delights[94] which are called concomitant

---

[93] St Teresa of Avila, *Interior Castle*, V Mansions, ch. 1, 4, 336.
[94] St Teresa of Avila says that there "is a very great difference" between consolations and spiritual delights (*Interior Castle*, III Mansions, ch. 2, 313). Through infused contemplation a person will often experience spiritual delights which are very different from those which are experienced through meditative prayer, and

phenomena; these spiritual delights can often accompany the prayer of infused contemplation when a person reaches a certain stage in the spiritual life. Thérèse mentions explicitly that she experienced transports *of love, flights of the spirit,* and *wounds of love*. Concomitant phenomena are not essential to infused contemplation; they are accidental, and distinct from it. These experiences usually accompany infused contemplation in the higher stages of the spiritual life.[95] Concomitant phenomena are not outside of the ordinary way of sanctity. In other words, they are not extraordinary; they are part of the normative spiritual journey toward greater union with God. In the spiritual life, any "infusion of charity" – no matter how great the intensity, including even divine touches – belongs to the "ordinary mode of divine action" because it is the "normal fruit of charity" and the seven gifts of the Holy Spirit.[96] In fact, any concomitant phenomena which favour greater union with God, or happen as a result of greater union, belong to the ordinary development of the "mystical life."[97] Transports of love, flights of the spirit, divine

---

which are referred to as consolations. St Teresa says: Consolations are experiences which we acquire through meditation and petitioning the Lord. God is of course involved because without "Him we can do nothing" (*Interior Castle,* IV Mansions, ch. 1, 317).

[95] Cf. Royo and Aumann, *Theology of Christian Perfection,* 549: "The prayer of union is usually accompanied by certain concomitant phenomena ... Although these phenomena are not produced at any definite moment…they are nevertheless manifested when the soul reaches this degree of prayer."

[96] Bl. Marie-Eugène, *I am a Daughter of the Church,* vol. II, translated by Sister M. Verda Clare, CSC (Allen, TX: Christian Classics, 1998), 245.

[97] Ven. Arintero, *Stages in Prayer,* 73.

touches, wounds of love, rapture, and ecstasy are concomitant phenomena which often accompany infused contemplation, and which "are all normal developments of a deepening communion with the Trinity."[98] On the other hand, graces which are considered as extraordinary are any type of grace, light, or favour that "neither proceed[s] from union itself, nor tend[s] principally and directly to produce it."[99] This would include such things as visions, and locutions, etc.[100]

Even though St Thérèse does not write much about experiencing various concomitant phenomena, she does experience them – not frequently, but we do find mention of them in her works.[101] When St Thérèse recounts these experiences, she draws very little attention to them. The following instances show that Thérèse does indeed experience various concomitant phenomena which accompany her infused contemplation.

Mother Agnes points out that Thérèse spoke to her of an occasion when she experienced a "flight of the

---

[98] Thomas Dubay, S.M., *Fire Within* (San Francisco: Ignatius Press, 1989), 100. Cf. Royo and Aumann: "There are four principal concomitant phenomena: Mystical touches, flights of the spirit, fiery darts of love and wounds of love" (*Theology of Christian Perfection*, 549).
[99] Ven. Arintero, *Stages in Prayer*, 73.
[100] Ven. Arintero, *Stages in Prayer*, 69-70. Marie-Eugène explains that St John of the Cross has only one desire when it concerns a soul that is receiving infused contemplation. That is that it will lead the person to "perfect union" with God. He advises us to be on guard when it comes to "supernatural phenomena that accompany infused contemplation but do not form part of it" (*I Want to See God*, 465-466).
[101] Jamart, *Spiritual Doctrine of St. Thérèse*, 253.

spirit." Mother Agnes explains: "During Matins she spoke to me about her prayers of former days, in the summer evenings during the periods of silence, and she understood then by experience what a 'flight of the spirit' was."[102] In *Story of a Soul*, Thérèse also mentions transports of love:

> Exteriorly my life appeared to be as usual. I studied, took lessons in drawing ... Above all, I was growing in love for God; I *felt* within my heart certain aspirations unknown until then, and at times I had veritable transports of love.[103]

Again, in one of her *Letters*, she mentions transports of love: "At the age of fourteen, I also ... experienced transports of love. Ah! how I loved God!"[104] Thérèse never makes any specific mention of rapture or ecstasy; however, St Teresa of Avila in the *Book of Her Life* says that in her opinion, transports are basically "the same as rapture and ecstasy."[105] So rapture,

---

[102] *LC*, July 11, 1, 87.
[103] Ms A 52r, 111-112 (emphasis added).
[104] *LC*, July 7, 2, 77. Cf. Miller, *The Trial of Faith*, 68-71, concerning Thérèse's mystical graces.
[105] St Teresa of Avila, *Life*, ch. 20, 1, 172. Royo and Aumann, explain the cause of ecstasy: "The efficient cause of mystical ecstasy is the Holy Ghost, working through his gifts. Ecstasy is appropriated to the Holy Spirit because it is an operation of love which sanctifies the soul, and the Holy Spirit is the Spirit of love. Operating through the gifts of wisdom and understanding, he uses the latter to illuminate faith and the former to arouse charity, until a most vehement love is aroused in the soul, causing the alienation of the senses" (Theology *of Christian Perfection*, 552). Arintero says, "Ecstasy is an excess of love and it is effected gradually and gently. Therefore the soul can often prevent it by trying to distract itself when it feels the ecstasy approaching, or at

ecstasy, and transports of love are all substantially the same, though they do have accidental differences.[106] Transports of love do not "cause the slightest change in the countenance of the person in whom they take place."[107] However, these transports of love can "inflame the soul with ardent desires of being consumed as a holocaust."[108] Thérèse had this ardent desire and some years later (after having experienced transports of love), she would compose her act of oblation (which will be described in the following chapter). In her act of oblation, Thérèse declares,

> In order to live in one single act of perfect Love, I offer myself as a victim holocaust to your merciful love.[109]

When Thérèse actually makes her Act of Oblation to Merciful Love, she experiences something called a *wound of love*.[110] Teresa of Avila says that these wounds

---

least the soul has time to hide or to assume an unassuming posture so that no one will be able to notice anything. Rapture is caused by an excess of light and wonder, and it comes suddenly and with great violence so that there is no way of resisting or preventing it. Ecstasy makes the person swoon and fall to the ground as if dead; rapture elevates one, transfigures, and tends to lift him into the air. The flight of the spirit is a rapture, in which the soul seems to be raised to unknown regions by an irresistible impulse" (*Mystical Evolution and Vitality of the Church*, vol. II, 265-266). See *ST* II-II, q. 175, a. 3, ad 1, for St Thomas' treatment of ecstasy.

[106] Dubay, *Fire Within*, 97.
[107] Ven. Arintero, *Mystical Evolution and Vitality of the Church*, vol. II, 177. Flights of love are synonymous with transports of love.
[108] Ven. Arintero, *Mystical Evolution and Vitality of the Church*, vol. II, 153.
[109] *Prayers* 6, Act of Oblation, 55.
[110] St John of the Cross describes these wounds as "secret touches

occur in the sixth mansions;[111] so Thérèse is no doubt in the sixth or seventh mansions when this occurs.

Thérèse experiences a wound of love one day when she is making the Stations of the Cross. When Thérèse is near the end of her life, Mother Agnes asks her to describe what happened when she made her Act of Oblation. Thérèse says:

> Well, I was beginning the Way of the Cross; suddenly, I was seized with such a violent love for [the good][112] God that I can't explain it except by saying it felt as though I were totally plunged into fire. Oh! *What fire and what sweetness* at one and the

---

of love, which like fiery arrows pierce and wound [the soul], leaving it wholly cauterized by the fire of love" (*Spiritual Canticle*, stanza 1, 17, 422). These wounds are the love sickness that the soul feels for God, and the only remedy for this "love-sickness" is God and more precisely the love of God. Unlike other sickness which takes a medicine contrary to the sickness; the sickness of love needs love as its cure (*Spiritual Canticle*, stanza 11, 11, 452). "No medicine can be gotten for these wounds of love except from the One Who causes them" (*Spiritual Canticle*, stanza 1, 20, 423). According to St Teresa of Avila, the soul which experiences these wounds of love is left with such a deep love for God that it has a great desire to continually praise Him. The desire to perform penances is very strong, however, even when great penances are performed the soul feels that it has not done much at all. It believes that even those who have suffered martyrdom have done little for God. It has a great desire to suffer and if there is no opportunity to suffer it complains to the Lord (*Interior Castle*, VI Mansions, ch. 4, 15, 384).

[111] See St Teresa of Avila, *Interior Castle*, VI Mansions, ch. 2, 366-370.

[112] In the French original, when she writes "God", Thérèse writes "le bon Dieu," but the official English translation omits the word "good" [bon]. See for example, Thérèse de Lisieux, *Oeuvres complètes* (Paris: Cerf DDB, 2006), 1027.

> same time! I was on fire with love and I felt that one minute more, one second more, and I wouldn't be able to sustain this ardor without dying.
>
> I understood then what the saints were saying about these states which they experienced so often. As for me, I experienced it only once and for one single instant, falling back immediately into my habitual state of dryness.[113]

St Teresa of Avila describes these wounds of love:

> the soul ... feels that it is wounded in the most exquisite way, but it doesn't learn how or by whom it was wounded. It knows clearly that the wound is something precious, and it would never want to be cured. It complains to its Spouse with words of love, even outwardly, without being able to do otherwise. It knows that He allows Himself to be enjoyed. And the pain is great, although delightful and sweet. And even if the soul does not want this wound, the wound cannot be avoided. But the soul, in fact, would never want to be deprived of this pain.[114]

St John of the Cross explains that the soul who receives a wound of love has

---

[113] *LC*, July 7, 2, 77 (emphasis added).

[114] St Teresa of Avila, *Interior Castle*, VI Mansions, ch. 2, 2, 367. St John of the Cross says that wounds of love "so inflame the will in its affection that it burns up in this flame and fire of love. So intense is this burning that the soul is seemingly consumed in that flame, and the fire makes it go out of itself, wholly renews it, and changes its manner of being, as in the case of the phoenix that burns itself in the fire and rises anew from the ashes" (*Spiritual Canticle*, stanza 1, 17, 422).

> a kind of immense torment and yearning to see God. So extreme is this torment that love seems to be unbearably rigorous with the soul, not because it has wounded her - she rather considers these wounds to be favorable to her health - but because it left her thus suffering with love, and did not slay her for the sake of her seeing and being united with him in the life of perfect love. In stressing or declaring her sorrow, she says, "After wounding me," that is, leaving me thus wounded, thus dying with wounds of love for you, you have hidden as swiftly as the stag.[115]

Wounds of love are not like other visits from God which satisfy and refresh the soul. God bestows them to wound the soul rather than to satisfy it. To wound, in the sense that by wounding the soul with His Love, which is delightful in itself, its longing to see the Lord is greatly increased. These wounds of love are so exquisite and cause such great delight that the soul feels a great yearning to see the Lord. The pain which arises from feeling the absence of God can be so strong, that if He was not sustaining the soul in this state, it would die.[116] "Love of God and desire for Him can increase so much that the natural subject is unable to endure it, and so there have been persons who have died from love."[117] These descriptions are important for understanding the connection between wounds of love and Thérèse's martyrdom of love, which will be considered in the final chapter.

---

[115] St John of the Cross, *Spiritual Canticle*, stanza, 1, 18-19, 422-423.
[116] St John of the Cross, *Spiritual Canticle*, stanza 1, 19, 423-424.
[117] St Teresa of Avila, *Way of Perfection*, ch. 19, 8, 111.

Thérèse sometimes experiences these various concomitant phenomena which accompany her infused contemplation; however, it is important to remember that these phenomena are not essential to infused contemplation. Attention has been given to these graces in order to reinforce the fact that St Thérèse is experiencing the heights of infused contemplation. Ordinarily, when a soul reaches the heights of contemplation, it experiences some kind of concomitant phenomena,[118] even if it is very seldom.

As we have seen, these graces seem to have accompanied Thérèse's contemplation on at least a few occasions. These concomitant phenomena confirm that she was indeed experiencing the full normal development of infused contemplation to an intense degree – which is indicative also of the operation of the gift of wisdom to a very high degree. The effects of infused contemplation are varied – in some souls they are very perceptible and in others they are less visible. In the life of Thérèse, the most perceptible mystical grace accompanying her infused contemplation is the wound of love. Most of the time, the effects of Thérèse's mystical state are much less perceptible than on the occasion of the wound of love; however, the "mystical state itself [is] no less real and she lack[s] none of the mystical graces essential to sanctification."[119] There is no doubt that Thérèse experiences the fullness of the operation of the gift of wisdom – and thus is imbued with a very high degree of infused contemplation. This re-enforces what has been explained above, that Thérèse is indeed in the

---

[118] Royo and Aumann, *Theology of Christian Perfection*, 549.
[119] Ven. Arintero, *Mystical Phenomena*, 51.

mystical state, and that she has a profound intimate union with the Lord through the operation of the gifts of the Holy Spirit, through infused contemplation, and hence the operation of the gift of wisdom.

Thérèse's prayer life can be misunderstood due to its purity and simplicity. "We might think it inconsequential, since it *is* so simple, yet it is precisely this simplicity that makes it perfect."[120] When a person is in the transforming union, phenomena such as ecstasy, flights of the spirit, etc. are very seldom experienced, or cease altogether.[121] Therefore, the absence of ecstasy, divine touches etc. – in other words the absence of concomitant phenomena[122] – does not mean that a person is not receiving a high degree of

---

[120] Bl. Marie-Eugène, *Under the Torrent of His Love*, 42-43.

[121] Ven. Arintero explains that when someone has reached the heights of perfection he or she has been strengthened and regenerated in such a way that any amount of light received from the Holy Spirit will very seldom cause ecstasies or raptures (*Mystical Evolution and Vitality of the Church*, vol. II, 229). Royo and Aumann also explain that in the highest degree of infused contemplation a person no longer experiences ecstasy. "The formal cause of ecstasy is infused contemplation in a very intense degree, although not the maximum degree. A less intense form of contemplation would not cause the suspension of the faculties of the soul nor of the bodily senses. Yet it need not be contemplation in the maximum degree of intensity, because the highest degree of infused contemplation does not produce any ecstasy" (*Theology of Christian Perfection*, 552).

[122] Royo and Aumann explain that concomitant phenomena are "transitory graces" which often accompany the "prayer of union." These concomitant phenomena are something different from the *gratiae gratis datae*, they are graces "which God grants at his good pleasure; they are nevertheless manifest when the soul reaches this degree of prayer. There are four principal concomitant phenomena: *mystical touches, flights of the spirit, fiery darts of love* and *wounds of love*" (*Theology of Christian Perfection*, 549).

infused contemplation; on the contrary, when a soul is very pure, infused contemplation becomes more simple. As a person advances in the spiritual life, contemplation becomes more pure, more unadorned. The absence or infrequent occurrence of concomitant phenomena, and even a sense of obscurity, is due to the fact that the

> divine light and its action are all the less felt as they are more noble and as the soul receiving them is purer. Second, because it is very lofty, this light or action of God produces a certain impression of deprivation or obscurity, for it reduces the natural powers to powerlessness.[123]

Hence, obscurity and an absence of "overflowing delight…becomes an indication of the elevated quality of the divine communications."[124] A thing is simple when it is unadorned, when there are no secondary elements, but only the thing's nature.[125] With regard to infused contemplation:

> …the simplified gaze is the only essential element of contemplation. Hence all the things we burden it with and believe necessary: dazzling lights, overflowing joy, even transports and ecstasies, no longer seem anything more than embellishments, secondary elements of which contemplation needs to be stripped so as to become more essentially and more perfectly itself, that is, purer and loftier.[126]

---

[123] Bl. Marie-Eugène, *Under the Torrent of His Love*, 138-139.
[124] Bl. Marie-Eugène, *Under the Torrent of His Love*, 140.
[125] Bl. Marie-Eugène, *Under the Torrent of His Love*, 42-43.
[126] Bl. Marie-Eugène, *Under the Torrent of His Love*, 127.

This is exactly how St Thérèse's contemplation is – simple, unadorned, and unembellished.[127]

Secrets

Through the operation of the gift of wisdom God makes Himself known and relished and reveals His Divine secrets.[128] The person who has a close friendship with God comes to know Him more and more, especially through infused contemplation and the operation of the gift of wisdom. St Thomas explains that "God reveals his secrets to us by letting us share in his wisdom,"[129] and "since true friendship is about sharing one's heart and mind with one's friend, God reveals His inmost secrets with His friends."[130] St Thomas explains that it "is a characteristic of the

---

[127] Bl. Marie-Eugène, *Under the Torrent of His Love*, 42-43. Not only was St Thérèse's contemplation simple; her whole spiritual life was simple. Describing her experiences in spiritual direction she says: "It was only with great effort that I was able to take direction, for I never became accustomed to speaking about my soul and I didn't know how to express what was going on within it. One good old Mother understood one day what I was experiencing, and she said laughingly during recreation: 'My child, it seems to me you don't have very much to tell your Superiors.' 'Why do you say that, Mother?' 'Because your soul is extremely *simple,* but when you will be perfect, you will be even *more simple*; the closer one approaches to God, the simpler one becomes'" (Ms A 70v, 151).

[128] Jamart, *Spiritual Doctrine of St. Thérèse,* 246.

[129] St Thomas Aquinas, *Super Ioan.*, cap. 15, lec. 3, n. 2016: "Deus autem faciendo nos participes suae sapientiae, sua secreta nobis revelat."

[130] Serge-Thomas Bonino, OP, "The Role of the Apostles in the Communication of Revelation according to *Lectura super Ioannem*

Holy Spirit to reveal the truth because it is love which impels one to reveal his secrets."[131] Therefore,

> the more a person wants to grasp the secrets of divine wisdom, the more he should try to get closer to Christ, according to: "come to him and be enlightened"(Ps 34:5). For the secrets of divine wisdom are especially revealed to those who are joined to God by love.[132]

As a person advances in the spiritual life, he or she gives everything to God and does not keep anything from Him. God teaches the soul His "wisdom and secrets."[133] God reveals and communicates His secrets to His intimate friends, to those souls that have a close intimacy with Him and truly love Him. Hence, when a person has grown so much in his or her relationship with God, He leads that person deeper and deeper into His mysteries. He begins to reveal the depths of

---

of St. Thomas Aquinas," in *Reading John with Saint Thomas*, 327. St Thomas explains: "For the true sign of friendship is that a friend reveals the secrets of his heart to his friend. Since friends have one mind and heart, it does not seem that what one friend reveals to another is placed outside his own heart" (*Super Ioan.*, cap. 15, lec. 3, n. 2016).

[131] St Thomas Aquinas, *Super Ioan.*, cap. 14, lec. 4, n. 1916: "Manifestare autem veritatem convenit proprietati Spiritus Sancti. Est enim amor qui facit secretorum revelationem."

[132] St Thomas Aquinas, *Super Ioan.*, cap. 13, lec. 4, n. 1807: "… quod quanto magis homo vult divinae sapientiae secreta capere, tanto magis conari debet ut propinquior fiat Iesu, secundum illud Ps. XXXIII, 6: *accedite ad eum, et illuminamini*. Nam divinae sapientiae secreta illis praecipue revelantur qui Deo iuncti sunt per amorem."

[133] St John of the Cross, *Spiritual Canticle*, stanza 27, 3, 518.

His love and instructs the soul in the very depth of its being.

These secrets come through infused contemplation and the gift of wisdom. This wisdom is called secret because it is a language spoken by God who is "Pure Spirit." Consequently, it is perceived by the spirit and not by the senses; therefore, it is "secret to the senses."[134] St John of the Cross explains:

> ...contemplation is the mystical theology which theologians call secret wisdom and which St Thomas says is communicated and infused into the soul through love. This communication is secret and dark to the work of the intellect and the other faculties. Insofar as these faculties do not acquire it but the Holy Spirit infuses it and puts it in order in the soul, as the bride says in the Canticle of Canticles [Ct. 2:4], the soul neither knows nor understands how this comes to pass and thus calls it secret.[135]

---

[134] St John of the Cross, *Dark Night*, bk II, ch. 17, 4, 369.

[135] St John of the Cross, *Dark Night*, bk II, ch. 17, 2, 368. St John of the Cross describes this secret wisdom: "Contemplation, consequently, by which the intellect has a higher knowledge of God, is called mystical theology, meaning the secret wisdom of God. For this wisdom is secret to the very intellect that receives it. St Dionysius on this account refers to contemplation as a ray of darkness ... Aristotle teaches that just as the sun is total darkness to the eyes of a bat, so the brightest light in God is complete darkness to our intellect. And he teaches in addition that the loftier and clearer the things of God are in themselves, the more unknown and obscure they are to us ...The Apostle also affirms this teaching: That which is highest in God is least known by men, [Rom. 11:33]" (*Ascent of Mount Carmel*, bk II, ch. 8, 6, 128). "Dark contemplation is the secret ladder: secret as is mystical theology that is communicated and infused into the soul through love." St Edith Stein, *Science of the Cross*, The Collected Works of Edith Stein,

Thérèse quotes St John of the Cross in *Story of a Soul* to describe this type of knowledge which is communicated to her in secret:

> On that glad night, in secret, for no one saw me, nor did I look at anything, with no other light or guide than the one that burned in my heart. This guided me more surely than the light of the noon to where he was awaiting me – him I knew so well – there in a place where no one else appeared.[136]

In a letter to her sister Céline, Thérèse describes that she sees nothing; however, her Beloved "instructs her soul." She says, "I myself see nothing ... but I say with Saint John of the Cross: 'My Beloved is in the

---

vol. VI, translated by Josephine Koeppel, OCD (Washington, D.C.: ICS Publications, 2002), 141.

[136] Ms A 49r, 105. St John of the Cross explains this secret wisdom: "Not only because of this inability to understand contemplation is it called 'secret' but also because of the effects it produces in the soul. The wisdom of love is not secret merely in the darkness and straits of the soul's purgation (for the soul does not know how to describe it) but also afterwards in the illumination, when it is communicated more clearly. Even then it is so secret that it is ineffable. Not only does a man feel unwilling to give expression to this wisdom, but he finds not adequate means or similitude to signify so sublime an understanding and delicate a spiritual feeling. Even if the soul should desire to convey this experience in words and think up many similitudes, the wisdom would always remain secret and still to be expressed. Since this interior wisdom is so simple, general, and spiritual that in entering the intellect it is not clothed in any sensory species or image, the imaginative faculty cannot form an idea or picture of it in order to speak of it; this wisdom did not enter through these faculties nor did they behold any of its apparel or color. Yet the soul is clearly aware that it understands and tastes that delightful and wondrous wisdom" (*Dark Night*, bk II, ch. 17, 3, 368-369).

mountains, and lonely, wooded valleys, etc.' And this Beloved instructs my soul, He speaks to it in silence, in darkness ..."[137]

There is another reason why this contemplation is called secret; it is because of the effects which it produces within the soul. These effects are so difficult to describe, that there are no adequate words to fully express this wisdom; it can be so "secret that it is ineffable."[138] These secrets can be very sublime and cannot be compared to anything here on earth; St Teresa of Avila explains that they are very different from all that can be seen and understood "here below." [139] However, as St John of the Cross says, "It is not secret to the soul itself... for within itself it has the experience of this intimate embrace;"[140] and through it a person is truly led "into the veins of the science of love."[141] Thérèse writing to her sister speaks of these secrets, this type of knowledge and wisdom which she receives from her friend and Spouse, and she explains how difficult it is to express what God has revealed. She knows that no words can describe such sublime communications:

> I am going to try to stammer some words, although I feel that it is impossible for human words to repeat things that the human heart can hardly sense... Dear Sister, how blessed we are to understand the intimate secrets of our Spouse.... I feel my powerlessness in repeating in earthly

---

[137] *GC* II, LT 135, 752.
[138] St John of the Cross, *Dark Night*, bk II, ch. 17, 3, 368-369.
[139] St Teresa of Avila, *Interior Castle*, VI Mansions ch. 2, 3, 367-368.
[140] St John of the Cross, *Living Flame of Love*, stanza 4, 14, 648.
[141] St John of the Cross, *Dark Night*, bk II, ch.17, 6, 370.

words the secrets of heaven. And, then, after having written out pages and pages, I would find that I had still not begun .... There are so many different horizons, so many infinitely varied nuances, that the palette of the heavenly Painter alone will be able, after the night of this life, to furnish me with colors capable of painting the marvels that He reveals to the eyes of my soul.[142]

At the beginning of Manuscript C of *Story of a Soul* which is addressed to Mother Agnes, Thérèse writes, "If she could express what she understands, you would hear a heavenly melody; but, unfortunately, I can have you listen to nothing but the stammering of a little child."[143] There are numerous texts in which Thérèse speaks of these secrets and this knowledge, which is obviously not a knowledge that has been derived from studies. Neither is it given through any kind of vision or locution; it is not something extraordinary, but something that comes from a connatural knowing, an infused knowledge which comes to her through infused contemplation, particularly through the operation of the gift of wisdom. Thérèse has absolute certainty that Jesus her Divine Spouse is teaching her in the depths of her soul, and infusing into her soul this wisdom and knowledge:

> Without showing Himself, without making His voice heard, Jesus teaches me in secret; it is not by means of books, for I do not understand what I am reading. Sometimes a word comes to console me,

---

[142] *GC* II, LT 196, 994-995. Cf. Ms B 1v, 189.
[143] Ms C 18v, 233.

such as this one which I received at the end of prayer (after having remained in silence and aridity): *"Here is the teacher whom I am giving you; he will teach you everything that you must do. I want to make you read in the book of life, wherein is contained the science of Love."* The science of Love, ah, yes, this word resounds sweetly in the ear of my soul and I desire only this science. *Having given all my riches for it*, I esteem it as *having given nothing* as did the bride in the sacred Canticles.[144]

Many of the Saints speak of this secret knowledge, which is not given the name secret because it is given to an elite few. This is not what Thérèse is suggesting and to believe this would certainly be contrary to the message of Thérèse. Rather, these secrets are communicated to the soul that gives itself to God without reserve, the person who remains humble in the sight of God. Thérèse also believes that Jesus is confiding these secrets to Marie.[145] In a letter to Céline, Thérèse refers to these secrets, this science of love that Jesus communicates to her sister when she says, "And now what science is He about to teach us? Has He not taught us all? … Let us listen to what He is saying to us …. Yes, it is there in the intimate retreat of the soul that He instructs us together, and one day He will show us the day which will no longer have setting."[146]

Thérèse is acutely aware that these secrets are something that God communicates to a soul sincerely seeking Him and one who has reached a certain level of detachment and humility. She understands that

---

[144] Ms B 1r, 187-188. See also *GC* II, LT 196, 994.
[145] *GC* II, LT 196, 993-994.
[146] *GC* II, LT 137, 761-762.

God reveals His secrets through a quasi-experiential knowledge to little souls – souls that remain detached and humble – she has unshakable confidence and certainty about this:

> Because I was little and weak He lowered Himself to me, and He instructed me secretly in the things of His love. Ah! Had the learned who spent their life in study come to me, undoubtedly they would have been astonished to see a child of fourteen understand perfection's secrets…![147]

Thérèse tastes and penetrates the mysteries of God with such clarity that she is able to express these truths and mysteries of the faith with precision and depth; yet she always maintains the simplicity of a child. In a letter to her sister Céline, Thérèse writes, "Together we grew up; together Jesus instructed us in His secrets, sublime secrets that He hides from the mighty and reveals to the little ones."[148] When Mother Marie de Gonzague gives Thérèse the job of helping one of the sisters with the training of novices, Thérèse remarks:

> You didn't fear, dear Mother, that I would lead your little lambs astray. My lack of experience and youthfulness did not frighten you in the least. Perhaps you remembered that *often the Lord is pleased to grant wisdom to the little ones,* and that one day, in a transport of joy, He blessed His *Father* for having hidden His secrets from the wise and

---

[147] Ms A 49r, 105.
[148] *GC* II, LT 127, 724.

prudent and for revealing them to the little ones.[149]

Benedict XV says that Thérèse's knowledge "came to her from the secrets which God reveals to children."[150] And St John Paul II, who declared St Thérèse a Doctor of the Church says:

> Shining brightly among the little ones to whom the secrets of the kingdom were revealed in a most special way is Thérèse of the Child Jesus and the Holy Face .... During her life Thérèse discovered "new lights, hidden and mysterious meanings"... and received from the divine Teacher that "science of love" which she then expressed with particular originality in her writings .... This science is the luminous expression of her knowledge of the mystery of the kingdom and of her personal experience of grace. [151]

Thérèse herself realises that the wisdom that she possesses is not of her own doing. Her own words clearly manifest that she has absolute confidence that she has received this science, these secrets, from Jesus alone. This is the quasi-experiential knowledge which comes through the operation of the gift of wisdom. She knows that it is only by God's grace that she is able to understand His Divine Mysteries. Thérèse understands and knows very well that God is teaching her in the secret of her heart, and that true wisdom comes from above. God does not want this wisdom to remain buried in the heart of Thérèse. His

---

[149] Ms C 3v-4r, 209 (emphasis added).
[150] Jamart, *Spiritual Doctrine of St. Thérèse*, 31.
[151] St John Paul II, *Divini Amoris Scientia*, 1.

plan is for her to share these secrets with the whole world. St John Paul II remarks in his apostolic letter *Divini Amoris:* "God did not want his secrets to remain hidden, but enabled Thérèse to proclaim the secrets of the King."[152]

Purification

In order for a person to grow in the spiritual life and to be able to receive these Divine secrets through the gift of wisdom and a high degree of infused contemplation, it is necessary that he or she be purified from unruly passions in order to be free to seek God. As the soul begins to receive infused contemplation, it is purified by the light and love it receives from God. St Thomas explains "that the more a soul is free of passions and is purged from affections for earthly things, the higher it rises in the contemplation of truth and tastes how sweet the Lord is."[153] God wants us to have a taste for heavenly things

---

[152] St John Paul II, *Divini Amoris Scientia*, 11.

[153] St Thomas Aquinas, *Super Ioan.*, cap. 1, lec. 11, n. 213: "Et inde est quod anima quanto magis est a passionibus libera, et purgata ab affectibus terrenorum, tanto amplius in contemplationem veritatis ascendit, et gustat quam suavis est dominus." St John of the Cross explains that in order that a person can receive God's wisdom, it is necessary that he or she has been purified. This is because "the spirit must be simple, pure, and naked as to all natural affections, actual and habitual, in order to be able to freely communicate in fullness of spirit with the divine wisdom, in which, on account of the soul's purity, the delights of all things are tasted in a certain eminent degree. Without this purgation the soul would be wholly unable to experience the satisfaction of all this

rather than earthly things; however, as St Thomas says, "just as a tainted tongue does not taste sweet flavors, so a soul tainted by the corruption of the world does not taste the sweetness of heavenly things."[154] For the person that is steeped in the pleasures of sense cannot understand the things of the Spirit of God.[155] When a soul is filled with self-love, with love of the world, and has not been purified from unruly passions, then the work of the Lord is hindered. St Thomas explains:

> For as the sun is said to enter a house, or to go out, according as its rays reach the house, so God is said to approach to us, or to recede from us, when we receive the influx of His goodness, or decline from Him.[156]

God wants to detach the soul from the things of the world so that it can grow in union with Him and experience the things of the Spirit. Thérèse un-

---

.abundance of spiritual delight. Only one attachment or one particular object to which the spirit is actually or habitually bound is enough to hinder the experience or reception of the delicate and intimate delight of the spirit of love which contains eminently in itself all delights" (St John of the Cross, *Dark Night*, bk II, ch. 9, 1, 346).

[154] St Thomas Aquinas, *Super Ioan.*, cap. 14, lec. 4, n. 1919: "Sicut lingua infecta non sentit bonum saporem propter corruptionem humoris, sic anima infecta a corruptione mundi, caelestium dulcedinem non gustat."

[155] St Thomas Aquinas, *Super I Ep. ad Cor.*, cap. 2, lec. 3, n. 114: "Quia igitur animalis homo ea quae sunt Spiritus Dei reputat stulta, ex hoc manifestatur quod ea non capit. Et hoc est quod dicit *stultitia enimt* est *illi*, scilicet animali. Iudicat enim esse stulta quae secundum Spiritum Dei aguntur."

[156] *ST* I, q. 9, a. 1, ad 3.

derstands the lure that the world can have:

> How can a heart given over to the affection of creatures be intimately united with God? I feel this is not possible. Without having drunk the empoisoned cup of a too ardent love of creatures, I *feel* I cannot be mistaken. I have seen so many souls, seduced by this *false light*, fly like poor moths and burn their wings, and then return to the real and gentle light of *Love* that gives them new wings which are more brilliant and delicate, so that they can fly towards Jesus, that Divine Fire "which burns without consuming."[157]

When a soul is detached from the things of the world, it is all the more beautiful. In the soul that has been purified from unruly appetites God dwells secretly within the soul with His intimate embrace:

> It is in the soul in which less of its own appetites and pleasures dwell where He dwells more alone, more pleased, and more as though in His own house, ruling and governing it. And He dwells more in secret, the more he dwells alone. Thus in this soul in which neither any appetite nor other images or forms, nor any affections for created things, dwell, the Beloved dwells secretly with an embrace so much the closer, more intimate, and interior, the purer and more alone the soul is to everything other than God. His dwelling is in secret, then, because the devil cannot reach the area of this embrace, nor can man's intellect understand how it occurs.[158]

---

[157] Ms A 38r-38v, 83.
[158] St John of the Cross, Living Flame of Love, stanza 4, 14, 648.

In order for a soul to make such a beautiful dwelling for the Lord and receive this infused contemplation, it must be detached from the pleasures of the world and desire to give every part of its life to God. So even though this contemplation is within the normal development of sanctity, the Lord does not bless a soul with this grace unless it is very serious about serving God and giving its whole self to Him. Describing infused contemplation, St Teresa of Avila insists, "Contemplation is something else, daughters …for this King doesn't give Himself but to those who give themselves entirely to Him."[159] St Thomas explains that some people love God but desire only to receive delightful experiences from Him; however, there are other people who prefer giving honour and glory to God over receiving these delights, and this is

---

[159] St Teresa of Avila, *Way of Perfection*, ch. 16, 4, 94-95. St Teresa of Avila points out that a sign of true humility is that "you do not think you deserve these favors and spiritual delights from the Lord or that you will receive them in your lifetime" (*Interior Castle*, IV Mansions, ch. 2, 9, 326). She says: "Perhaps we don't know what love is…it doesn't consist in great delight but in desiring with strong determination to please God in everything" (IV Mansions, ch. 1, 7, 319). "For perfection as well as its reward does not consist in spiritual delights but in greater love and in deeds done with greater justice and truth" (III Mansions, ch. 2, 10, 313). St Teresa describing those who desire infused contemplation says that these people think they can ask God for favours because they believe it is due to them, but the Lord seeing that they lack humility "very seldom grants such persons favors, and rightly so. He sees clearly that they are not ready to drink from the chalice" (*Way of Perfection*, ch. 18, 6, 104). We often ask the Lord for gifts and different favours. However, we should realise how blessed we are to be able to repay Him in some way for all that He has done for us (III Mansions, ch. 1, 8, 308).

a "love of friendship."[160] To always desire to please the heart of God, and to desire to give more than to receive, "this attitude is what merits the name 'love.'"[161]

Thérèse never looks to the Lord for consolation; rather she always wants to console her Beloved Spouse.[162] Thérèse is a true friend of God; she gives herself to God without reserve. While Thérèse gives herself entirely to the Lord, she realises that there are few souls who really want to give everything to Him; many Christians are more interested in what they can receive from Him. She says that "many serve Jesus when he is consoling them, but *few* consent to keep company with *Jesus sleeping* on the waves or suffering in the garden of agony! ... Who, then, will be willing to serve Jesus for Himself?"[163] She exclaims:

> Ah! I *feel it more than ever before*, Jesus is parched, for He meets only the ungrateful and indifferent among His disciples in the world, and among His own disciples, alas, He finds few hearts who

---

[160] St Thomas Aquinas, *Super Ep. ad Phil.* cap. 1, lect. 3: "Primum enim desiderium excitat in nobis dilectio Dei, secundum dilectio proximi: maius autem et melius est desiderium primum, igitur, et cetera. Respondeo. Dicendum est quod duplex est dilectio Dei, scilicet dilectio concupiscentiae, qua vult frui Deo et delectari in ipso, et hoc est bonum hominis. Item est dilectio amicitiae, qua homo praeponit honorem Dei etiam huic delectationi, qua fruitur Deo, et haec est perfecta charitas." St Teresa of Avila says that if someone is a "true person of prayer and aims to enjoy the delights of God, he must not turn his back upon the desire to die for God and suffer martyrdom" (*Way of Perfection*, ch. 12, 2, 82).

[161] St Teresa of Avila, *Way of Perfection*, ch. 6, 7, 64.

[162] Fulton Sheen, *St. Thérèse: A Treasured Love Story* (Irving TX: Basilica Press 2007), 82.

[163] *GC* II, LT 165, 862.

surrender to Him without reservations, who understand the real tenderness of His infinite Love.[164]

Thérèse knows very well that there are "many degrees of perfection and each soul [is] free to respond to the advances of Our Lord, to do little or much for Him."[165] From a young age, Thérèse learns that all the things of the earth are passing away and that Jesus is the only one to whom a person should attach himself or herself. When Thérèse is young, she has an experience which greatly impacts how she looks at the things of this world. It is an occasion when her father has given her a little lamb as a gift. Unfortunately, the lamb dies after being only a few days old because the place where it was born was too cold for the little lamb. Thérèse has been hoping to see the lamb leap and jump around; however this does not happen. In a letter to Marie (her Godmother), Thérèse describes how this event impacts her spiritual life:

> You don't realise, dear Godmother, how much the death of this little animal made me reflect. Oh! Yes! on this earth we must attach ourselves to nothing, not even the most innocent things, for they fail you at the moment when you are least expecting it. It is only what is eternal that can content us.[166]

Thus, at a very early age, Thérèse learns to be detached from the things of the world. She says, "I find nothing on earth that makes me happy; my heart

---

[164] Ms B 1v, 189 and *GC* II, Lt. 196, 995-996 (emphasis added).
[165] Ms A 10r-10v, 27.
[166] *GC* I, LT 42, 396.

is too big, nothing that is called happiness in this world can satisfy it. My mind takes flight to Eternity!"[167] St Thomas explains that due to the operation of the gift of wisdom a person no longer has a taste for anything worldly, but rather a taste for what is heavenly.[168] Things that taste sour to worldly people will be found sweet to those who truly love the Lord.[169] As a result of the operation of the gift of wisdom, Thérèse asks God to "put a drop of bitterness on all earthly delights," because after having tasted the sweetness of Divine goodness through the operation of the gift of wisdom nothing else could satisfy her.[170] It is only God's grace that brings this transformation; it is the Spirit that, as St Thomas says, "makes us know all things by inspiring us from within, by directing us and lifting us up to spiritual things."[171] This transformation had taken place within the heart of Thérèse so that even when the beautiful things of the world surrounded her, they did not captivate her heart.[172] God had given her a taste for heavenly things and this would never leave her.

This whole transformation happens through the Holy Spirit's action in a person's life. However, this

---

[167] *GC* II, LT 245, 1129.
[168] ST II-II, q. 46, a. 1 ad 4.
[169] St Teresa of Avila, *Way of Perfection*, ch. 10, 4, 77.
[170] Martinez, *Sanctifier*, 192-193. St Thérèse's mother Zélie also understood this perfectly well: "Life is not a bed of roses; God wills this to detach us from earth and draw our thoughts to heaven" (*GC* II, Extracts, 39 March 1873, 1205).
[171] St Thomas Aquinas, *Super Ioan.*, cap. 14, lec. 6, n. 1959: "Facit autem nos scire omnia interius inspirando, dirigendo, et ad spiritualia elevando."
[172] *GC* I, LT 30, 308.

does not take place unless the person also co-operates and accepts his or her daily crosses. The cross helps in the whole interior transformation, and without the cross, a person cannot reach such a transformation in God. Of course, God would want to spare us of this suffering; but a person can never reach holiness and perfect union with God without having undergone many trials. Thérèse explains:

> Alas, it does pain Him to give us sorrows to drink, but He knows this is the only means of preparing us to "know Him as *He knows Himself* and to become *God ourselves.*" Oh! what a destiny. How great is our soul....[173]

In order for a soul to reach the very heights of contemplation, it has to pass through the night of the senses and the night of the spirit. This happens as a result of the operation of the gifts of knowledge and understanding, and also through the operation of the gift of wisdom. At various stages in the spiritual life, God saturates the soul with His light and love in order to purify the soul; the soul experiences this light and love as something bitter until it has been purified and is able to "taste the ineffable sweetness of the God of all consolation."[174]

---

[173] *GC* I, LT 57, 450. St Teresa of Avila says that in the sixth mansions, trials and suffering can be intense, but she explains that these are all meant to increase a person's "desire to enjoy the Spouse. And His Majesty, as one who knows our weakness, is enabling the soul through these afflictions and many others to have the courage to be joined with so great a Lord and to take Him as its Spouse" (*Interior Castle* VI Mansions, ch. 4, 1, 378).

[174] Ven. Arintero, *Mystical Evolution and Vitality of the Church*, vol. II, 430.

These negative experiences come "from the soul's own weakness and imperfection. Without this purgation it cannot receive the divine light, sweetness, and delight of wisdom."[175] When God begins to infuse His light and love in these nights, it does not come without suffering, and hence, many will turn back. This contemplation and these nights can be difficult, and many will abandon the road on which God wishes to lead them. Thérèse experienced the dark night, and she obviously did not abandon the path that God had prepared for her. Thérèse vividly describes this dark night:

> I was in a sad desert, or rather my soul was like a fragile boat delivered up to the mercy of the waves

---

[175] St John of the Cross, *Dark Night*, bk II, ch. 10, 4, 351. St John of the Cross says that a person's "intellect, clouded by the appetites, becomes dark and impedes the sun of either natural reason or supernatural wisdom from shining within and completely illuminating it...This is like saying the faculties of my soul are disordered. For the intellect (as the murky air in relation to the sun's light) is incapable of receiving the illumination of God's wisdom; and the will is incapable of an embrace of pure love of God" (*Ascent of Mount Carmel*, bk I, ch. 8, 1-2, 89). St John of the Cross explains why a person must undergo trials in order to reach the highest stages of the spiritual life: "The reason these trials are necessary in order to reach this state is that this highest union cannot be wrought in a soul that is not fortified by trials and temptations and purified by tribulations, darkness, and distress, just as a superior quality liqueur is poured only into a sturdy flask which is prepared and purified. By these trials the sensory part of the soul is purified and strengthened and the spiritual part is refined, purged, and disposed.... Through these trials, in which God places the spirit and the senses, the soul in bitterness acquires virtues, strength, and perfection, for virtue is made perfect in weakness [2 Cor. 12:9] and is refined through the endurance of suffering" (*Living Flame of Love*, stanza 2, 25-26, 604).

having no pilot. I knew Jesus was there sleeping in my boat, but the night was so black that it was impossible to see Him; nothing gave me any light, not a single flash came to break the dark clouds. No doubt, lightning is a dismal light, but at least if the storm had broken out in earnest I would have been able to see Jesus for one passing moment. But it was night! The dark night of the soul! I felt I was alone in the garden of Gethsemane like Jesus, and I found no consolation on earth or from heaven; God Himself seemed to have abandoned me.[176]

No matter how difficult this night is for Thérèse, she never despairs, and she allows Jesus to go on sleeping in her boat. In one of her poems, Thérèse writes, "Living on Love, when Jesus is sleeping, is rest on stormy seas. Oh! Lord, don't fear that I'll wake you. I'm waiting in peace for Heaven's shore ...."[177] These nights are of such great benefit to souls, but unfortunately many people became frightened when faced with such trials. People think that they will not be able to suffer what is necessary in order to be purified and reach such a high degree of union with the Lord; they forget or do not understand that God will give them the grace. For this reason, they want to turn back instead of advancing along the road to sanctity.

Not surprisingly, if a person were to read St John of the Cross, he or she may feel doubly discouraged. For example, in regard to the means by which a person advances on the road to sanctity, St John of the Cross writes: "To love is to strip oneself for God of all that is

---

[176] Ms A 51r, 109.
[177] PN 17, 9, 91.

not God!" A person reading this could feel that St John of the Cross' description of love is simply beyond what that person is able to do. On the other hand, when St Thérèse describes what love is, she says "To love is to give all and even oneself." This seems much more palatable than the definition given by St John of the Cross; however, the substance is really no different. Thérèse's definition seems much more positive and appealing. It is not that Thérèse asks less than John of the Cross, but her way of describing the road to holiness seems much gentler and doable.[178]

Ida Görres in her book *The Hidden Face* says she believes that St Thérèse "underwent the same experiences as John of the Cross and expressed simply what he expounded."[179] St Thérèse describes her experiences from a different angle. Like St John of the Cross, she also wants to point out the way that leads to union with God, the "summit of the mount of Love, transforming union with God."[180] However, Thérèse's emphasis is different – for St Thérèse, the "naked cross of detachment will be hidden under the rose petals of gentle love all intent on giving."[181] Hence, one could say that St Thérèse adds something to the teaching of St John of the Cross, something that is very appealing to *little souls*. She gives the perfect solution, by saying that God will carry these souls as long as they remain

---

[178] Gabriel of St Mary Magdalene, OCD, "St. Thérèse's 'Little Way' and the Teachings of St. John of the Cross," *Spiritual Life*, vol. 2, n. 2 (June 1956): 88.
[179] Ida F. Görres, *The Hidden Face*, 250.
[180] Gabriel of St Mary Magdalene, "St. Thérèse's 'Little Way' and the Teachings of St. John of the Cross," 86.
[181] Gabriel of St Mary Magdalene, "St. Thérèse's 'Little Way' and the Teachings of St. John of the Cross," 88.

little.[182] For St Thérèse, the way of spiritual childhood is the way of love and simplicity, through which she reaches the heights of perfection. She explains, "perfection seems simple to me, I see it is sufficient to recognize one's nothingness and to abandon oneself as a child into God's arms."[183]

St Thérèse's *Little Way* – A Perfect Preparation for Infused Contemplation and the Operation of the Gift of Wisdom

St Thérèse's *Little Way* is a perfect preparation for infused contemplation which is caused by the operation of the gifts, especially the gift of wisdom; it is the way of total trust and abandonment. From a very young age Thérèse is being prepared by God to reach the heights of union with Him. Her childlike trust in God is unshakable and her simplicity gives her complete confidence in Him. She does not trust her own strength but relies on God for everything. This childlike trust permeates her life of prayer which she always puts into the hands of God. Thérèse believes that by remaining humble and recognising one's own human weakness, a person is much more disposed to the grace of God working in his or her life. She declares:

---

[182] Gabriel of St Mary Magdalene, "St. Thérèse's 'Little Way' and the Teachings of St. John of the Cross," 91.
[183] *GC* II, LT 226, 1094.

> Even if I had accomplished all the works of St. Paul, I would still believe myself to be a "useless servant." But it is precisely this that makes up my joy, for having nothing, I shall receive everything from God.[184]

Thérèse has great confidence that God will give her what she needs, and in this way she moves the heart of God. Her spirituality of abandonment and confidence in God incites the outpourings of the Holy Spirit.[185] Thérèse exclaims, "Oh! how I would like to be able to make you understand what I *feel*!... It is confidence and nothing but confidence that must lead us to Love."[186]

God wants to lavish the soul with His grace and love. The way of Thérèse, the *Little Way* is a way of abandoning oneself to God as a little child.[187] Through this total abandonment and reliance on God's grace, the Lord works in and through her. The *Little Way* is not so much about what the soul does, as it is about how the soul relies completely on God. When a soul begins to receive infused contemplation, it will often have the temptation to rely on its own active form of prayer rather than allowing God to work in it by infusing His light and love. However, the person who is already accustomed to following the *Little Way* finds the transition from a more active form of prayer to a more passive form much easier – because the soul is

---

[184] *LC*, June 23, 67.
[185] Bl. Marie-Eugène, Under the Torrent of His Love, 129. St Thomas says, "confidence is hope with firm expectation and without fear" (*Super Ep. ad Hebr.*, cap. 3 lec. 1, n. 169).
[186] *GC* II, LT 190, 1000 (emphasis added).
[187] Bl. Marie-Eugène, *Under the Torrent of His Love*, 129.

already accustomed to abandoning itself to God and relying on Him for everything. For this reason, Thérèse's *Little Way* is the perfect preparation for infused contemplation and the operation of the gift of wisdom. This *Little Way*, which is open to all souls, can be a perfect way for the soul to be disposed for the reception of the outpouring of grace. Arintero explains:

> ...the "little way" ...is an appeal *to all souls for infused contemplation,* and the best preparation for it; for the basis of the "little way" is humility, spiritual poverty ... The *little child* seeing himself so poor and miserable, flees from himself and throws himself into the arms of God in Whom he places all his hope.[188]

Thérèse relies on God for everything; she knows that without God's grace she can do nothing. Her *Little Way*, the way of humility, trust, and abandonment, gives God the room to mould and work within the soul. In recognising one's own human weakness and abandoning oneself to God, a person allows God to work in his or her daily life and in the life of prayer. Thérèse has the deep conviction that it is not so much about what a person can do, but what God can do in that person. If the person remains open to the grace of God, He – Who can do infinitely more than we could ever hope for – takes over.

Thérèse has a profound understanding of the theology of grace. It is unlikely that she read any of the works of St Thomas Aquinas;[189] nevertheless, her

---

[188] Ven. Arintero, *Mystical Phenomena*, 48.
[189] In one book which Thérèse had read and thoroughly enjoyed,

understanding of grace is consistent with St Thomas' theology of grace – God has been teaching Thérèse in the depths of her soul. In other words, she has arrived at this understanding not through study, but because God Himself has taught her through a connatural way of knowing which comes as a result of the operation of the gift of wisdom.

Thérèse is highly aware of how God works in a soul that is open and willing to entrust itself to Him.[190] She abandons herself to God and is always sensitive to the promptings of the Holy Spirit,[191] Who blesses her with very clear lights and an abundance of grace, Who permeates every area of her life. For St Thomas, "mystical passivity" is the "apex of the Spirit's action."[192] Thérèse is completely abandoned to God; she is "wholly possessed by the Divine Spirit, instructed by the heavenly Master, moved and directed by a higher instinct."[193] The prayer of infused

---

called *The End of the Present World and the Mysteries of the Future Life*, there are a number of references to St Thomas Aquinas. See Charles Arminjon, *The End of the Present World and the Mysteries of the Future Life*, translated by Martin Research Associates (Illinois: Martin Books Edition, 1968). This book made a great impression on Thérèse – she says that reading this book "was one of the greatest graces in [her] life," and that "the impressions" she received were "too deep to express in human words" (Ms A 47v, 102).

[190] St Thomas says, that on the part of the soul, one can receive more grace than another, because it has prepared well to receive grace and whoever is "better prepared for grace, receives more grace." We cannot just look for the primary reason here though, because it is God who gives His gifts as He wills (*ST* I-II, q. 112, a. 4).

[191] André Combes, *St. Thérèse and Suffering: The Spirituality of St. Thérèse in its Essence*, translated by Msgr. Philip E. Hallett (Dublin: M.H. Gill and Son, Ltd., 1951), 60-61.

[192] Chenu, *Aquinas and His Role in Theology*, 50.

contemplation is primarily the action of God working in the soul to heal and vivify it and to lead it to the heights of holiness. The response of the soul ought always to be "expressed by the *fiat* of perfect abandonment."[194]

We have seen that the *Little Way*, which above all is the way of the loving trust of a little child, is the perfect preparation for infused contemplation. The soul that is not so accustomed to abandoning itself to God or being open to God's grace may be less disposed to receive this more passive type of prayer. When God begins to infuse His light and love into a soul through the prayer of infused contemplation, it may be difficult for this soul to give up its usual active prayer of meditation; for this reason, many people do not advance in their prayer life. Sometimes, more passive prayer can cause people to feel that they are being lazy, and instead of abandoning themselves to the Holy Spirit, they rely more on their own efforts. They try to persist with a more active form of prayer by trying to meditate actively, when in fact, God wants to lead them into a more passive form of prayer. For this reason, they do not remain open to the Spirit's action working in the soul through the prayer of infused contemplation. This is unfortunate because of the huge benefits that a soul receives as a result of infused contemplation. On the other hand, if a person

---

[193] Ven. Arintero, *Mystical Phenomena*, 33.
[194] Garrigou-Lagrange, Christian Perfection and Contemplation, 100. St John of the Cross explains the action of the Holy Spirit in the soul who is open to His Spirit: "By reason of his being so fully disposed, he usually remains for a long time in contemplation" (Living Flame of Love, stanza 1, 33, 593).

is already practising the way of loving abandonment and trust in God's mercy, the usual struggle that accompanies the transition from a more active type of prayer to the passive prayer of infused contemplation can be less difficult precisely because the person is already accustomed to abandoning himself or herself into the hands of God. The *Little Way* of Thérèse is the way of a little child who sleeps in its Father's arms. The soul that can be truly child-like and allow the Lord to take over its life of prayer will "live the mysteries of salvation ... will taste them [and] contemplate them with admiration."[195]

Experiencing the Indwelling through the Operation of the Gift of Wisdom

When a person has advanced considerably in the spiritual life, it may happen that he or she experiences the presence of God dwelling within the soul. According to St Thomas, this quasi-experiential knowing and awareness of the indwelling of the Trinity happens through the gift of wisdom,[196] which enables us to know God present within us in a quasi-experiential manner.[197] Thérèse often experiences the

---

[195] Garrigou-Lagrange, Three Ages of the Interior Life, vol. II, 435.
[196] *ST* I, q. 43, a. 5, ad 2. Garrigou-Lagrange explains that in the mystical state a person can have the feeling that God dwells within his or her soul and this springs from the gift of wisdom. At other times a person can feel abandoned or separated from God and this is due more to the gift of understanding (*Three Ages of the Interior Life*, vol. II, 317).
[197] Garrigou-Lagrange, *Three Ages of the Interior Life*, vol. II, 467-468.

presence of Jesus within her soul – Jesus has become Thérèse's constant guide and teacher – and her awareness of the presence of Jesus becomes increasingly more intense.[198] She describes this experience in a letter to Céline:

> Jesus calls us, He wants to look at us at His leisure, but *He is not alone; with Him, the two other Persons of the Blessed Trinity come to take possession of our soul....* Jesus had promised it in days gone by when He was about to reascend to His Father and our Father. He said with ineffable tenderness: "If anyone loves me, he will keep my word, and my Father will love him, and we will come to him, and we will make in him our abode."[199]

Jesus is enlightening and teaching Thérèse, and she experiences Him present within her soul at each moment:

> I understand and I know from experience that: "the kingdom of God is within you." Jesus has no need of books or teachers to instruct souls; He teaches without the noise of words. Never have I heard

---

John F. Dedek in his article "Quasi experimentalis cognitio" points out that "Thomas insisted that the just man's knowledge of the divine Persons sent to inhabit his soul must needs be not merely informed faith but knowledge accompanied by charity, that is to say, experimental knowledge. Moreover, such knowledge belongs to wisdom, since the spiritual taste and connaturality resulting from the affective union with God through charity afford the just man a basis for a correct estimation of God and His creatures" ("Quasi experimentalis cognition, 386).

[198] Frederick L. Miller, *The Trial of Faith of St. Thérèse of Lisieux* (New York: Alba House, 1998), 157-158.

[199] *GC* II, LT 165, 1894, 861-862 (emphasis added).

> Him speak, but I *feel that He is within me at each moment;* He is guiding and inspiring me with what I must say and do. I find just when I need them certain lights that I had not seen until then ...[200]

This quasi-experiential knowledge is something that Thérèse continues to experience throughout her short life. Again, she says:

> I have frequently noticed that Jesus doesn't want me to lay up provisions; He nourishes me at each moment with a totally new food; *I find it within me without my knowing how it is there.* I believe it is Jesus himself hidden in the depths of my poor little heart: He is giving me the grace of acting within me, making me think of all He desires me to do at the present moment.[201]

Thérèse is certain that God is present within her soul; this is possible only through the operation of the gift of wisdom.[202] Through this gift Thérèse actually "felt charity" enter into her soul.[203] Of course, Thérèse is in a state of grace and therefore already has charity present within her soul. What she is describing here is consistent with St Thomas' explanation of a soul receiving an increase in grace and perceiving this

---

[200] Ms A 83v, 179 (emphasis added).
[201] Ms A 76r, 165 (emphasis added).
[202] A. Gardeil, OP, *Le Saint-Esprit dans la vie chrétienne.* (Juvisy Seine-&-Oise: Cerf, 1934), 160-161: "Sainte Thérèse sortait de cette oraison avec la certitude qu'elle était allée en Dieu, présent en elle. Il n'y a que la Sagesse qui puisse appliquer ainsi notre esprit à la substance de Dieu dans le fond de notre âme, mais elle nous conduit jusque-là."
[203] Ms A 45v, 99.

increase by way of a quasi-experiential knowledge through the operation of the gift of wisdom. According to St Thomas, it is possible for us to have such a perception when we progress in virtue or receive an increase in grace.[204] This "perception implies a certain experimental knowledge; and this is properly called wisdom [sapientia], as it were a sweet knowledge."[205]

St Thérèse is aware that Jesus is "acting in and through her by means of charity."[206] She says, "Yes, *I feel* it. When I am charitable, it is Jesus alone who is acting in me and the more united I am to Him, the more also do I love my Sisters."[207] When Jesus fills St Thérèse with His love, she responds by extending this love to others, so that she is loving with His love, and she experiences Jesus acting in and through her. This is an effect of the operation of the gift of wisdom. She knows that by receiving Love she can then be used as

---

[204] *ST* I, q. 43, a. 6, ad 2: "The invisible mission takes place...as regards progress in virtue or increase of grace.
Hence Augustine says (De Trin. iv, 20), that 'the Son is sent to each one when He is known and perceived by anyone, so far as He can be known and perceived according to the capacity of the soul, whether journeying towards God, or united perfectly to Him.' Such invisible mission, however, chiefly occurs as regards anyone's proficiency in the performance of a new act, or in the acquisition of a new state of grace as for example... the fervor of charity leading a man to expose himself to the danger of martyrdom, or to renounce his possessions, or to undertake any arduous work."
[205] *ST* I, q. 43, a. 5, ad 2.
[206] Miller, *The Trial of Faith,* 166.
[207] Ms C 12v, 220 (emphasis added).

God's instrument to lavish others with His love.[208] As Benedict XVI says in his encyclical *Deus Caritas Est*, God

> has loved us first and he continues to do so; we too, then, can respond with love. God does not demand of us a feeling which we ourselves are incapable of producing. He loves us, he makes us see and experience his love, and since he has "loved us first," love can also blossom as a response within us.[209]

When St Thérèse has the experience of Jesus dwelling within her soul, she often feels that He is there dwelling as one who is asleep. Just before Thérèse enters Carmel, she is experiencing dryness and aridity in prayer. She is still aware that Jesus is present in the very depths of her soul; however, He is "present as one asleep – and, as asleep, dreaming of Thérèse."[210] St Thérèse describes this experience as Jesus "sleeping" in His boat; in other words, He is sleeping in her soul. She understands He is hidden within her, even though she feels she is in darkness. In *Story of a Soul, Manuscript A,* which is addressed to Mother Agnes, she writes:

> I should have spoken to you about the retreat preceding my Profession, dear Mother, before speaking about the trial I have mentioned; it was

---

[208] When a person grows in charity, he or she receives an "essential increase of charity" which means that the soul now has the "ability to produce an act of more fervent love" (*ST* II-II, q. 24, a. 4, ad 3).
[209] Benedict XVI, *Deus Caritas Est*, 17.
[210] Miller, *The Trial of Faith*, 157-158.

far from bringing me any consolations since the most absolute aridity and almost total abandonment were my lot. Jesus was sleeping as usual in my little boat; ah! I see very well how rarely souls allow Him to sleep peacefully within them. Jesus is so fatigued with always having to take the initiative and to attend to others that He hastens to take advantage of the repose I offer to Him. He will undoubtedly awaken before my great eternal retreat, but instead of being troubled about it this only gives me extreme pleasure.[211]

St John of the Cross also describes how Jesus dwells in a soul as if asleep and how He awakens from time to time:

> ... within itself it has the experience of this intimate embrace. It does not however, always experience these awakenings, for when the Beloved produces them, it seems to the soul that He is awakening in its heart, where before He remained as though asleep. Although it was experiencing and enjoying Him, this took place as though with a loved one who is asleep, for knowledge and love is not communicated mutually while one is still asleep.
>
> Oh, how happy is this soul which ever experiences God resting and reposing within it! Oh, how fitting it is for it to withdraw from things, flee from business matters, and live in immense tranquillity,

---

[211] Ms A 75v, 165. St Teresa of Avila says the way to walk along the "path of love" is to serve Christ and refuse to seek spiritual delights. There are some people that desire to walk along this path, and not only do they refuse to seek spiritual delights, but they actually beseech God "not to give them these favors during their lifetime" (*Interior Castle*, IV Mansions, ch. 2, 9, 326).

so that it may not even with the slightest speck of dust or noise disturb or trouble its heart where the Beloved dwells.

He is usually there, in this embrace with His bride, as though asleep in the substance of the soul. And it is very well aware of Him and ordinarily enjoys Him. Were He always awake within it, communicating knowledge and love, it would already be in glory. For if, when He does waken, scarcely opening His eyes, He has such an effect on the soul, what would it be like were He ordinarily in it fully awake?[212]

Here, St John of the Cross is describing Jesus present within the soul that has reached a high degree of holiness, the state of union. Describing those who are in a state of grace but have not yet reached such a high degree of perfection, St John of the Cross says:

His dwelling is secret to them, even as though He does not dwell in them. They do not experience Him ordinarily, except when He grants them some delightful awakening.[213]

---

[212] St John of the Cross, *Living Flame of Love*, stanza 4, 14 -15, 648-649.

[213] St John of the Cross, *Living Flame of Love*, stanza 4, 16, 648-649: "Although He is not displeased with other souls that have not reached this union, for after all they are in the state of grace, yet insofar as they are not well disposed, His dwelling is secret to them, even as though He does not dwell in them. They do not experience Him ordinarily, except when He grants them some delightful awakening. But such an awakening is not of the kind and high quality, nor is it comparable to these, nor as secret to the intellect and the devil, which are still able to understand something through the movement of the senses. For the senses are not

St Thérèse's words express the description given by St John of the Cross about those who have reached the state of union. Thérèse experiences the Lord resting within her soul; she is happy to leave Jesus sleeping. In her poem *Living on Love*, she writes:

> Living on Love when Jesus is sleeping,
> Is rest on stormy seas.
> Oh! Lord, don't fear that I'll wake you.
> I'm waiting in peace for Heaven's shore…[214]

St Thérèse even has the experience of Jesus dwelling deep within her soul when she is experiencing intense aridity and darkness.[215] She says, "I felt (in the center of my heart a great calm through Jesus, little Jesus) that I was suffering for Jesus… (He was in my heart)."[216] Even when Thérèse is experiencing her trial of faith near the end of her life, she has the constant awareness of Jesus "dwelling and acting in her soul."[217]

Through the operation of the gift of wisdom a person can experience the Trinity deep within the soul in a way that is more often than not very subtle. The awareness of God dwelling within the soul is not something extraordinary. It is within the ordinary path of sanctification because it is made possible

---

fully annihilated until the soul reaches this union, and they still have some activity and movements concerning the spiritual, since they are not yet totally spiritual."

[214] PN 17, 9, 91.
[215] Jamart, *Spiritual Doctrine of St. Thérèse*, 243.
[216] *GC* I, LT 38A, 380.
[217] Miller, *The Trial of Faith*, 173.

through the operation of the gift of wisdom and can be experienced by all those who truly give themselves to God with their whole heart, mind, and strength.

The Gift of Wisdom Perfects Charity

Love is never static – "love is never 'finished' and complete; throughout life, it changes and matures."[218] St Thomas says that "charity is so encompassing that there will always be something left through which one might improve"[219] and that "even the perfect can make progress in charity."[220] As the Catechism puts it, "Charity is the soul of the holiness to which all are called."[221] The gift of wisdom helps to perfect the virtue of charity and helps this virtue reach tremendous heights – it can raise a person to heroism. By remaining open to God's grace and the gifts of the Holy Spirit, Thérèse reaches the heights of perfection, especially through the operation of the gift of wisdom. Thérèse had always practised loving God; her desire was always to please God in everything, and she was extremely pure in all her intentions. Thérèse's one desire in life was to do all that she could for God in order that He would be loved more. Her actions were never motivated by fear, but only love: "My nature

---

[218] Benedict XVI, *Deus Caritas Est*, 17.
[219] *St Thomas Aquinas, Super I Ep. ad Thess*, cap. 4, lec.1: "Est enim charitas tam magna, quod semper restat quo proficiendum sit."
[220] *ST* II-II, q. 24, a. 9, ad 3.
[221] *CCC* 826. See also *Lumen Gentium*, 40: "All the faithful of Christ of whatever rank or status, are called to the fullness of the Christian life and to the perfection of charity."

was such that fear made me recoil; with love not only did I advance, I actually flew."[222]

Thérèse is the Saint of Love, and her mission is to be love in the Church: "I understood that without *love* all works are nothing, even the most dazzling, such as raising the dead to life and converting peoples."[223] Thérèse understands that all of the works that are done here on earth are nothing without charity, that nothing in this life is more important than growth in charity, love of God and neighbour. She understands that "charity must not remain hidden in the bottom of the heart."[224] Thérèse explains what it is that makes her happy: "I felt *charity* enter into my soul, and the need to forget myself and to please others; since then I've been happy."[225]

Thérèse has a profound understanding that she does not have to perform great works, and that what is important is that she do all things with great love. She is aware that this is what pleases Jesus: "it is the heart that the eyes of Jesus are always looking at!"[226] Thérèse is faithful in all things, even the smallest of things, which to us might seem insignificant; and even when she experiences tremendous aridity, she continues to practise great charity. St John of the Cross says that God esteems very highly all our works that are done in hardships and aridity.[227] A sign of heroic charity is "radiating goodness toward all amid the

---

[222] Ms A 80v, 174.
[223] Ms A 81v, 175.
[224] Ms C 12r, 220.
[225] Ms A 45v, 99.
[226] *GC* I, LT 73, 496.
[227] St John of the Cross, *Spiritual Canticle*, stanza, 30, 5, 528.

greatest of difficulties."[228] By remaining open to God's grace and being faithful even during very difficult periods, Thérèse reaches a very high degree of love for God and neighbour. Concerning this high degree of charity, St John of the Cross explains:

> The purer and more refined a soul is in faith, the more infused charity it possesses, and the more charity it has the more the Holy Spirit illumines it and communicates His gifts, because charity is the means by which they are communicated.[229]

Thérèse is filled with the gifts of the Holy Spirit, and through the operation of the gift of wisdom, Thérèse's love is perfected. She begins to taste true happiness here on earth, and through the help of the gift of wisdom her charity continues to blossom. "The light of the gift of wisdom sets the heart on fire with love and in that way returns to the principle from which it emanated, completing the divine circle."[230] In other words, the gift of wisdom flows from charity and leads back to charity. Through the operation of this gift, the heart is enflamed with love and thus wisdom completes its divine circle.

The gift of wisdom is a most precious gift. It is the highest of the seven gifts, and it is the gift which is most suited to setting the heart aflame with love.[231] Through the operation of this gift, the "heart melts

---

[228] Garrigou-Lagrange, *Three Ages of the Interior Life*, vol. II, 469.
[229] St John of the Cross, *Ascent of Mount Carmel*, bk II, ch. 28, 6, 205.
[230] Martinez, *Sanctifier*, 189.
[231] Àngel de les Gavarres, *Thérèse, Little Child of God's Mercy*, 353.

under the great fire of God's familiarity."[232] Charity becomes so ordered through the gift of wisdom, and the soul loves God so much, that it has truly reached the summit of Christian perfection.[233] Thérèse had truly reached the heights of union with God. She never performed dazzling works; in fact, she lived in silence and in simplicity. However, she had reached a very high degree of perfection, which did not go unnoticed in Carmel. Marie of the Sacred Heart (Marie Martin) says:

> Generally speaking, the Servant of God did not attract any attention during her lifetime. Her virtue consisted principally in doing the ordinary things extraordinarily well. Those who observed her more closely, however, noticed an absolutely rare degree of perfection in her.[234]

The gift of wisdom was highly operative throughout the life of Thérèse and increased in proportion to her growth in charity and holiness. The operation of the gift of wisdom – perfecting charity – will become more evident and will be manifested more fully in the next two chapters.

---

[232] Vonier, *The Spirit and the Bride*, 190-191.
[233] Ven. Arintero, *Mystical Phenomena*, 38.
[234] Christopher O'Mahony, *St. Thérèse of Lisieux by those who knew her*, 103.

Ordering Others According to Divine Rules - The Charism of Wisdom

Sermo Sapientiae is the charism of wisdom by which a person is able to direct the affairs of others "according to Divine rules."[235] When this charism is given to a person who is in a state of grace, it is joined to the gift of wisdom.[236] In other words, when the gift of wisdom is operating in a very high degree, there can be an overflow of this gift which manifests itself as a charism. St Thomas explains that some people

> receive a higher degree of the gift of wisdom, both as to the contemplation of Divine things (by both knowing more exalted mysteries and being able to impart this knowledge to others) and as to the direction of human affairs according to Divine rules (by being able to direct not only themselves but also others according to those rules).[237]

This charism of wisdom – which is an overflowing of the operation of the gift of wisdom – is often operating in the life of St Thérèse; she is able to help and instruct others because of this charism. St John

---

[235] *ST* II-II, q. 45, a. 5.
[236] Jacobus M. Ramirez, OP, *De Donis Spiritus Sancti deque Vita Mystica*, 337-339. Garrigou-Lagrange points out that "St Thomas, 'Doctor Communis' as he is called in Pius XI's encyclical *Studiorum Ducem*, is pre-eminent among theologians because he attained the secrets of this twofold wisdom, he received in a very high degree the special grace which St Paul calls *sermo sapientiae*" (Garrigou-Lagrange, *Christian Perfection and Contemplation*, 1).
[237] *ST* II-II, q. 45, a. 5.

Paul II, in his apostolic letter *Divini Amoris*, points out that Thérèse has a

> special charism of wisdom. This young Carmelite, without any particular theological training, but illumined by the light of the Gospel, feels she is being taught by the divine Teacher who, as she says, is "the Doctor of Doctors" ... What strikes us most about the Saint is her infused wisdom, that is to say, her lucid, profound and inebriating absorption of the divine truths and mysteries of faith ... That assimilation was ... due to a charism of wisdom from the Holy Spirit.[238]

For example, as novice mistress, Thérèse entrusts herself entirely to Jesus, confident that He will give her all that she needs:

> I have recalled to you, dear Mother, the first work Jesus and you saw fit to accomplish through me. This was the prelude of those which were to be confided to me. When I was given the office of entering into the sanctuary of souls, I saw immediately that the task was beyond my strength. I threw myself into the arms of God as a little child and, hiding my face in His hair, I said: "Lord I am too little to nourish Your children; if You wish to give through me what is suitable for each, fill my little hand and without leaving Your arms or turning my head, I shall give Your treasures to the soul who will come and ask for nourishment."[239]

---

[238] John Paul II, *Divini Amoris Scientia*, 7.
[239] Ms C 22r, 237-238.

Thérèse throws herself into the arms of the Lord and counts on Him to provide what is needed; in this way, she is assured that the novices will receive the instruction that they need. Thérèse knows that Jesus is speaking through her, and it is because of this that she has the confidence to guide these novices: "'I *feel*,' she told them, 'that when I am telling you these things, I am not mistaken and that Jesus is speaking through my mouth.'"[240] Here, the bold confidence, which is a hallmark of the gift of wisdom, can be seen alongside the clear ability to direct souls for Jesus (which is the manifestation of the charism). Thérèse understands that God likes to use us as His instruments:

> He [the Lord] is always using His creatures as instruments to carry on His work in souls. If a piece of canvas painted on by an artist could think and speak it certainly would not complain at being constantly touched and retouched by the brush, and would not envy the lot of that instrument, for it would realize it was not to the brush but to the artist using it that it owed the beauty with which it was clothed. The brush, too, would not be able to boast of the masterpiece produced with it, as it knows that artists are not at a loss; they play with difficulties, and are pleased to choose at times weak and defective instruments.
>
> My dear Mother, I am a little brush that Jesus has chosen in order to paint His own image in the souls you entrusted to my care. An artist doesn't use only one brush, but needs at least two; the first is the more useful and with it he applies the general tints

---

[240] Jamart, *Spiritual Doctrine of St. Thérèse*, 245-246.

and covers the canvas entirely in a very short time; the other, the smaller one, he uses for the details.

Mother, you are the precious brush that the hand of Jesus lovingly holds when He wishes to do a *great work* in souls of your children, and I am the very *small brush* He deigns to use afterward for the smallest details.[241]

Thérèse also has a profound understanding that God loves us so much that He wants to let us share in the cultivation of souls, in the work of bringing souls closer to heaven. She sees this as a huge gift from God:

> God has no need for anyone to carry out His work, I know, but just as He allows a clever gardener to raise rare and delicate plants, giving him the necessary knowledge for this while reserving to Himself the care of making them fruitful, so Jesus wills to be helped in His divine cultivation of souls.[242]

When the Lord works in and through Thérèse, she has no doubt that the help she gives to others comes from Jesus. In a letter to her sister Céline, she writes:

> I find that Jesus is very good in allowing my poor letter to do you some good, but, I assure you I am not making the mistake of thinking I have anything to do with it… All the most beautiful discourses of the greatest saint would be incapable of making one *single* act of love come from a heart that Jesus did not possess. He alone can use His lyre, no one

---

[241] Ms C 20r -20v, 235.
[242] Ms A 53r, 113.

else can make its harmonious notes sound; however, Jesus uses all means, all creatures are at His service, and He loves to use them during the night of life in order to hide His adorable presence, but He does not hide Himself in such a way that He does not allow Himself to be divined. In fact, *I really feel that often He gives me some lights*, not for myself but for His little exiled dove, His dear spouse.[243]

Thérèse always remains humble, no matter how much the Lord uses her to enlighten other souls; she never seeks anything extraordinary in the spiritual life. Thérèse believes that God working deep within a soul is what is most impressive, most secure, and less open to deception. One day, Thérèse goes to visit Mother Geneviève, who is sick at the time. Thérèse has been undergoing a severe trial. When Thérèse arrives at Mother Geneviève's room she is unable to enter because only two sisters are allowed in the room at one time. When Thérèse turns to leave, Mother Geneviève says to Thérèse "Wait, my little child, I'm going to say just a little word to you; every time you come you ask for a spiritual bouquet. Well, today, I will give you this one: Serve God with *peace* and *joy*; remember, my child, *Our God is a God of peace*."[244] Thérèse is moved to tears and experiences great consolation. She wants to find out more about the revelation from Mother Geneviève; however much to Thérèse's surprise, Mother Geneviève says that she has not received any revelation. Thérèse says:

> Then my admiration was greater still when I saw

---

[243] *GC* II, LT 147, 813 (emphasis added).
[244] Ms A 78r, 169-170.

the degree to which Jesus was living within her and making her act and speak. Ah! that type of sanctity seems the *truest* and the *most holy* to me, and it is the type that I desire because in it one meets with no deceptions.[245]

Thérèse remarks that Mother Geneviève has been "made holy by the practice of the hidden virtues, the ordinary virtues."[246] This is the same road Thérèse wants to follow; she seeks after God in the ordinary things. Even if God had given Thérèse visions or locutions, if she had raised the dead, to love God with a sincere heart and to practice the virtues with great humility would always remain for her the most important things in the spiritual life. Marie-Eugène of the Child Jesus remarks:

> God's hold on a soul that is unaware of it, seemed to Saint Therese of the Child Jesus the most desirable form of sanctity because the most simple. Is it not also the highest? At least, it is the one that shows best how the Spirit of God is "more active than all active things: and reaches everywhere by reason of her purity."[247]

This is the way that the Lord works in the soul of Thérèse. He instructs her and guides her for the good of her own soul, the novices she is leading, and all those who would learn from her teaching and example. She understands that the lights she has received are "always increasing for the good of her

---

[245] Ms A 78r, 169-170.
[246] Ms A 78r, 169.
[247] Bl. Marie-Eugène, *I Want to See God*, 344.

soul and for the enlightenment and counsel of innumerable others."[248] Thérèse is given an amazing insight in regard to leading the novices:

> Jesus gave me a simple means of accomplishing my mission. He made me understand these words of the Canticle of Canticles: *DRAW ME, WE SHALL RUN after you in the odor of your ointments.* O Jesus, it is not even necessary to say: "*When drawing me, draw the souls whom I love!*" This simple statement "Draw me" suffices; I understand, Lord that when a soul allows herself to be captivated *by the odor of your ointments*, she cannot run alone, all the souls whom she loves follow in her train; this is done without constraint, without effort, it is a natural consequence of her attraction for You. Just as a torrent, throwing itself with impetuosity into the ocean, drags after it everything it encounters in its passage, in the same way, O Jesus, the soul who plunges into the shoreless ocean of Your Love, draws with her all the treasures she possesses. Lord, You know it, I have no other treasure than the souls it has pleased You to unite to mine.[249]

> I feel that the more the fire of love burns within my heart, the more I shall say: "*Draw me,*" the more also the souls who will approach me (poor little piece of iron, unless if I withdraw from the divine furnace), the more these souls *will run swiftly on the odor of the ointments of their Beloved,* for a soul that is burning with love cannot remain inactive.[250]

---

[248] Ven. Arintero, *Mystical Phenomena,* 35-36.
[249] Ms C 33v-34r, 254.
[250] Ms C 36r, 257.

Thérèse exclaims, "Dear Mother, this is my prayer. I asked Jesus to draw me into the flames of His love, to unite me so closely to Him that He live and act in me."[251] Thérèse penetrates the Divine mysteries with such clarity and depth that she can express the things that she has discovered with the "language of a child. She possesse[s] the science of salvation to a high degree and [is] able to impart it with rare perfection."[252]

Blessed are the Peacemakers

St Thomas states that peace is the ultimate effect of the gift of wisdom.[253] Hence, one would expect to see this effect especially in a soul who is experiencing the very heights of the operation of this gift. St Thérèse enters Carmel on 9 April 1888. She says that when the doors of Carmel closed behind her and her desires were finally accomplished: "My soul experienced a *PEACE* so sweet, so deep, it would be impossible to express it. For seven years and a half that inner peace has remained my lot, and has not abandoned me in the midst of the greatest trials."[254] Thérèse has such a profound peace within her heart that she says:

> My heart is filled with God's will, and when someone pours something on it, this doesn't penetrate its interior; it's a nothing which glides off

---

[251] Ms C 36r, 257.
[252] Bl. Marie-Eugène, *Under the Torrent of His Love*, 99.
[253] *ST* II-II, q. 45, a. 6.
[254] Ms A 69r-69v, 148.

easily, just like oil which can't mix with water. I remain always at profound peace in the depths of my heart: nothing can disturb it.[255]

In fact, her "heart is peaceful like a tranquil lake or a serene sky."[256] Even when things do not appear serene on the outside, Thérèse always exhibits that interior peace which is an effect of a high degree of the operation of the gift of wisdom. During a struggle she has with one of the sisters in Carmel, Thérèse says, "I was as much at peace as if I were at prayer."[257] This deep peace never leaves Thérèse; she remains at peace during struggles with others, through illness and trials, and even in her final struggles near the end of her life – peace reigns in her heart. She says, "It's all God's tenderness to me: exteriorly, I'm loaded with gifts; interiorly, I'm always in my trial (*of faith*) … but also in peace."[258] To have true peace is beyond a person's own ability; it is something that only Divine "wisdom and love can produce."[259] The gift of wisdom enkindles the fire of love so deeply within the heart

---

[255] *LC*, July 14, 9, 97-98.
[256] *GC* II, LT 245, 1129.
[257] *LC*, April 18, 1, 38.
[258] *LC*, September 8, 186. Jamart says "we must not think that her trial was solely for the purification of her soul. Thérèse herself attributed to it an apostolic purpose. She offered it to God to obtain the light of divine faith for the unbelievers and to make reparation for the faults committed against that virtue. That she might merit these graces for sinners 'she accepted to eat nothing but the bread of affliction, until the time when it would please Jesus to introduce her into His glorious kingdom.' Her trials… lasted until the end of her life" (*Spiritual Doctrine of St. Thérèse*, 239). See also Miller, *The Trial of Faith*, 191- 207.
[259] Martinez, *Sanctifier*, 305.

that nothing can disturb the soul's peace. Through the operation of the gift of wisdom, Thérèse experiences this profound sense of peace: "I'm always happy, for I always manage in the midst of the tempest to preserve interior peace."[260] She explains to Sr Marie of the Eucharist, "It's especially because I am in great peace that I am happy; as for feeling an immense joy as we sometimes do when our heart beats with happiness, oh! no… I'm in peace, that's why I'm happy."[261]

As stated above, when peace is the effect of the gift of wisdom operating in a very high degree, this peace cannot be disturbed. This is clearly manifested in the life of St Thérèse. For example, she says, "Although Jesus is giving me no consolation, He is giving me a peace so great that it is doing me more good!"[262] On a couple of occasions when Thérèse is going through tremendous suffering, near the end of her life, she exclaims, "Yes, but peace, too, peace!"[263] Again she says, "I have great peace in my heart."[264] Even on the very last day of Thérèse's life, when she is close to death and enduring great physical suffering, she says: "Ah, what darkness! However, I am still at peace."[265]

The truly peaceful person rests "tranquilly in divine simplicity."[266] Thérèse always remains in constant peace deep within her soul because of her

---

[260] *LC*, April 18, 1, 37.
[261] *LC*, August 17, 287. From Sister Marie of the Eucharist to M. Guerin, 287.
[262] *GC* I, LT 76, 504.
[263] *LC*, August 21, 1, 160.
[264] *LC*, August 27, 3, 171.
[265] *Story of a Soul, Epilogue*, 266.
[266] Martinez, *Sanctifier*, 305-306.

"perfect union with God."[267] A person can reach such an advanced state in the spiritual life that nothing can disturb him or her; this is the peace that comes from the operation of the gift of wisdom. When this type of peace has been established within, it is because the person has a deep union with God. St Augustine explains that when this peace has been "established and strengthened" within a person, then even persecution cannot shake the edifice of the soul that has been made so strong, and "hence there follows: "Blessed are they which are persecuted for justice' sake: for theirs is the kingdom of heaven."[268]

When this type of peace has been established, the soul never wants to renounce such a deep peace. It never wants to lose what has been gained through its progress in the spiritual life; therefore whatever trials come its way, it never turns away from this peace and union with God. For this reason, St Thomas says:

> The eighth beatitude is a confirmation and declaration of all those that precede. Because from the very fact that a man is confirmed in poverty of spirit, meekness, and the rest, it follows that no persecution will induce him to renounce them. Hence the eighth beatitude corresponds, in a way, to all the preceding seven.[269]

And because the "eighth beatitude is a confirmation of all the beatitudes, so it deserves all the rewards of

---

[267] Àngel de les Gavarres, *Thérèse: The Little Child of God's Mercy*, 320.
[268] St Augustine, *Commentary on the Lord's Sermon on the Mount*, bk 1, ch. 2, 9.
[269] *ST* I-II, q. 69, a. 3, ad 5.

the beatitudes. Hence it returns to the first, that we may understand all the other rewards to be attributed to it in consequence."[270] This is "the circle of the Gospel's happiness."[271] Hence, the eighth beatitude is a "summary of everything that goes before with accent on suffering and firm adherence to God's will."[272] When one remains constantly humble and at peace even in the face of torment and persecution, this is certainly the true and "full perfection of Christian life. It is realized especially in the last trials undergone by perfect souls which God purifies by making them work for the salvation of their neighbour."[273] Thérèse would have gladly undergone any type of persecution for love of her Beloved Spouse. She was subject to many kinds of trials and temptations throughout her short life, and in the last year of her life, she struggled with strong temptations against faith. She had great trials; however, peace continued to reign in the very depth of her soul. This deep peace comes from the operation of the gift of wisdom.

Conclusion

In this chapter, the many effects of the operation of the gift of wisdom have been shown to be clearly manifest in the life of St Thérèse of Lisieux. When this gift of the Holy Spirit is operating in a high degree, the soul

---

[270] *ST* I-II, q. 69, a. 4, ad 2.
[271] Jacques Maritain, *The Range of Reason*, 219.
[272] Brennan Robert Edward, *The Seven Horns of the Lamb*, 17-18.
[273] Garrigou-Lagrange, *Three Ages of the Interior Life*, vol. I, 171.

experiences a sort of connaturality with Divine things; it receives knowledge from Jesus in a quasi-experiential way. Consequently, it has great confidence that this knowledge is from God. For this reason, St Thérèse exhibits extraordinary confidence in the infinite love and mercy of God. In regard to the mystical life, as has been stated earlier, "the full normal actualization of the gift of wisdom deserves the name infused contemplation, properly so called."[274] It has been shown that St Thérèse enjoyed a very high degree of infused contemplation, and that through this contemplation, Jesus taught her His Divine Secrets, including the *Little Way*. Moreover, evidence has been presented to verify that St Thérèse did indeed experience the indwelling of the Holy Trinity, and that she experienced the concomitant phenomena that often accompany infused contemplation. It has been shown that she was given the charism of wisdom, an overflowing of the gift of wisdom, and that she enjoyed the peace which is a consequence of the gift of wisdom operating in a very high degree. Finally, it has been stated that St Thérèse reached the heights of charity through the operation of the gift of wisdom. What remains is to focus on this perfecting of charity – to such a degree that God's *Little Flower* would offer her life in imitation of Christ as a martyr of love. This full blossoming of wisdom's effect on charity will be the focus of the next chapter and final chapter.

---

[274] Garrigou-Lagrange, *Three Ages of the Interior Life*, vol. II, 339.

5

THE FULL FLOWERING OF THE GIFT OF WISDOM IN THE LIFE OF ST THÉRÈSE

The goal of this fifth chapter is to show the full blossoming of the operation of the gift of wisdom in St Thérèse's life – following the order of her life and showing the growth in the operation of this gift; and her death as a martyr of love will be treated in the sixth chapter. Examining the important events in the life of St Thérèse manifests a progressive growth in the perfection of charity, and her desire to be conformed to Christ; these significant moments give a clear indication of the operation of the gift of wisdom perfecting the theological virtue of charity in the soul of Thérèse. These events lead up to the moment of Thérèse's death when her charity has reached remarkable heights and she is finally brought to the point of dying as a martyr of love.

The Lover and the Beloved

As we grow in the spiritual life, our acts of "charity are accompanied in a proportionate degree by the act of the gift of wisdom."[1] Thérèse's charity had reached the heights of sanctity as a result of wisdom's

---

[1] Garrigou-Lagrange, *Three Ages of the Interior Life*, vol. II, 467-468.

perfecting influence on charity, and she desired to be more and more conformed to her Beloved. The desire to be more conformed to Christ is especially due to the operation of the gift of wisdom. Through this gift, we come to know God as the Beloved. This can be compared to "the poetic experience whereby a person is grasped strongly and yet inarticulately by the beautiful."[2] When the gift of wisdom operates, charity is perfected, and we desire to become more and more conformed to Christ, the Beloved. St Thomas says that it is "a characteristic of true love that it draws the one loved to love the one who loves him,"[3] and that "love is perfected by the lover being drawn to the beloved."[4] Thérèse is continually drawn into a deeper love relationship with her Beloved Lord, and the more she is drawn, the more she increases in charity and is given the capacity to love more deeply. She is consumed by love and the more pure and unbounded her charity, the more she desires to be conformed to her Beloved. As Thérèse reaches the heights of perfection, all her thoughts, all her actions, are done out of her perfect love for the Lord. Without the operation of the gift of wisdom, Thérèse's charity would never have reached such heights.

---

[2] Heath R. Thomas, "The Gift of Wisdom," 201.
[3] St Thomas Aquinas, *Super Ioan.*, cap. 14, lec. 5, n. 1934: "Habet enim hoc verus amor ut amatos ad amantis dilectionem trahat."
[4] *ST* I-II, q. 66, a. 6, ad 1.

Suffering – Conformity to Christ

If we want to be more conformed to Christ, we also must carry the Cross. If we want to share in Christ's glory, suffering cannot be avoided; we must follow the way of the Cross so that "being made conformable to the sufferings and death of Christ, we are brought into immortal glory."[5] To be more conformed to Christ will bring us more into union with Christ crucified, and our sufferings will be transformed when they are offered in union with Him. St Thomas says: "it is not enough just to suffer in some way, but this must be done by following Christ, that is, by suffering for his sake."[6] By God's design, authentic love always involves sacrifice.[7] There is a "sense in which love must be prepared to express itself in suffering,"[8] but suffering without love would be of no value, because it is only through love that suffering becomes meritorious. "Only love is truly able to restore the order which has been compromised by sin and it alone gives value to suffering."[9] Through the gift of wisdom, not only can we come to appreciate the

---

[5] *ST* III, q. 49, a. 3, ad 3.
[6] St Thomas Aquinas, *Super Ioan.*, cap. 21, lec. 5, n. 2635: "...quia non sufficit qualitercumque pati, sed solum sequendo Christum, idest propter ipsum."
[7] Martinez, *Sanctifier*, 102.
[8] Simon Tugwell, OP, *The Beatitudes: Soundings in Christian Traditions* (Springfield, IL: Templegate Publishers, 1980), 133.
[9] P. Lucien-Marie de Saint Joseph, OCD, "Le Martyre d'Amour," in *Études Carmélitaines: Limites De L'Humain* (Paris: Desclée de Brouwer, 1953), 330-331: "Seul l'amour peut véritablement restaurer l'ordre compris par le péché et seul il donne sa valeur à la souffrance comme il lui confère le mérite."

value of suffering, but we can reach a stage where we also have a love of the Cross and suffering in union with Christ crucified. Through the gift of wisdom, the soul understands the great privilege of being able to suffer and is even able to desire to suffer in union with the Lord and for His sake. "All the saints who have loved suffering ... have been under the influence of this gift."[10] By way of the gift of wisdom, God perfects Thérèse's charity and fills her soul with the desire to be conformed to her Beloved Christ Crucified. She is happy to accept all types of suffering, even the most difficult: she believes that "Love can do all things, and the most difficult things don't appear difficult to it."[11] Thérèse embraces her suffering with great love – not suffering for the sake of suffering but suffering united to Christ on the Cross – a redemptive suffering.

Suffering Becomes Sweet and Desirable

When we contemplate the mystery of the Cross, the mystery of "Christ dying for love of us," we can come to have a certain love of suffering.[12] As we advance in the spiritual life, we become more and more aware of the treasure of the Cross. The Holy Spirit reveals to us His Divine secrets, and slowly begins to remove the "veil that hides from human eyes the holy, the unutterable and divine revelation of the Cross."[13] The

---

[10] Martinez, *Sanctifier*, 193.
[11] *GC* I, LT 65, 468.
[12] Garrigou-Lagrange, *Three Ages of the Interior Life*, vol. II, 467-468.
[13] Martinez, *Sanctifier*, 108.

Holy Spirit often "fills souls with light to help them penetrate the mystery of the Cross, he also enkindles in them an ardent and passionate love for suffering."[14] Through the gift of wisdom a person is able to penetrate and understand the Cross and all its riches, so that suffering becomes sweet and desirable.[15] The soul that has reached a considerable degree of holiness can appreciate "the Cross of Jesus; at times, it even finds therein spiritual sweetness and a 'peace which surpasses all understanding.'"[16] This gift gives a certain sweetness to suffering, and makes all that is bitter sweet. St Augustine says, "Love makes all hard and repulsive tasks easy and next to nothing."[17] St Thomas also teaches that through the operation of the gift of wisdom, the bitter becomes sweet and the labour rest.[18] Through the operation of the gift of wisdom, a person sees that the Cross can be sweet because it has "something of the divine, something of Jesus; it is the straight and luminous ladder by which we mount to heaven."[19] Thérèse declares,

> Lord, suffering
> Becomes delight
> When the soul leaps
> Towards you forever.[20]

---

[14] Martinez, *Sanctifier*, 108.
[15] Martinez, *Sanctifier*, 193-194.
[16] Garrigou-Lagrange, *Christian Perfection and Contemplation*, 308-309.
[17] St Augustine, *De Verbis Domini*, Sermone 70, as quoted in *ST* I-II, q. 114, a. 4, ad 2.
[18] *ST* II-II, q. 45, a. 3, ad 3.
[19] Martinez, *Sanctifier*, 193.
[20] PN 28, 6, 143.

Thérèse had united all her sufferings to Jesus; she used to sing: "*'You have given me DELIGHT, O Lord, in ALL Your doings.'* For is there a *joy* greater than that of suffering out of love for You?"[21] She exclaims, *"Oh! How sweet is the way of Love!* How I want to apply myself to doing the will of God always with the greatest self-surrender!"[22] It is love that gives us strength and which makes us capable of giving all for the One who is loved. In *The Imitation of Christ*, the book which Thérèse treasured in her young years and knew by heart, there is a beautiful explanation of how love bears all suffering and how at times, suffering can even seem sweet:

> Love is a mighty power, a great and complete good; Love alone lightens every burden, and makes the rough places smooth. It bears every hardship as though it were nothing, and renders all bitterness sweet and acceptable. The love of Jesus is noble, and inspires us to great deeds; it moves us always to desire perfection. Love aspires to high things, and is held back by nothing base ... Nothing is sweeter than love, nothing stronger, nothing higher, nothing wider, nothing more pleasant, nothing fuller or better in heaven or earth; for love is born of God, and can rest only in God, above all created things.[23]
>
> Why, then, do you fear to take up the Cross, which is the road to the kingdom? In the Cross is salvation; in the Cross is life; in the Cross is

---

[21] Ms C 7r, 214.
[22] Ms A 84v, 181 (emphasis added).
[23] Thomas A. Kempis, CRSA, *The Imitation of Christ* (London: Penguin Books, 1952), 97-98.

protection against our enemies; in the Cross is infusion of heavenly sweetness; in the Cross is strength of mind; in the Cross is joy of spirit; in the Cross is excellence of virtue; in the Cross is perfection of holiness. There is no salvation of soul, nor hope of eternal life, save in the Cross.[24]

Through the effect of the operation of the gift of wisdom, suffering is made sweet; it is only through Thérèse's love and the gift of wisdom, that she comes to love suffering. To live a life in love and union with God brings moments of joy and moments of suffering, and sometimes there can be a mingling together of bitter and sweet; this is the Christian life – a life lived in communion with Jesus. St Thérèse frequently experiences sweetness in suffering throughout the ups and downs of her short life: "Life is burdensome. What bitterness ... but what sweetness."[25] She says that even God's "bitter chalice seemed delightful."[26] In fact Thérèse reaches the point of saying to Mother Agnes when she is only a few months away from her death: "Oh! don't be troubled about me, for I have come to a point where I cannot suffer any longer, because all suffering is sweet to me."[27] Without the gift of

---

[24] Kempis, *The Imitation of Christ*, 85.
[25] *GC* I, LT 57, 450.
[26] Ms A 71r, 152. St Teresa of Avila says that a person can feel that the Cross that God sends is both delicate and heavy. It is delicate because it is something that is very pleasing to the soul. However, it is also heavy because there are times when it seems that this Cross can no longer be carried. But even though this burden is felt, the person would not want to be freed from this burden unless it meant that he or she could be with God (*Life*, ch. 16, 5, 150).
[27] *LC*, May 29, 52.

wisdom, such a high degree of charity and love of suffering would be impossible. This sweetness, this intense love of the Cross, comes when the soul has reached a high degree of union with Christ, and in a sense, sees through the eyes of God. In a letter Thérèse had written to a missionary, she gives the following advice: "When you find suffering sweet and when you love it for the love of Jesus Christ, you will have found paradise on earth."[28] And in a poem, she writes about the best way to embrace the sufferings that are sent our way:

> If sometimes bitter suffering
> Should come to visit your heart,
> Make it your joy: To suffer for God...
> what sweetness!...
> Then Divine tenderness
> Will make you soon forget
> That you walk on thorns.
> Rather you will believe that you are flying...[29]

The Cross is Salutary for Believers but Seems Foolish to the Eyes of the World

Thérèse exclaims, "Oh! how the divine thoughts are above ours!"[30] On a natural level, one shudders in the face of suffering and may want to run away. The

---

[28] *GC* II, LT 221, 1069. The missionary brother was P. Adolphe Roulland. In this text Thérèse is quoting from the *Imitation of Christ*.
[29] PN 10, 8, 69.
[30] *GC* II, LT 226, 1092.

world sees love of the Cross as complete madness, and suffering is greatly misunderstood. St Thomas says, "The reason why the word of the Cross, which is salutary for believers, seems foolish to others, [is] because they are devoid of wisdom."[31] For "the wisdom of this world...considers the things of this world in such a way that it does not reach divine truth."[32] Thérèse, on the other hand, has penetrated into the mystery of suffering; she understands that the joys of the world are fleeting. She writes in a letter to a missionary priest, "The joy that worldlings seek in the midst of pleasures is only a fleeting shadow, but our joy sought and tested in works and sufferings is a very sweet reality, a foretaste of the happiness of heaven."[33] She also knows that the worldly cannot understand the mystery of suffering. In a letter to her sister Céline, she writes:

> Winter is suffering; suffering misunderstood, misjudged, looked upon as useless by profane eyes, but as fruitful and powerful in the eyes of Jesus and the angels who, like the vigilant bees, know how to gather the honey contained within the mysterious and multiple calyxes that represent souls or rather the children of the virginal little flower...Céline, I

---

[31] St Thomas Aquinas, *Super I Ep. ad Cor.* 1-3, n. 49: Haec est ergo causa quare verbum crucis quod est salutiferum credentibus, quibusdam videtur stultitia, quia sunt ipsi sapientia privati.

[32] St Thomas Aquinas, *Super I Ep. ad Cor.* 3-3, n. 179. Sapientia ergo mundi, quae sic rebus intendit, ut ad divinam veritatem non pertingat, *stultitia est apud Deum*.

[33] GC II, LT 221, 1069. The missionary was P. Adolphe Roulland. Combes explains that "angels who are pure spirit in a way envy us because they cannot suffer with and for Jesus" (*St Thérèse and Suffering*, 91).

would need volumes to write all I am thinking about my little flower...for me it is so perfect an image of your soul.[34]

In another letter to Céline, she writes:

> We have only the short moment of this life *to give* to God .... and He is already preparing to say: "Now, my turn..." What a joy to suffer for Him who loves us unto *folly* and to pass as *fools* in the eyes of the world.[35]

The Benefits a Soul can Receive through Suffering

In *Story of a Soul,* St Thérèse writes, "I can speak these words of the Spiritual Canticle of St John of the Cross: ... After I have known it *LOVE* works so in me that whether things go well or badly love turns them to one sweetness transforming the soul in *ITSELF.*"[36] There are so many benefits that can come from suffering out of love for God.[37] On one occasion St Thomas said to his students, "I have learned more from my crucifix than from my books."[38] In the following text, St John of the Cross describes beautifully the benefits that can come to a soul through suffering:

---

[34] *GC* II, LT 132, 741.
[35] *GC* II, LT 168, 882.
[36] Ms A 83r, 178-179.
[37] St Teresa of Avila, *Interior Castle,* VI Mansions, ch. 1, 7, 362.
[38] Benedict M. Ashley, *Thomas Aquinas: The Gifts of the Spirit,* 11.

> Suffering is the means of her penetrating further, deep into the thicket of the delectable wisdom of God. The purest suffering brings with it the purest and most intimate knowing, and consequently the purest and highest joy, because it is a knowing from further within … If we could but now fully understand how a soul cannot reach the thicket and wisdom of the riches of God, which are of many kinds, without entering the thicket of many kinds of suffering, finding in this her delight and consolation; and how a soul with an authentic desire for divine wisdom, wants suffering first in order to enter this wisdom by the thicket of the Cross!... The gate entering into these riches of His wisdom is the Cross, which is narrow, and few desire to enter by it.[39]

Thérèse desires to advance on the narrow road that leads to Jesus. She suffers so much throughout her short life, but this suffering is borne with much joy, and the gift of wisdom shines brightly in her life. Without this gift, Thérèse could never have expressed these sentiments. In one of Thérèse's poems *My Joy!* she writes,

> Truly I'm so happy.
> I always have my way …
> How could I not be joyful
> And not show my cheerfulness?
> My joy is to love suffering.
> I smile while shedding tears.
> I accept with gratitude
> The thorns mingled with the flowers.[40]

---

[39] St John of the Cross, *The Spiritual Canticle*, stanza 36, 12-13, 549.
[40] PN 45, 2,185.

She exclaims, "Joy is to be found only in suffering and in suffering without any consolation!"[41] In Thérèse's writing, there is a clear indication of the operation of the gift of wisdom as it perfects charity to a heroic degree. Nevertheless, Thérèse is always consistent in keeping with her *Little Way*, even with regard to suffering. Her way is to accept the sufferings that come; she embraces these sufferings with great love for Jesus. She explains how she would never ask God for suffering:

> I would never want to ask God for greater sufferings. If He increases them, I will bear them with pleasure and with joy because they will be coming from Him. But I'm too little to have any strength through myself. If I were to ask for sufferings, these would be mine, and I would have to bear them alone, and I've never been able to do anything alone.[42]

She counts on God to help her through all of her trials and sufferings:

> God has always come to my aid; he has helped me and led me by the hand from my childhood. I count upon Him. I'm sure He will continue to help me until the end. I may really become exhausted and worn out, but I shall never have too much to suffer; I'm sure of this.[43]

---

[41] *GC* I, LT 76, 504.
[42] *LC*, August 11, 3, 145. Cf. Conrad de Meester, OCD, *The Power of Confidence*, translated by Susan Conroy (New York: Alba House, 1998), 325.
[43] *LC*, May 27, 2, 50.

Progression from Suffering with Tears to Desiring Suffering and Finally Finding Joy in Suffering

When Thérèse was a small child, she suffered a lot; at this age, suffering filled her with sadness. How-ever, as Thérèse advances in years and in the spiritual life, suffering becomes her joy. She says, "I have suffered very much since I was on earth, but, if in my childhood I suffered with sadness, it is no longer in this way that I suffer. It is with joy and peace. I am truly happy to suffer."[44] Thérèse goes from *bearing* her sufferings, to feeling that she is given the *desire* to suffer. She then is given the *strength* to suffer, and finally, she is given the *desire to suffer for the salvation of sinners* – eventually dying as a *martyr of love.*

Thérèse's sister Marie does not seem to think that God would lead Thérèse down the path of suffering. She expresses her sentiment by telling Thérèse that "God would carry [her] as a child."[45] God does indeed always carry Thérèse as a child; however, she is not spared from suffering – in fact, her whole little life is strewn with suffering. From Thérèse's own words, it is clear that she grows to love and desire suffering. Through the effect of the gift of wisdom, she sees its immense value. She says:

> ...each soul [is] free to respond to the advances of Our Lord, to do little or much for Him, in a word, to *choose* among the sacrifices He [is] asking. Then,

---

[44] Ms C 4v, 210.
[45] Ms A 36r, 79.

as in the days of my childhood, I cried out: "My God '*I choose all!*' I don't want to be a *saint by halves*, I'm not afraid to suffer for You, I fear only one thing: to keep my own *will*; so take it, for '*I choose all*' that you will!"[46]

From a very early age God is preparing His little bride so that she can reach the heights of holiness and full union with Him. The following significant moments in the life of Thérèse manifest how her heart changes in regard to suffering.

First Communion – Thérèse Receives the Desire to Suffer

Thérèse prepared very well for her First Holy Communion. In fact, she had been preparing for a few years, and she longed to receive Jesus. Describing the day of her First Communion she says, "For a long time now Jesus and poor little Thérèse *looked at* and understood each other. That day, it was no longer simply a *look*, it was a fusion; they were no longer two, Thérèse had vanished as a drop of water is lost in the immensity of the ocean. Jesus alone remained; He was the Master, the King."[47] The very next day Thérèse received a great desire to suffer:

---

[46] Ms A 10r-10v, 27.
[47] Ms A 35r, 77. Cf. Àngel de les Gavarres, *Thérèse: The Little Child of God's Mercy*, 61. Thérèse had a profound understanding of the importance of receiving communion as often as possible. In a letter to Marie Guérin, Thérèse "urged her cousin to put aside the scruples that were keeping her from Communion: 'Dear little

> The day after my Communion... I felt born within my heart a *great desire* to suffer, and at the same time the interior assurance that Jesus reserved a great number of Crosses for me. I felt myself flooded with consolations so *great* that I look upon them as one of the *greatest* graces of my life.[48]

Thérèse says that since this time, she "had a perpetual desire to suffer."[49] She explains:

> Suffering became my attraction; it had charms about it which ravished me without my understanding them very well. Up until this time, I had suffered without *loving* suffering, but since then I felt a real love for it. I also felt the desire of loving only God, of finding my joy only in Him.[50]

With an increase in sanctifying grace as a result of receiving her First Holy Communion, and an increase in the operation of the gift of wisdom (which perfects her charity), Thérèse is given an ardent love and desire for suffering. However, Thérèse does not yet find joy in suffering, and she is not thinking "of making suffering [her] joy." She says, "This is a grace that was

---

sister, receive Communion often, very often...That is the *only remedy* if you want to be healed, and Jesus hasn't placed this attraction in your soul for nothing.' When this letter was read to Pope Pius X in 1910, he cried out, 'This is most opportune! It's a great joy for me,' and he told the vice-postulator of the cause, Msgr de Teil, 'We must hurry this cause.'" Carroll Eamon, "Thérèse and the Mother of God" in *Experiencing Saint Thérèse Today*, Carmelite Studies V (Washington, D.C., ICS Publications, 1990), 86.

[48] Ms A 36r, 79. Cf. Àngel de les Gavarres, *Thérèse: The Little Child of God's Mercy*, 61.
[49] *LC*, July 31, 13, 123.
[50] Ms A 36r-36v, 79.

given to me later on."[51] She explains that until that time arrived, joy was

> like a spark hidden beneath the ashes, and like blossoms on a tree that must become fruit in time. But seeing my blossoms always falling, that is, allowing myself to fall into tears whenever I suffered, I said to myself with astonishment and sadness: But I will never go beyond the stage of desires![52]

Thérèse had received a new grace on the day of her First Communion. Up until this time, Thérèse had suffered greatly; yet as she says, she had not desired suffering. On the day of her First Communion, she receives the desire to suffer; nevertheless, suffering still often ends in tears.

Confirmation – Thérèse Receives the Strength to Suffer

Soon Thérèse would receive another grace – in the Sacrament of Confirmation:

> I was prepared with great care to receive the visit of the Holy Spirit, and I did not understand why a greater attention was not paid to the reception of this sacrament of *Love* ... I did not experience an impetuous wind at the moment of the Holy Spirit's descent but rather this *light breeze* which the prophet Elias heard on Mount Horeb. On that day,

---

[51] *LC,* July 31, 13, 123.
[52] *LC,* July 31, 13, 123.

> I received the strength to *suffer*, for soon afterwards the martyrdom of my soul was about to commence.[53]

On the day of Thérèse's Confirmation, she receives the strength to suffer. As the desire to suffer all for Jesus is an effect of the gift of wisdom, so the *feeling* of the added strength to bear all such sufferings is indicative of an even greater action of the Holy Spirit by way of the gift of wisdom. At this point, one may object by saying that this is not the gift of wisdom – but rather, the gift of fortitude. It is true that fortitude is involved in the endurance of sufferings when they occur. However, here, our emphasis is not actually on *how it is* that Thérèse endures suffering, but rather on *what* Thérèse is experiencing at the moment of her Confirmation. She is *experiencing* the Holy Spirit's descent upon her. She *feels* not an "impetuous wind" but a "light breeze." Further, since she is not experiencing suffering at this moment, what she is really describing is the *quasi-experiential knowing* that is the hallmark of the gift of wisdom. She *knows* by this *experience* that at this moment she has been given the strength to suffer and that another significant change has taken place. Our Lord has given Thérèse a new grace – this is the day when she begins to have the strength to suffer. Whereas suffering had filled Thérèse with sadness before, now she has a great strength to suffer; this would help her throughout the rest of her short life here on earth.

---

[53] Ms A 36v-37r, 80.

Christmas Grace – Thérèse Receives the Desire to Suffer for Souls

Even though she had already received strength to be able to suffer, at the age of fourteen, Thérèse still remained fragile and unable to overcome her extreme sensitivities. Then, on Christmas Eve, she was given a huge grace which changed her forever. Thérèse calls this her "conversion." She was changed in an instant and from that day her excessive sensitivity disappeared; all that remained was a healthy and delicate sensitivity to the inspirations of the Holy Spirit.[54] She says, "On that *night of light* began the third period of my life, the most beautiful and

---

[54] From the time that Thérèse's mother died right up until the age of fourteen, Thérèse was extremely sensitive and could cry at the drop of a hat. However, an event took place that was to change Thérèse forever. It was Christmas Eve and the Martins had just attended Midnight Mass. Their usual custom was that the children would leave out their shoes to be filled with presents. Even though Thérèse was now fourteen years old, Céline still wanted her little sister to have the pleasure of receiving presents because this custom had filled her and Thérèse with so much happiness when they were younger. However, this year Louis Martin was very tired after Midnight Mass and Thérèse overheard her father saying that "fortunately this will be the last year!" – meaning the last year to fill their shoes with presents. Thérèse being so sensitive would normally have been terribly upset by these words. But contrary to what Céline expected, Thérèse kept back her tears and ran downstairs to her father to take out all her little presents. She did this so joyfully that Céline could not believe her eyes. This event sounds small, but it has great significance; after this event, Thérèse had changed. Her propensity to extreme sensitivity had disappeared; she had changed in an instant (Ms A 45r, 98). Looking back on her life Thérèse said: "When I think of the past, my soul overflows with gratitude when I see the favors I received from heaven. They have made such a change that I hardly recognize myself" (Ms A 43r, 91).

the most filled with graces from heaven. The work I had been unable to do in ten years was done by Jesus in one instant."[55]

At this time, Thérèse also found that she had received a great desire to save souls. She began to have a great desire to offer up her sufferings for the conversion of sinners and to forget herself. This indicates just how intense her love had become. She says, "I experienced a great desire to work for the conversion of sinners, a desire I hadn't felt so intensely before... I felt myself consumed with a *thirst for souls*."[56] This *feeling*, this quasi-experiential knowledge, and the further refining of her desire for suffering – in conformity with the Only Begotten Son – coupled with the obvious increase in charity, point clearly to the operation of the gift of wisdom. She says, "Jesus *took the net Himself*, cast it, and drew it in filled with fish. He made me a fisher of *souls*."[57] One Sunday following this experience, Thérèse was looking at a picture of Jesus on the Cross; she was impacted by the sight of the blood that was falling "to the ground without anyone's hastening to gather it up."[58] She says:

> I was resolved to remain in spirit at the foot of the Cross and to receive the dew. I understood I was then to pour it out upon souls. The cry of Jesus on the Cross sounded continually in my heart: *"I thirst!"* These words ignited within me an

---

[55] Ms A 45v, 98.
[56] Ms A 45v, 99.
[57] Ms A 45v, 99.
[58] Ms A 45v, 99.

unknown and very living fire. I wanted to give my Beloved to drink and I felt myself consumed with a *thirst for souls*. As yet, it was not the souls of priests that attracted me, but those of *great sinners*; I *burned* with the desire to snatch them from the eternal flames.[59]

Through the operation of the gift of wisdom, Thérèse understands the immense value of suffering and longs to help God in the redemption of souls. Her constant desire is to bring souls to Jesus. In a letter to her sister Céline, she remarks, "Alas, He is not far; He is there, very close. He is looking at us, and He is *begging this* sorrow, this agony from us. He needs it for souls and for our soul."[60] The desire to give her whole self for the salvation of souls continues throughout her life. In her Act of Offering to Merciful Love, she offers herself and says that she desires "to work for the glory of Holy Church by saving souls on earth and liberating those suffering in purgatory."[61] Then at the end of her life, Thérèse offers up her very self in her *martyrdom of love*.

After Entering Carmel

Through infused contemplation and the operation of the gift of wisdom, Thérèse had reached the point where she not only accepted suffering and overcame the most difficult trials, but she had grown to love and desire suffering. She had an intense desire to suffer for

---

[59] Ms A 45v, 99.
[60] *GC* I, LT 57, 450.
[61] *Prayers* 6 (Act of Oblation), 53.

the salvation of souls, to win souls for her Beloved Spouse.

At the age of fifteen, Thérèse enters the Carmelite convent in Lisieux. She comes to Carmel "to save souls and especially to pray for priests."[62] She says, "It is for this purpose I became a Carmelite nun; being unable to be an active missionary, I wanted to be one through love and penance just like Saint Teresa, my seraphic Mother."[63] In a letter to her sister Pauline, she writes, "I desire only one thing when I am in Carmel, it is always (to preserve my place) to suffer for Jesus."[64] Thus, she becomes a missionary for souls from the Cloister of Carmel.

In Carmel, Thérèse contemplated the suffering Face of Jesus and said: "Ah! I desired that, like the Face of Jesus, 'my face be truly hidden, that no one on earth would know me.' I thirsted after suffering and longed to be forgotten."[65] Thérèse contemplates both God's Love and His Mercy, recognising the immense Love and Mercy of God which He has shown for us by sending His only Begotten Son. God manifests this Love and Mercy both on the Cross and in the Crib.[66] When Thérèse receives the habit in Carmel on 10 January 1889, she takes the name *St Thérèse of the Child Jesus and the Holy Face*. She has the name *the Holy Face* added to her religious name.[67] There is a tendency to speak of *St Thérèse* as *Thérèse of the Child Jesus* without

---

[62] Ms A 69v, 149.
[63] *GC* II, LT 189, 956.
[64] *GC* I, LT 43A, 399.
[65] Ms A 71r, 152.
[66] Jean Clapier, *Aimer jusqu'à mourir d'amour: Thérèse de Lisieux et le mystère pascal par Jean Clapier* (Paris: Cerf, 2003), 455.
[67] Miller, *Trial of Faith*, 124.

considering the second part of her name, *the Holy Face*. Although the second part of Thérèse's religious name is seldom mentioned, it should not be forgotten. It is essential to understanding the whole life of Thérèse because her life was a constant assimilation of the mystery of suffering united to love.[68] In fact "devotion to the Holy Face was, for Thérèse, the crown and complement of her love for the Sacred Humanity of Our Lord."[69] Céline writes:

> It was from the contemplation of the agonizing Face of Jesus that Thérèse drew strength for all those courageous acts of exalted virtue which characterized her life: it was in the meditation of the humiliated Face of Jesus that she learned to exercise herself in humility and detachment from creatures, in love of suffering and in generous self-

---

[68] Don Giuseppe Scarpellini, *Santa Teresa di Gesù Bambino e la scoperta del Volto Santo* (Rimini, Italy: Mostra a cura di Scarpellini Don Giuseppe), 3: "Molti, quando si parla di S. Teresa di Lisieux, pensano solo ad una parte del suo nome, assunto all' entrata al Carmelo: *Teresa di Gesù Bambino*, non considerando la seconda parte del nome da lei scelto al momento della sua Vestizione (10 gennaio 1889): *Teresa del Volto Santo*... La vita di Teresa è stata un approfondimento e un'assimilazione costante del mistero d'amore e di sofferenza; d'amore nella sofferenza, della sofferenza unita all'amore, e pienamente assunta nell'amore salvifico di Gesù. Effettivamente i due aspetti del suo nome in religione, esprimono una sola e medesima realtà essenziale del mistero di Dio manifestatosi nell'Incarnazione redentrice del Figlio. Il Volto Santo è in qualche modo l'estensione temporale dell'Amore divino inizialmente contemplato nel Bambino di Betlemme."
[69] Sister Geneviève of the Holy Face (Céline Martin), *My Sister Saint Thérèse*, translated by the Carmelite Sisters of New York of Conseils et Souvenirs (Rockford, IL: Tan Books and Publishers, Inc., 1997), 111.

sacrifice; this love was the motive force of her zeal for the salvation of souls.[70]

Thérèse wanted always to console her Beloved Spouse, to dry the tears from His eyes. She says:

> Living on Love, is wiping your Face,
> It's obtaining the pardon of sinners,
> O God of Love! May they return to your grace,
> And may they forever bless your Name....[71]

She expresses the love she has for the Lord and His Adorable Face and how she desires to be conformed to His image in one of her prayers when she writes,

> O Adorable Face of Jesus, the only Beauty that captivates my heart, deign to imprint in me your Divine Likeness so that you may not behold the soul of your little bride without seeing Yourself in her.[72]

And in a play she had written in Carmel in the section entitled, *A Mirror*, she writes:

> Ah! be the living image
> The pure Mirror of your Spouse,
> The Divine brightness of His Face
> He wants to contemplate in you!...[73]

---

[70] Sister Geneviève of the Holy Face (*Céline Martin*), *My Sister Saint Thérèse*, 111.

[71] PN 17, 11, 91.

[72] *Prayers* 16, 104.

[73] St Thérèse of Lisieux, *The Plays of Saint Thérèse of Lisieux*, translated by Susan Conroy and David J. Dwyer (Washington, D.C.: ICS Publications, 2008), *A Mirror*, 240. Henceforth cited as *Plays*.

Benedict XVI, at an audience in St Peter's square, pointed out how the illness of Thérèse's father caused her a great deal of suffering and "led her to contemplation of the Face of Jesus in his Passion." He says, "Thus, her name as a religious – Sister *Thérèse of the Child Jesus and of the Holy Face* – expresses the programme of her whole life, in communion with the central mysteries of the Incarnation and the Redemption."[74]

In Carmel, Thérèse's desire to suffer for souls continues. Religious life is exactly how she has imagined it to be:

> Yes, suffering opened wide its arms to me and I threw myself into them with love. I had declared at the feet of Jesus-Victim, in the examination preceding my Profession, what I had come to Carmel for: "I came to save souls and especially to pray for priests." When one wishes to attain a goal, one must use the means; Jesus made me understand that it was through suffering that He wanted to give me souls and my attraction for suffering grew in proportion to its increase.[75]

Thérèse's every thought, every beat of her heart, is concerned with the salvation of souls; she desires only to love and to win for Jesus the souls for whom He is thirsting. She embraces everything with great love, trust, and abandonment, and is strengthened by the infinite love that God has poured into her heart. She tries to use every occasion that presents itself, no

---

[74] Benedict XVI, General Audience, St Peter's Square, 6 April 2011, "St. Thérèse of Lisieux."
[75] Ms A 69v, 149.

matter how small, to offer a pleasing sacrifice to the Lord; she never wastes a moment. She exclaims, "Ah! let us profit from the *short moment* of life ... *together* let us please Jesus, let us save souls for Him by our sacrifices."[76] In a letter to her sister Pauline, Thérèse expresses similar sentiments:

> Life passes so quickly that truly it must be better to have a very beautiful crown and a little trouble than (not) to have an ordinary one without any trouble and then for a suffering borne without joy, when I think that for all eternity I shall love God better. Then in suffering, one can save souls. Ah! Pauline, if during my life I could have suffered, to offer one soul to God, one soul that would be snatched from the fire of hell, oh! how happy I would be. Really, how could one complain about suffering when one sees the fruit of suffering.[77]

For Thérèse there is nothing more beneficial and beautiful than working for the salvation of souls. She says, "While awaiting this blessed eternity that will open up for us in a short time, since life is only a day, let us work together for the salvation of souls."[78] Thérèse has a profound understanding of the immense gift that God has given to us by letting us share in His plan of salvation. She explains beautifully how Jesus wants us to help Him save souls:

> What a mystery! ... Is not Jesus all powerful? Are not creatures His who made them? Why, then, does Jesus say: "Ask the Lord of the harvest that he send

---

[76] *GC* II, LT 241, 1117.
[77] *GC* I, LT 43A, 399.
[78] *GC* II, LT 226, 1095.

some workers"? Why? ... Ah! It is because Jesus has so incomprehensible a love for us that He wills that we have a share with Him in the salvation of souls. He wills to do nothing without us. The Creator of the universe awaits the prayer of a poor little soul to save other souls redeemed like it at the price of all His Blood ...[79]

Jesus' "suffering has fully atoned for our sins;" He "gave more to God than was required to compensate for the offense of the whole human race."[80] Nevertheless, He has given us the beautiful gift of being able to share in the redemption of souls.[81] Each

---

[79] *GC* II, LT 135, 753.

[80] *ST* III, q. 48, a. 2: "By suffering out of love and obedience, Christ gave more to God than was required to compensate for the offense of the whole human race. First of all, because of the exceeding charity from which He suffered; secondly, on account of the dignity of His life which He laid down in atonement, for it was the life of one who was God and man; thirdly, on account of the extent of the Passion, and the greatness of the grief endured... And therefore Christ's Passion was not only a sufficient but a superabundant atonement for the sins of the human race."

[81] St Thomas gives the example of St Paul and explains what it means when he says: "'in my flesh I complete what is lacking in Christ's afflictions.' At first glance these words can be misunderstood to mean that the passion of Christ was not sufficient for our redemption, and that the sufferings of the saints were added to complete it. But this is heretical, because the blood of Christ is sufficient to redeem many worlds: 'He is the expiation for our sins, and not for ours only but also for the sins of the whole world' (1 Jn 2:2). Rather, we should understand that Christ and the Church are one mystical person, whose head is Christ, and whose body is all the just, for every just person is a member of this head: 'individually members' (1 Cor. 12:27). Now God in his predestination has arranged how much merit will exist throughout the entire Church, both in the head and in the members, just as he has predestined the number of the elect. And among these

person in his or her suffering can "become a sharer in the redemptive suffering of Christ."[82] Thérèse understands that "it is not our merits but those of our Spouse, which are *ours*, that we offer to Our Father who is in heaven."[83] To win souls for Jesus is one of Thérèse's greatest joys. She says: "It is so sweet *to help Jesus* by our light sacrifices, to help Him save souls that He bought at the price of His Blood and that are awaiting only our help in order not to fall into the abyss."[84] She says, "Let us not refuse Him the least sacrifice. Everything is so big in religion…to pick up a pin out of love can convert a soul. What a mystery!... Ah! It is Jesus alone who can give such a value to our actions; let us love Him with all our strength."[85]

Thérèse continues to contemplate the immense

---

merits, the sufferings of the holy martyrs occupy a prominent place. For while the merits of Christ, the head, are infinite, each saint displays some merits in a limited degree. This is why he says, I complete what is lacking in Christ's afflictions, that is, what is lacking in the afflictions of the whole Church, of which Christ is the head. I complete, that is, I add my own amount; and I do this in my flesh, that is, it is I myself who am suffering. Or, we could say that Paul was completing the sufferings that were lacking in his own flesh for what was lacking was that, just as Christ had suffered in his own body, so he should also suffer in Paul, his member, and in similar ways in others. And Paul does this for the sake of his body, which is the Church that was to be redeemed by Christ: 'That he might present the Church to himself in splendor, without spot or wrinkle' (Eph 5:27). In the same way all the saints suffer for the Church, which receives strength from their example 'afflictions are still lacking, because the treasure house of the Church's merits is not full, and it will not be full until the end of the world'" (Super *Ep. ad Col.* cap. 1, lec. 6).

[82] St John Paul II, *Salvifici Doloris*, 19.
[83] *GC* II, LT 129, 729.
[84] *GC* II, LT 191, 966.
[85] *GC* II, LT 164, 855.

value of suffering out of love for Jesus. She continues to grow in charity and love of suffering precisely because of the effect that the gift of wisdom has on charity. In a letter to her sister Céline, she says: "Ah! Céline, let us not forget souls, but let us forget ourselves for them."[86] This shows the intensity of Thérèse's love – it has grown to the point of being heroic. St Thomas says that the effect of love can be so intense that a person will "surrender not only temporal but also spiritual goods and even himself, for his neighbor's sake."[87] Thérèse wants to give everything for the sake of poor souls: "I hold nothing in my hands. Everything I have, everything I merit is for the Church and for souls. If I were to live to eighty, I will always be as poor as I am now."[88] She explains:

> If I had been rich, I would have found it impossible to see a poor person going hungry without giving him my possessions. And in the same way, when I gain any spiritual treasures, feeling that at this very moment there are souls in danger of being lost and falling into hell, I give them what I possess, and I

---

[86] *GC* II, LT 130, 733.

[87] *ST* II-II, q. 184, a. 2, ad 3: St Thomas Aquinas says "intensity of love ... is shown by the things which man despises for his neighbor's sake, through his despising not only external goods for the sake of his neighbor, but also bodily hardships and even death...[And] as to the effect of love, so that a man will surrender not only temporal but also spiritual goods and even himself, for his neighbor's sake, according to the words of the Apostle (2 Corinthians 12:15), 'But I most gladly will spend and be spent myself for your souls.'"

[88] *LC*, July 12, 3, 91.

have not yet found a moment when I can say: Now I'm going to work for myself.[89]

It is evident that the gift of wisdom has given Thérèse a deep experiential knowledge of the mysteries of her Divine Spouse and her charity has reached tremendous heights. She is becoming more perfectly conformed to Christ each day. Such a profound love of the Cross speaks volumes of the immense love Thérèse has for the Lord, and one cannot help but marvel at her wisdom, clarity, and unreserved acceptance of everything the Lord desires to give her. The Cross is sweet to her because here, she can show Jesus how much she loves Him. Through her unreserved love for the Lord, she is able to draw graces from the Cross and help in the Lord's plan of salvation. Her life is full of different types of suffering from the beginning of her life to the end. It is only through the gift of wisdom that charity can reach such heights. Thérèse's charity continues to mature as the years go by in Carmel, and her relationship with Jesus continues to blossom.

Act of Oblation

In what is called her *Act of Oblation*,[90] Thérèse offers herself as a Victim Holocaust to God's merciful love:

---

[89] *LC*, July 14, 2, 96.
[90] *Prayers* 6 (Act of Oblation), 53-55 & *Story of a Soul, Appendices*, 276-277.

> In order to live in one single act of perfect Love, I OFFER MYSELF AS A VICTIM OF HOLOCAUST TO YOUR MERCIFUL LOVE, asking You to consume me incessantly, allowing the waves of *infinite tenderness* shut up within You to overflow into my soul, and that thus I may become a *martyr of Your Love,* O my God! May this martyrdom, after having prepared me to appear before You, finally cause me to die and may my soul take its flight without any delay into the eternal embrace of *Your Merciful Love.*

St Thérèse was 23 years old when she made this offering. She had already reached a very high degree of holiness, and she was being conformed to Christ more and more:

> To be holy is to be Jesus Crucified; to be like Him … To be holy is to be victim, it is to offer oneself as a sacrifice of adoration, as a holocaust of love to the heavenly Father; to offer oneself immaculate through the Holy Spirit as victim, altar, and priest.[91]

Even though Thérèse suffers for sinners out of love for God, as her short life continues, she reaches a moment when she desires to give God even more. Thérèse's love cannot be contained; she is consumed by love alone. She wants to give to Jesus without reserve; she wants to love Him with her whole heart, her whole being. Thérèse has a profound awareness of how much God wants to lavish His children with love. She understands the heart of Jesus Her Spouse and the Infinite Mercy of His love, a love that He wants to share with all of His friends; but so few are

---

[91] Martinez, *Sanctifier,* 313.

ready to share in this love. Thérèse says, "This year, June 9, the feast of the Holy Trinity, I received the grace to understand more than ever before how much Jesus desires to be loved."[92] Thérèse sees that God's love is continually rejected and unknown and that people make the mistake of turning to creatures to seek love and affection rather than running into the arms of God to receive His tender and infinite love.[93] She exclaims, "Ah! how little known are the *goodness*, the *merciful love* of Jesus."[94]

In the times that Thérèse lived, there was a huge focus on the justice of God.[95] Jansenism was rampant in France. The Jansenists were so preoccupied with people's need of grace and their inability to dispose themselves to it, that they distorted Christianity in such a way that it made people both pessimistic and scrupulous. Therefore, "under the pretext of making Christians more worthy of God's love and mercy, the Jansenists alienated them from God."[96] Rarely was

---

[92] Ms A 84r, 180.
[93] Ms A 84r, 180.
[94] *GC* II, LT 261, 1165.
[95] Jean Guitton, *The Spiritual Genius of Saint Thérèse of Lisieux*, translated by Felicity Leng (Kent: Burns & Oates, 1997), 23. Guitton remarks: "It is surprising, given the atmosphere of the times, to find not a hint of even latent Jansenism in the Martin family compared with other Catholic families in the same sector of the French middle class of that period" (*The Spiritual Genius of Saint Thérèse of Lisieux*, 23).
[96] Aumann, *Christian Spirituality in the Catholic Tradition*, 231. Guitton notes that "Apart from the bastion of extreme Jansenism at Port-Royal itself, the atmosphere of the seventeenth century was permeated with a more diffuse form of Jansenism. It was found in the great preacher Bossuet himself, and little by little it seeped into the very fabric of French Catholic culture and life" (*The Spiritual Genius*, 24).

God seen as a God of Love, and during much of this period, the thought of a mystic was rare and suspect.[97] Many Christians tried to win God over by trying to merit everything and never trusting in God's Mercy. However, despite the fact that Jansenism plagued France and there were even signs of a "Jansenistic spirituality" in the Carmelite convent at Lisieux and a sense that the God of Love and Mercy was unknown, there were no traces of a Jansenistic spirituality in the life of the Martin family.[98] Rather, Thérèse was raised in a household that believed that God wants to lavish us with His Love and Mercy; He is a God Who gives "beyond all demands and rights."[99]

The contact that Thérèse had with those who focused on the "idea of divine justice must have contributed heavily to making her think about the coexistence of justice and mercy in God."[100] Many people were offering themselves as victim souls to God's Justice in order to take upon themselves the punishments reserved for sinners. "To offer oneself to the justice of God to take on chastisements reserved for the guilty cannot be but the fruit of a great love for God and for sinners."[101] This great offering seemed

---

[97] Bl. Marie-Eugène, *Torrent*, 8.
[98] Miller, *Trial of Faith*, 2. Miller notes: "Her parents, so healthy in their religious observance, had been carefully formed by several anti-Jansenistic Jesuits. Also, through Zélie Martin, the balanced spirituality of St Francis de Sales exercised a strong influenced in the Martin home" (*Trial of Faith*, 2).
[99] Bl. Marie-Eugène, *Torrent*, 23.
[100] Conrad de Meester, *The Power of Confidence*, 343.
[101] Philipe de la Trinité, "Le Thomisme de Sainte Thérèse de l'Enfant-Jésus en matière de Rédemption," VT 8 (1962), 5: "S'offrir à la justice de Dieu pour porter les châtiments réservés aux coupables, ne peut être que le fruit d'un grand amour et de Dieu

very generous to Thérèse, but she was not at all attracted to making this offering herself. She was filled with a desire to offer herself to God's Merciful Love instead of focusing on the attribute of His Justice.[102] Contrary to the harsh penances of her time, an overemphasis on the Justice of God, and an extreme suspicion towards anything that might appear to be of a mystical nature, Thérèse focused on the Mercy of God. She says, "It seems to me that if all creatures had received the same graces I received, God would be feared by none but would be loved to the point of folly; and through *love,* not through fear, no one would ever consent to cause Him any pain."[103] St John Paul II, in his encyclical *Dives in Misericordia,* says that "believing in this love means *believing in mercy*. For mercy is an indispensable dimension of love; it is as it were love's second name and, at the same time, the specific manner in which love is revealed and effected."[104] Thérèse could not understand how a God of love could be so feared; she says, "My way is all confidence and love. I do not understand souls who fear a Friend so tender."[105] So contrary to fearing the justice of God, Thérèse felt that God's justice was for her a source of joy, and confidence – she explains why when she says:

---

et des pécheurs, et ne peut donc partir que d'une intention *subjectivement* grande et généreuse - c'est vrai-mais saint Thérèse était loin de s'y sentir portée... " as quoted in Jean Clapier, *Aimer jusqu'à mourir d'amour,* 431.

[102] Ms A 84r, 180.
[103] Ms A 83v, 180.
[104] St John Paul II, Dives *in Misericordia,* 7.
[105] *GC* II, LT 226, 1093.

> I know one must be very pure to appear before the God of all Holiness, but I know, too, that the Lord is infinitely just; and it is this justice which frightens so many souls that is the object of my joy and confidence. To be just is not only to exercise severity in order to punish the guilty; it is also to recognize right intentions and to reward virtue. I expect as much from God's justice as from His mercy. It is because He is just that "He is compassionate and filled with gentleness, slow to punish, and abundant in mercy, for He knows our frailty. He remembers we are only dust. As a father has tenderness for his children, so the Lord has compassion on us!!"[106]

Thérèse "helped to heal souls of the rigours and fears of Jansenism, which tended to stress God's justice rather than his divine mercy."[107] God destined that she would live in a time when there was an emphasis on the Justice and wrath of God rather than His Love and Mercy. God raises up Saints through the ages to bring a certain message to the world. Each Saint reflects a particular message or points to one of God's perfections. Each soul is unique; each has its place. Thérèse had a particular mission to reveal God's Love and Mercy to the world:

> I understand ... that all souls cannot be the same, that it is necessary there be different types in order to honor each of God's perfections in a particular way. To me He has granted His *infinite Mercy* and

---

[106] GC II, LT 226, 1093.
[107] St John Paul II, Divini *Amoris Scientia*, 8.

through it I contemplate and adore the other divine perfections!¹⁰⁸

Thérèse was brought into the world to remind us of God's Love and Mercy. She had a profound understanding that "God never acts only according to His justice without being merciful, because the same traits of His justice are also those of His mercy."¹⁰⁹ In other words, "God is just through love and with love; His justice is a justice of love."¹¹⁰ Thérèse explains further:

> After so many graces can I not sing with the Psalmist: *"How GOOD is the Lord, his MERCY endures forever!"...* To me He has granted His *infinite Mercy,* and *through it* I contemplate and adore the other divine perfections! All these perfections appear to be resplendent *with love;* even His Justice (and perhaps this even more so than the others) seems to me clothed in *love.* What a sweet joy it is to think that God is *Just,* i.e., that He takes into account our weakness, that He is perfectly aware of our fragile nature. What should I fear then? Ah! must not the infinitely just God, who deigns to pardon the faults of the prodigal son with so much kindness, be just also toward me who "am with Him always"? ¹¹¹

---

¹⁰⁸ Ms A 83v, 180.

¹⁰⁹ Jean Clapier, *Aimer jusqu'à mourir d'amour,* 434: "Dieu n'agira jamais selon la justice sans être miséricorde. Car les traits mêmes de sa justice sont ceux de la miséricorde."

¹¹⁰ Philippe de la Trinité, "De Saint Thomas d'Aquin à Sainte Thérèse de l'Enfant-Jésus," 386: "Dieu est juste par amour et avec amour, la justice de Dieu est une justice d'amour."

¹¹¹ Ms A 83v-84r, 180. Cf. Conrad de Meester, *The Power of Confidence,* 343 & Jean Clapier, *Aimer jusqu'à mourir d'amour,* 433.

Quasi-Experiential Knowledge of Divine Mercy – Contemplation and the Gift of Wisdom

Through the operation of the gift of wisdom "the mind under the impulse of the Spirit judges, that is, sees and tastes, how all God's works are traceable to his mercy; it *tastes* the difference between love and justice in God."[112] Marie-Eugène of the Child Jesus says that it was through Thérèse's contemplation that she was led to make her Act of Oblation and was given a deep penetration into the infinite Mercy of God.[113] She had a connatural understanding of God's Mercy, an experiential knowledge "which was almost second nature to her."[114] She had a continuous loving knowledge of God and a simple loving contemplative gaze. She discovered both God's Love and His Mercy experientially and had a deep understanding that God is the God of Infinite Mercy; she not only knew this, she tasted it. St John of the Cross explains that a soul can receive a type of knowledge wherein one of God's attributes is experienced in such a sublime way that this can never be forgotten – he says this

---

[112] Heath R. Thomas, "The Gift of Wisdom," 201.

[113] Bl. Marie-Eugène, *Under the Torrent of His Love*, 76; see also *Torrent*, 45.

[114] Bl. Marie-Eugène, *Under the Torrent of His Love*, 35. Garrigou-Lagrange explains that a soul who has reached a very high degree of charity knows God "with a knowledge which is quasi-experimental and almost continuous;" it is a knowledge which "proceeds from the gift of wisdom" (*Three Conversions of the Spiritual Life*, 93-94).

"communication is pure contemplation."[115] This gaze of pure contemplation has become so simple for Thérèse that "everything in God ... stands out in this one light and is reflected in a single mirror, that of infinite Mercy;"[116] this infinite Mercy is the attribute of God which is most beautiful to Thérèse.

St Thomas Aquinas – Mercy

St Thomas says:

> ... the effect of the divine mercy is the foundation of all the divine works. For nothing is due to anyone, except on account of something already given him gratuitously by God. In this way the divine omnipotence is particularly made manifest, because to it pertains the first foundation of all good things.[117]

Thérèse had reached this deep understanding of God's Mercy through her pure contemplation and the gift of wisdom. Her understanding is no different than the teaching of St Thomas Aquinas who says, "the work of divine justice always presupposes the work of mercy; and is founded thereupon."[118] In other

---

[115] St John of the Cross, *Ascent of Mount Carmel*, bk II, ch. 26, 3, 194.
[116] Bl. Marie-Eugène, *Torrent*, 101. St John Paul II says: "Mercy in itself, as a perfection of the infinite God, is also infinite" (*Dives in Misericordia*, 13).
[117] *ST* I, q. 25, a. 3, ad 3.
[118] *ST* I, q. 21, a. 4: "Now the work of divine justice always presupposes the work of mercy; and is founded thereupon. For nothing is due to creatures, except for something pre-existing in

words, "all the Divine works are marked by a seal of justice and mercy but before and above is that of mercy."[119] St Thomas says that "on account of His infinite goodness, it is more proper to God to have mercy and to spare, than to punish."[120] He explains:

> God acts mercifully, not indeed by going against His justice, but by doing something more than justice; thus a man who pays another two hundred pieces of money, though owing him only one hundred, does nothing against justice, but acts liberally or mercifully. The case is the same with

---

them, or foreknown. Again, if this is due to a creature, it must be due on account of something that precedes. And since we cannot go on to infinity, we must come to something that depends only on the goodness of the divine will – which is the ultimate end. We may say, for instance, that to possess hands is due to man on account of his rational soul; and his rational soul is due to him that he may be man; and his being man is on account of the divine goodness. So in every work of God, viewed at its primary source, there appears mercy. In all that follows, the power of mercy remains, and works indeed with even greater force; as the influence of the first cause is more intense than that of second causes. For this reason does God out of abundance of His goodness bestow upon creatures what is due to them more bountifully than is proportionate to their deserts: since less would suffice for preserving the order of justice than what the divine goodness confers; because between creatures and God's goodness there can be no proportion." Cf. Philippe de la Trinité, "De Saint Thomas d'Aquin à Sainte Thérèse de l'Enfant-Jésus," 383; Jean Clapier *Aimer jusqu'à mourir d'amour*, 433; André Combes "Saint Thérèse de Lisieux et Saint Thomas de Aquin," 176.

[119] Philippe de la Trinité, "De Saint Thomas d'Aquin à Sainte Thérèse de l'Enfant-Jésus," 383: "Toutes les oeuvres divines sont *à la fois* marquées du sceau de la justice et de celui de la miséricorde, mais *d'abord et avant tout* de celui de la miséricorde."

[120] *ST* II-II, q. 21, a. 2. Cf. André Combes, "Saint Thérèse de Lisieux et Saint Thomas de Aquin," 177-178.

one who pardons an offence committed against him, for in remitting it he may be said to bestow a gift...Hence it is clear that mercy does not destroy justice, but in a sense is the fullness thereof. And thus it is said: "Mercy exalteth itself above judgment" (James 2:13).[121]

God's Mercy does not contradict His justice in anyway but goes beyond it.[122] Hence Thérèse and Thomas hold and teach the same doctrine regarding the Divine attributes of Justice and Mercy; and although St Thomas was a highly educated Dominican scholar, St Thérèse reached this understanding solely through a connatural knowing which comes from the operation of the gift of wisdom.

Living on Love

Seeing that God's Love is often rejected, Thérèse is inspired to offer herself to God during Mass on the Feast of the Holy Trinity, 9 June 1895, as a victim of holocaust to God's Merciful Love. She feels strongly that not only is God's justice in need of victims, God's Merciful Love is also in need of little victims.[123] Before

---

[121] *ST* I, q. 21, a. 3, ad 2. Cf. Jean Clapier, *Aimer jusqu'à mourir d'amour*, 434.

[122] Jean Clapier, *Aimer jusqu'à mourir d'amour*, 434: "Par ailleurs, la signification et la mise en pratique d'une *justice de miséricorde* ne contredisent en rien les exigences intrinsèques de le seule justice, mais elles les dépassent dans 'une plénitude de justice.'"

[123] Ms A 84r, 180. In question eight of the *Little Catechism of the Act of Oblation of St Thérèse of the Child Jesus,* it is explained that "*By the word Victim,* St Thérèse meant to denote a *complete oblation of herself*

Thérèse is able to make her Act of Offering she has to ask permission from Mother Agnes de Jesus, the Prioress (Pauline). She asks to offer herself to God so that His love which has been rejected will consume her.[124] Thérèse is granted permission, and she offers herself as a victim to God's Merciful Love. After that day she is never the same – "oceans of graces" flood her soul.[125] She says after that day, "Everything that I do, my actions, my looks, everything, since my Offering, is done through love."[126]

Thérèse had a great love for God from a very early age, but after this offering, her heart burned with love: "Ah! How I loved God! But it wasn't at all as it was after my Oblation to Love; it wasn't a real flame that

---

to Divine Love; she desired that all personal life should disappear, as though it were absorbed by this Love. Again, she used the expression *Victim of Love* in opposition to *Victim of Justice* in a spontaneous outburst from her sensitive heart; she did not wish the most beautiful attribute of God to be less favored than the other, which has long had its victims." In question nine it says that "Holocaust, to the Saint's mind, means that the soul 'plunged in the rapturous fire of God's Infinite Love' aspires, ardently desires, to be *wholly consumed*, and to be so transformed as to *become fire* herself at the permanent contact of the Divine Fire." *Little Catechism of the Act of Oblation of St Thérèse of the Child Jesus*, translated by Michael Collins, AM, in collaboration with Carmel of Kilmacud, Co. Dublin (Westminster, Maryland: The Newman Press, 1949), 6-7. Speaking of the Act of oblation André Combes comments "This text, so important in the history of the spiritual life, has been many times published and commented. No commentary has greater authority than the *Petit catéchisme de l'acte d'offrande*, edited by the Carmel of Lisieux with a facsimile of Thérèse's manuscript." André Combes, *Spirituality of St Thérèse*, 52-53.

[124] Ms A 84r, 181.
[125] Ms A 84r, 181.
[126] *LC*, August 8, 2, 141.

was burning me."[127] She explains:

> ... at each moment this Merciful Love renews me, purifying my soul and leaving no trace of sin within it and I need have no fear of purgatory. I know that of myself I would not merit even to enter that place of expiation since only holy souls can have entrance there, but I also know that the Fire of Love is more sanctifying than is the fire of purgatory. I know that Jesus cannot desire useless sufferings for us, and that He would not inspire the longings I *feel* unless He wanted to grant them.[128]

After this offering Thérèse is consumed by the love of God; by offering herself to Merciful Love Thérèse expresses her desire of loving and pleasing God in all things. She explains that to offer oneself to God's Merciful Love means a person is abandoning himself

---

[127] *LC*, July 7, 2, 77.
[128] Ms A 84r-84v, 181 (emphasis added). Marie-Eugène of the Child Jesus explains that Saint John of the Cross "speaks practically the same language as Saint Teresa. It is a soul wounded by love that he too presents to us at the beginning of the *Spiritual Canticle* and in the *Living Flame of Love*. The inflowings of divine love, received passively in contemplation, constitute the dark night of the spirit, which he so magnificently terms 'the dark night of loving fire.' It is the same flame, that is, the Holy Spirit, who, against the day when He will glorify it, now penetrates the substance of the soul in order to purify. These assaults of love in the soul can be compared to a material fire that attacks a log of wood, envelops it, penetrates its substance, and transforms it into fire. This comparison translates very well the experience of the flames of love that Saint Thérèse of the Child Jesus had after her act of oblation to Merciful Love. In a few words she expresses it: 'From that day I have been penetrated and surrounded with love. Every moment this Merciful Love renews me and purifies me, leaving in my soul no trace of sin'" (*I am a Daughter of the Church*, 213).

or herself to whatever God wants to send out of love. It means the ability to love the good God more and more, and to make up for souls who do not want to love Him. "It is to compensate the good God for the refusal which His creatures oppose to the Love that He desires to shower upon them."[129] By offering herself to Merciful Love Thérèse expresses her desire of loving and pleasing God in all things. She offers her daily sacrifices to God, but not only her daily sacrifices, she offers her very self.[130] Thérèse offers herself as a sacrifice, a complete oblation to God.[131] This marks a new stage in the life of Thérèse. Jesus had laid down His life for her, and Thérèse desires to give her whole life to Him in a total sacrificial gift of self: "To him, who had given his life for her, she could only want to give hers in return, totally. For *love is to give all and to give oneself ... Love for love.*"[132]

By offering herself as a victim holocaust, Thérèse is not suggesting that she be completely destroyed in suffering and in pain, but rather, that any obstacles that stand in the way of God's action of love may be taken away and destroyed. Her full and complete giving of self to God as a victim of love is a giving of

---

[129] *Little Catechism of the Act of Oblation of St Thérèse of the Child Jesus*, question 1, 4.

[130] Louis Liagre, *Retreat with Saint Thérèse*, translated by Dom P. J. Owen (Westminster, Maryland: The Newman Press, 1961), 120.

[131] "Oblatio, onis, f. – an offering, presenting, a giving or bestowing gratuitously, gift." Roy J. Deferrari, Mary Inviolata Barry, and Ignatius McGuiness, *A Lexicon of St Thomas Aquinas*.

[132] Guy Gaucher, OCD, *The Story of a Life, St. Thérèse of Lisieux*, translated by Sr Anne Marie Brennan (San Francisco: Harper and Row Publishers, 1987), 148.

self in total abandonment to God's Will.[133] Sister Geneviève of the Holy Face (Thérèse's blood sister) says:

> The soul offering herself to love is not asking for suffering, but yielding herself up entirely to the designs of love, she is accepting in advance all that divine providence will send her by way of joys, labours and trials; at the same time, she counts on infinite mercy to enable her to sanctify her crosses by an enduring spirit of joy.[134]

Thérèse "had not offered to suffer but to love. Everything in her offering was inspired by love and for love."[135] The "soul offers itself to love in order *to live in an act of love*...all that is done, all the acts of virtue are reduced to a single common denominator: love."[136] By making this act of offering a person opens

---

[133] André Combes, *St. Thérèse and Suffering*, 100.

[134] Sister Geneviève of the Holy Face, (Céline Martin) *My Sister Saint Thérèse*, 84-85: "When the Liturgical Office of Saint Thérèse of the Child Jesus was given to the Church the summarized ninth lesson of Matins contained these words: ' ... *inflamed with the desire of suffering*, she offered herself, two years before her death, as a victim to the merciful love of God.' But Mère Agnès de Jésus (our sister) had no rest until she obtained, from the Sacred Congregation of Rites, a modification of this text. It was solely due to her intervention that finally, on May 2, 1932, the substitute phrase was published in the *Acta Apostolicae Sedis* '... on fire with divine love...' which is a faithful expression of Thérèsian thought."

[135] Herbert Schmidt, *St Thérèse - A Martyr of Love* (Copyright Rev. Herbert Schmidt, 1989), 95.

[136] Father Camillus, OCD, "The Act of Oblation to Merciful Love," *Spiritual Life*, vol. XII, n. 2, Summer Issue, Discalced Carmelite Fathers of the Province of the Immaculate Heart of Mary, Washington Province, (1966): 116.

himself or herself up to all that God wants to communicate to his or her soul; and since it is by responding to God's grace that a person grows in sanctity, there is no better way to be open to God than by offering all to Him in an act of love. By offering oneself to God's merciful love a "person is proposing *'to live in an act of perfect love.'*"[137]

It is evident that Thérèse goes from desiring to suffer, (her emphasis being on the love of suffering), to desiring only to love God and to fulfil His Will. In other words, there is a certain shift from an emphasis on suffering to an emphasis on love and abandonment. As a person progresses in the spiritual life, the focus becomes more on total abandonment to the Will of God. Now Thérèse is not thinking of or desiring suffering. She says:

> Neither do I desire any longer suffering or death, and still I love them both; it is *love* alone that attracts me, however. I desired them for a long time; I possessed suffering and believed I had touched the shores of heaven, that the little flower would be gathered in the springtime of her life. Now, abandonment alone guides me. I have no other compass! I can no longer ask for anything with fervor except the accomplishment of God's will in my soul without any creature being able to set obstacles in the way.[138]

Thérèse's whole focus now is love and abandonment to God's will. It is not that Thérèse wants to exclude or lessen her suffering; but if it were absent

---

[137] Camillus, "The Act of Oblation to Merciful Love," 112.
[138] Ms A 83r, 178.

from her life she would not ask for it. She sees suffering as "far lower than this other good which even here below can include it and give it all its meaning, viz., love."[139] Thérèse no longer has any particular desire for suffering; rather, "this act transcends the desire for suffering ... [so that all is] at the free disposition of God's infinite love."[140] Therefore even though the words *victim, martyrdom,* and *holocaust*, seem to be suggesting this, these words are simply expressing the "effect of love in a soul that is afire and consumed by that love. St John of the Cross, speaking of souls that are consecrated to love, expresses himself in similar terms in his *Spiritual Canticle* and his Living *Flame of Love.*"[141]

The Desire to be a Victim of Love Suffices

In order to offer oneself as a holocaust to God's Merciful Love, it is not necessary for one to be strong or full of virtues. On the contrary, Thérèse insists that

---

[139] André Combes, *St. Thérèse and Suffering,* 99-100. Combes points out that at "the date when Thérèse tells us, without regret, that she no longer possesses the desire for suffering, six or seven months had passed since her act of oblation to the merciful love of God. Since that act of June 9th, 1895, her sole desire had been to live and to die in martyrdom to the love of God."

[140] André Combes, *St. Thérèse and Suffering,* 100.

[141] Jamart, *Spiritual Doctrine of St. Thérèse,* 156. See, St John of the Cross, *Living Flame of Love,* stanza 9 and *Spiritual Canticle,* stanza 1, 2.

the weaker one is, the more the Lord will be able to work:

> understand that to love Jesus, to be His *victim of love*, the weaker one is, without desires or virtues, the more suited one is for the workings of this consuming and transforming Love.... The *desire* alone to be a victim suffices, but we must consent to remain always poor and without strength, and this is the difficulty.[142]

St Thérèse, however, does not want us to believe that virtue is of little importance. Rather she wants to emphasise that we should not become discouraged because of a lack of virtue. It is important that we recognise and acknowledge our weakness;[143] God then helps the humble soul and pours out His grace. Hence, in order to offer oneself as a victim of Divine Love it is not necessary to be perfect; rather, it is necessary to be aware of one's littleness and to have total dependence on God.[144] Thérèse offers God "her poverty ... that emptiness of her poor created heart and by her desire opens it before Him as widely as she can; she offers Him that empty vessel for Him to fill."[145] She says that to enjoy the treasures of Jesus "one must humble oneself, recognise one's nothingness, [but] that is what many souls do not want to do."[146] Thérèse understands that it is love, trust, and abandonment which moves the heart of God and

---

[142] *GC* II, LT 197, 999.
[143] Simon Tugwell, OP, "Jean Pierre de Caussade, Saint Thérèse of Lisieux," *Doctrine and Life*, vol. 33, n.1 (1983): 338.
[144] Conrad de Meester, *The Power of Confidence*, 344.
[145] Louis Liagre, *A Retreat with Saint Thérèse*, 120.
[146] *GC* II, LT 261, 1165.

leads a soul to sanctity. God grants mercy to those who trust the Lord with the abandonment of a little child:

> I understand so well that it is only love that can make us pleasing to God, that this love is the only good that I ambition. Jesus is pleased to show me the only road which leads to this divine furnace, and this road is the *abandonment* of the little child who sleeps without fear in his Father's arms.... "Whoever is a *little one*, let him come to me" said the Holy Spirit through the mouth of Solomon, and this same Spirit of Love has said again: "Mercy is granted to little ones." ... Ah! if all weak and imperfect souls felt what the littlest of all souls feels, the soul of your little Thérèse, not one would despair of reaching the summit of the mountain of love, since Jesus does not ask for great actions but only abandonment and gratitude.[147]

Thérèse is inviting other little souls to make this Act of Oblation; she appeals to God's Merciful Love and His compassionate heart to help all "weak souls" and to "regard their insignificance with pity."[148] Thérèse says, "God cannot be satisfied, until He has raised to His Sacred Heart even the least of us; and there, like a runaway lamb, at the shepherd's bosom we may rest, held tenderly captive, victims of His divine love."[149]

---

[147] *GC* II, LT 196, 994.
[148] Sister Geneviève of the Holy Face, (Céline Martin), *My Sister Saint Thérèse*, 80-81. Céline says that her sister St Thérèse "did not identify the martyrdom of love with that call to suffering which distinguishes the victims of God's justice." (*My Sister Saint Thérèse*, 80).
[149] Sister Geneviève of the Holy Face, (Céline Martin) *My Sister Saint Thérèse*, 80-81.

A Way of Trust and Confidence that can Lead to the Heights of Perfection

Thérèse's offering to Merciful Love is not a one-time offering but rather a continuous offering to the Lord through her ongoing abandonment and confidence in God.[150] It is a way of total confidence and trust in the God of mercy, "a way of confidence which leads to the experience of love."[151] God loves the "blind hope" that Thérèse has "in His mercy."[152] Thérèse explains:

> I am only a child, powerless and weak, and yet it is my weakness that gives me the boldness of offering myself as VICTIM of Your Love, O Jesus! In times past, victims, pure and spotless, were the only ones accepted by the Strong and Powerful God. To satisfy Divine *Justice,* perfect victims were necessary, but the *law of Love* has succeeded to the law of fear, and Love has chosen me as a holocaust, me, a weak and imperfect creature. Is not this choice worthy of *Love*? Yes, in order that Love be fully satisfied, it is necessary that It lower Itself, and that It lower Itself to nothingness and transform this nothingness into *fire*.[153]

Thérèse has immense love and trust, and a deep recognition of her poverty before the Lord. She is well disposed for the Lord to work deep within her soul transforming her and bringing her to the heights of perfection. By recognising her weaknesses from a

---

[150] Conrad de Meester, *The Power of Confidence*, 176.
[151] Conrad de Meester, *The Power of Confidence*, 344.
[152] *GC II*, LT 197, 999.
[153] Ms B 3v, 195.

very early age, Thérèse has been open to the workings of the grace of God in her life. She does not look at herself, but always to the God of mercy Who showers her with His love. She reaches such a high degree of perfection through God's grace and the working of His seven-fold gift, especially the gift of wisdom.

From the effect that the gift of wisdom has on charity "comes peace; and from peace, or harmony among the component parts of the supernatural organism, comes our sharing in the sonship of God."[154] Thérèse's confidence and her offering to Merciful Love is the perfect expression of spiritual childhood and of being an adopted daughter of the King. In his apostolic letter, *Divini Amoris Scientia*, St John Paul II explains:

> Thérèse experienced divine revelation, going so far as to contemplate the fundamental truths of our faith united in the mystery of Trinitarian life. At the summit, as the source and goal, is the merciful love of the three Divine Persons, as she expresses it, especially in her *Act of Oblation to Merciful Love*. At the root, on the subject's part, is the experience of being the Father's adoptive children in Jesus; this is the most authentic meaning of spiritual childhood, that is, the experience of divine filiation, under the movement of the Holy Spirit.[155]

There is clear evidence of her sense of God's mercy in Thérèse's whole spiritual doctrine.[156] Her message

---

[154] Robert Edward, Brennan, *The Seven Horns of the Lamb, A Study of the Gifts Based on Saint Thomas Aquinas*, 86.
[155] St John Paul II, *Divini Amoris Scientia*, 8.
[156] Philippe de la Trinité, "De Saint Thomas d'Aquin à Sainte Thérèse de l'Enfant-Jésus," 384.

always reminds us of the God of Love and Mercy. She always gently points us toward Him, showing us that God's love and mercy are inseparable.

Vocation of Love/ The Little Doctrine

It was not long after Thérèse had made her Act of Oblation to Merciful Love that she discovered her *Little Way* and that her *vocation in the Church is love*. Since the day of her offering to Merciful Love, Thérèse was being consumed more and more by the Love of God. Manuscript B of *Story of a Soul* expresses some of Thérèse's most intimate thoughts. It is in this Manuscript that one can see Thérèse's *Little Doctrine*. She writes by addressing her thoughts to Jesus and so it is in this manuscript that one really gets a glimpse of Thérèse's intimate relationship with Jesus her Spouse.

Thérèse was already practising this *Little Way*, the way of love, from an early age. However, Jesus had yet to reveal to Thérèse that this would be the central point of her life and the message that she would impart to the whole Church. Thérèse recounts her thoughts on the sixth anniversary of her union with Jesus (her profession in Carmel) – she feels within herself the vocation of the "WARRIOR, THE PRIEST, THE APOSTLE, THE DOCTOR, THE MARTYR," and she asks, "O Jesus, my Love, my Life, how can I combine these contrasts? How can I realise the desires of my poor *little soul*?"[157] Reading First Corinthians,

---

[157] Ms B 2v-3r, 192.

Thérèse finds her answer:

> During my meditations, my desires caused me a veritable martyrdom, and I opened the Epistles of St Paul to find some kind of answer. Chapter 12 and 13 of the First Epistle to the Corinthians fell under my eyes. I read there, in the first of these chapters, that *all* cannot be apostles, prophets, doctors, etc., that the Church is composed of different members, and that the eye cannot be the hand at *one and the same time*.[158]

Thérèse still wanted more answers; she felt that her desires had not been fulfilled. However, she did not become discouraged, but continued to read. It was the next sentence that gave Thérèse consolation: *"Yet strive after the BETTER GIFTS, and I point out to you a yet more excellent way."* Thérèse exclaims, "The Apostle explains how all *the most PERFECT gifts* are nothing without *LOVE. That Charity is the EXCELLENT WAY that leads most surely to* God;" she is finally at rest.[159]

Thérèse had not recognised herself in any of the descriptions given by St Paul, or rather she had desired to see herself in all of them. It is charity that finally gives Thérèse the key to her vocation; she cries out:

> I understood that if the Church had a body composed of different members, the most necessary and most noble of all could not be lacking to it, and so I understood that the Church *had a heart and that this Heart was BURNING WITH LOVE. I understood it was Love alone* that made the Church's

---

[158] Ms B 3r, 193-194.
[159] Ms B 3v, 194.

members act, that if *Love* ever became extinct, apostles would not preach the Gospel and martyrs would not shed their blood, I understood that LOVE COMPRISED ALL VOCATIONS, THAT LOVE WAS EVERYTHING, THAT IT EMBRACED ALL TIMES AND PLACES ... IN A WORD, THAT IT WAS ETERNAL![160]

Then, in the excess of my delirious joy, I cried out: O Jesus, my Love... my *vocation*, at last I have found it... MY VOCATION IS LOVE![161]

O my Jesus! I love You! I love the Church, my Mother! I recall that *"the smallest act* of PURE LOVE *is more value to her than all other works together."*[162]

Thérèse's *Little Way* was Given to Her Through a Knowledge of Love

Thérèse had found her vocation in the Church ... Thérèse knew so well that it is love that moves the

---

[160] Ms B 3v, 194. Cf. *CCC* 826.

[161] Ms B 3v, 194.

[162] Ms B 4v, 197. Here Thérèse is referring to what St John of the Cross writes in *The Spiritual Canticle*: "It should be noted that until the soul reached this state of union of love, she should practice love in both the active and contemplative life. Yet once she arrives, she should not become involved in other works and exterior exercises that might be of the slightest hindrance to the attentiveness of love toward God, even though the work be of great service to God. For a little of this pure love is more precious to God and the soul and more beneficial to the Church, even though it seems one is doing nothing, than all these other works put together" (St John of the Cross, *Spiritual Canticle*, stanza 29, 2, 523).

an ordinary love but like the Saints who did foolish things for Him."[185]

Christian Perfection and the Way of Abandonment

Christian perfection consists in following the Lord's will, and loving Him with our whole heart. Thérèse wanted to be a Saint, she wanted to reach the heights of perfection; she understood that love was the means to obtain it. She says, "I know no other means of reaching perfection but (love)... Love, how well our heart is made for that!"[186] She explains, "I find perfection very easy to practice because I have understood it is a matter of taking hold of Jesus by His Heart."[187]

Despite the fact that Thérèse has reached the heights of holiness, she looks upon herself as a very small and weak soul, and yet she is content to remain "weak and little."[188] She believes she is a "poor little thing who would return to nothingness if [Jesus'] divine glance did not give [her] life from one moment to the next."[189] She says, "I understand so well that it is only love that can make us pleasing to God, that this love is the only good that I ambition. Jesus deigned to show me the road that leads to this Divine Furnace,

---

[185] GC II, LT 225, 1090.
[186] GC I, LT 109, 641.
[187] GC II, LT 191, 965-966.
[188] Ms B 5r, 199.
[189] Ms B 5v, 199.

and this road is the *abandonment* of the little child who sleeps without fear in its Father's arms."[190] In a letter to her sister Marie, she writes:

> You are mistaken … if you believe that your little Thérèse walks always with fervor on the road of virtue. She is weak and very weak, and every day she has a new experience of this weakness, but Marie, Jesus is pleased to teach her, as He did St Paul, the science of rejoicing in her infirmities. This is a great grace, and I beg Jesus to teach it to you, for peace and quiet of heart are to be found there only.[191]

Even after "seven years in the religious life," Thérèse says, "I still am weak and imperfect."[192] She is highly aware of her need of God's grace and of her own shortcomings. She exclaims, "O my Jesus! …Is there a soul more *little*, more powerless than mine?"[193] However, she is forever confident that if she remains faithful to God, He will always work in her and accomplish His will in and through her: "Ah! how sweet it is to abandon oneself into His arms without fear or desire."[194] She understands that everything is a gift and God is happy with those that maintain the humility of a child. In a letter to her Sister Geneviève, she writes:

> Let us esteem ourselves as little souls whom God must sustain at each moment. When He sees we

---

[190] *GC* II, LT 196, 994; Ms B 1r, 188.
[191] *GC* I, LT 109, 641.
[192] Ms A 32r, 72.
[193] Ms B 3r, 193.
[194] *GC* II, LT 263, 1173.

are very much convinced of our nothingness, He extends His hand to us. If we still wish to attempt doing something *great* even under the pretext of zeal, Good Jesus leaves us all alone. "But when I said: 'My foot has stumbled,' your mercy, Lord, strengthened me!... Ps. 93." Yes, it suffices to humble oneself, to bear with one's imperfections. That is real sanctity![195]

Thérèse relies on God for everything and abandons herself into the arms of Jesus. She is always happy to remain little, to remain poor in the eyes of the world. She understands very well that to remain small and humble, relying on God for all things, running into His arms like a daughter does to her father, is a sure way to reach the heights of sanctity.

Thérèse Believes all Souls Can Follow Her Little Way

Thérèse has no doubt that all souls can follow her *Little Way* and reach the summit of the spiritual life if they remain humble and put all of their hope and trust in God. "This loving confidence and abandonment [is] the fundamental attitude of Theresian spirituality."[196] When she is asked how she would like to "teach souls" she says, "It's the way of spiritual childhood,

---

[195] *GC* II, LT 243, 1122.
[196] Bl. Marie-Eugène, *Under the Torrent of His Love*, 109.

it's the way of confidence and total abandon."[197] She exclaims:

> O Jesus! why can't I tell all *little souls* how unspeakable is Your condescension? I feel that if You found a soul weaker and littler than mine, which is impossible, You would be pleased to grant it still greater favors, provided it abandoned itself with total confidence to Your Infinite Mercy ... I beg You to cast Your Divine Glance upon a great number of *little* souls. I beg You to choose a legion of *little* Victims worthy of Your LOVE![198]

Thérèse believes that weak souls can reach the heights of perfection and that true sanctity consists in remaining humble, recognising one's nothingness and the need to have confidence in God. The Theresian spirituality is a way of learning to accept one's own weaknesses and to rely on God in all things. It is important not to confuse this spirituality with one that sees no need for co-operating with God's grace; one must always have the good will to co-operate.[199] The *Little Way* of Thérèse is a perfect preparation for God to work, through His grace and through the seven gifts of the Holy Spirit – it is a way which recognises that without God we can do nothing. It is the way of total abandonment into the arms of Jesus. Jean-Pierre Caussade in his book *Abandonment to Divine Providence* says that if we try our best to quietly go about our duties each day and "follow any impulse coming from God, if we peacefully submit to the influence of grace,

---

[197] *LC*, Additional Conversations, July, 257. Cf. Bl. Marie-Eugène, *Under the Torrent of His Love* 109.
[198] Ms B 5v, 200.
[199] Bl. Marie-Eugène, *Under the Torrent of His Love,* 129.

we are making an act of total abandonment."[200] Thérèse "shows us the courageous way of abandonment into the hands of God to whom she entrusts her littleness."[201] It is the hero that conquers in battle, the "saint is the one who lets God conquer in him."[202] This is exactly what Thérèse does. She has an acute awareness and understanding that growth in the spiritual life is not so much about what a person does; rather, it is about God, Who sanctifies and brings the soul to perfection. All that a person needs to do is to have the trust of a child sleeping in its father's arms. Fr Gabriel of St Mary Magdalen explains that Thérèse "seems to have understood with deep penetration how the work of the sanctification of the soul is above all, the work of God. This, I believe, is the basic idea in the 'little way', the foundation for the perfect surrender of the child who trusts wholly in its father."[203]

Thérèse knows that all she has received is a gift from God. It is because she constantly drinks from the abundant river of God's grace that Thérèse is able to do all things with such great love. God first gives us the grace to love, and when we co-operate with this grace, we can do all things with great love. Benedict XVI in his encyclical *Deus Caritas Est* says:

> Anyone who wishes to give love must also receive love as a gift. Certainly, as the Lord tells us, one can

---

[200] Jean-Pierre de Caussade, SJ, *Abandonment to Divine Providence*, translated by John Beevers (New York: Double Day, 1975), 66.
[201] St Paul VI, *Gaudete in Domino*, IV.
[202] Bl. Marie-Eugène, *Under the Torrent of His Love*, 47.
[203] Gabriel of Saint Mary Magdalen, *Le Message de la petite Thérèse*, 19, as quoted in *Mystical Phenomena*, 49.

become a source from which rivers of living water flow (cf. Jn 7:37-38). Yet to become such a source, one must constantly drink anew from the original source, which is Jesus Christ, from whose pierced heart flows the love of God (cf. Jn 19:34).[204]

Thérèse constantly drinks from these streams of living water, and she wants all souls to do the same. She longs for others to love God as she has loved Him; she wants all souls to know that they can follow her *Little Way* and that they can abandon themselves like a child into the arms of Love – this is her desire and what she knows to be her mission. Just before her death, she says:

> I feel that I'm about to enter into my rest. But I feel especially that my mission is about to begin, my mission of making God loved as I love Him, of giving my little way to souls. If God answers my desires, my heaven will be spent on earth until the end of the world. Yes, I want to spend my heaven in doing good on earth.[205]

---

[204] Benedict XVI, *Deus Caritas Est*, 7.
[205] *LC*, July 17, 102.

6

GOD'S LITTLE MARTYR OF LOVE

Martyrdom of Love

Through the working of the Holy Spirit and by way of the gift of wisdom, Thérèse is being refined more and more by Jesus Himself, and her desire to be conformed to Christ continues to develop. This section will manifest the full blossoming of the effect of the gift of wisdom on charity and how God has brought His little flower to the summit of love.

In the works of St Thérèse, we find the expressions *Martyr of Love* and *dying of love*.[1] As we shall see in this chapter, a soul that dies as a *martyr of love* has reached the stage of the transforming union;[2]

---

[1] See for example Ms C 7v, 214; *Story of a Soul,* Act of Oblation, 277; GC II, LT 182, 927; *LC,* July 4, 2, 73; July 11, 6, 89 and July 14, 4, 97.

[2] St John of the Cross explains that when a person has reached the transforming union, he or she has reached a very high state of union with God; it is the highest state attainable in this life. Through this union the soul and God have as it were become one. This spiritual marriage "is total transformation in the Beloved in which each surrenders the entire possession of self to the other with a certain consummation of the union of love. The soul thereby becomes divine, becomes God through participation, insofar as is possible in this life" (*Spiritual Canticle,* stanza 22, 3 497). He says that very few people reach this state (*Spiritual Canticle,* stanza 26, 4, 512). This high state of transforming union, however high a state it is, is still part of the normal development

between this soul and God, there is only a very thin veil which is keeping the soul from flying off to heaven. When the soul dies as a *martyr of love*, the very thin veil is broken through *love*.

Even before Thérèse entered Carmel, she had desired to be a martyr, and this desire continued to develop within Carmel. But in Carmel she did not just use the word *martyr* – she used the expression *martyr of love* – she wanted to be consumed by God's fire of love and eventually die as a *martyr of love*. From a young age Thérèse speaks of her desire to be a martyr and *feels* that her desires are going to be answered. On a visit to Rome with her father and her sister Céline, she visits the Colosseum. Here the thing that Thérèse desires to do most is to kiss the spot where the martyrs had shed their blood. She says: "My heart was beating hard when my lips touched the dust stained with the blood of the first Christians. I asked for the grace of being a martyr for Jesus and felt that my prayer was answered!"[3] She explains: "*Martyrdom* was the dream of my youth and this dream has grown with me within Carmel's cloisters... I cannot confine myself to desiring *one kind* of martyrdom. To satisfy me I need *all*."[4] She also says:

---

of grace, it is not something extraordinary but within the normal way of sanctity.

[3] Ms A 61r, 131. The day Thérèse prayed that she would be given the "grace of martyrdom" and felt certain that God would answer her prayers was 14 November 1887 (André Combes, *St. Thérèse and Suffering*, 114).

[4] Ms B 3r, 193. Here we see the echoes of Thérèse's childhood, when she was asked by her sister Léonie which toy she would like to have from her box. "I choose all" was the reply. "One day, Léonie, thinking she was too big to be playing any longer with

> Like You, my Adorable Spouse, I would be scourged and crucified. I would die flayed like St Bartholomew. I would be plunged into boiling oil like St John; I would undergo all the tortures inflicted upon the martyrs. With St Agnes and St Cecilia, I would present my neck to the sword, and like Joan of Arc, my dear sister, I would whisper at the stake Your Name, O JESUS. When thinking of the torments which will be the lot of Christians at the time of Anti-Christ, I feel my heart leap with joy and I would that these torments be reserved for me. Jesus, Jesus, if I wanted to write all my desires, I would have to borrow Your *Book of Life,* for in it are reported all the actions of all the saints, and I would accomplish all of them for You.[5]

On the day of Thérèse's religious profession, she had placed a note over her heart which read "Jesus, may I die a martyr for You. Give me martyrdom of heart or of body, or rather give me both!"[6] Thérèse's love is so great that she cannot confine herself to desiring one type of martyrdom, and she eventually turns to the *martyrdom of love.* The Lord had shown her that through the martyrdom of love, her dream of

---

dolls, came to us with a basket filled with dresses and pretty pieces for making others; her doll was resting on top. 'Here, my little sister, *choose*; I'm giving you all this.' Céline stretched out her hand and took a little ball of wool that pleased her. After a moment's reflection, I stretched out mine saying: 'I choose all!' and took the basket without further ceremony. Those who witnessed the scene saw nothing wrong and even Céline herself didn't dream of complaining." St Thérèse herself exclaims, "This little incident of my childhood is a summary of my whole life" (Ms A, 10r & 10v, 27).

[5] Ms B 3r, 193.
[6] *Story of a Soul,* Appendices, 275.

martyrdom would be answered.

Thérèse understands that love encompasses all things, and therefore, through the martyrdom of love, she sees that all her desires will be fulfilled. In her Act of Oblation to Merciful Love she writes:

> In order to live in one single act of perfect Love, I OFFER MYSELF AS A VICTIM OF HOLOCAUST TO YOUR MERCIFUL LOVE, asking You to consume me incessantly, allowing the waves of *infinite tenderness* shut up within You to overflow into my soul, and that thus I may become a *martyr* of Your *Love*, O my God! May this martyrdom, after having prepared me to appear before You, finally cause me to die and may my soul take its flight without delay into the eternal embrace of *Your Merciful Love*.[7]

The expression *martyrdom of love* actually means that a person gives up his or her very life. Thérèse wants to imitate as far as possible the death of Jesus, and so she constantly asks the Lord to let Love finally take her life.[8] *Jean Clapier* in his book *Aimer jusqu'à*

---

[7] *Story of a Soul*, Appendices, 277.
[8] St Thomas says that "the perfect notion of martyrdom requires that a [person] suffer death for Christ's sake" (*ST* II-II, q. 124, a. 4). Thérèse does speak of a type of "martyrdom of the heart," however this does not fully encompass all that she means by martyrdom of love. By martyrdom of the heart, she is referring to a slow daily martyrdom, referring to the interior sufferings endured in our daily lives. Thérèse speaks about interior sufferings and how they can be a real Cross. She says: "What is a real Cross is the martyrdom of the heart, the interior suffering of the soul, and this, which no one sees" (*GC* II, LT 167, 872). When Thérèse speaks of *Martyrdom of Love* she is not simply referring to

mourir d'amour says that when a person dies as a martyr of love, he or she mystically reproduces the act of Christ's Love dying on the Cross.[9] The Theresian understanding of "to die of love" is a conforming of oneself to the Paschal Sacrifice of Christ. It is a death which is brought about by God Who "attracts hearts to collaborate with His works of salvation"[10] – it is a redemptive death.[11]

Previous sufferings borne with love, by a person who will eventually die as a martyr of love, are all preparations for this final death of love "and are virtually contained in it."[12] The gift of self in the martyrdom of love "becomes the choicest offering that a spouse of Christ can present to her crucified Lord."[13] This gift of self is the most absolute expression of love that one can give; it is the ultimate gift of love.[14] Thérèse had offered her whole self to God to the point

---

a daily martyrdom of the heart but a martyrdom which will eventually take her life.

[9] Jean Clapier, *Aimer jusqu'à mourir d'amour*, 503: "Cette *"mort d'amour"* reproduit mystiquement, dans l'aujourd'hui terrestre, l'acte d'amour du Christ en sa passion, expirant sur la croix."

[10] Jean Clapier, *Aimer jusqu'à mourir d'amour*, 496: "Nous préciserons ensuite la compréhension thérésienne du *"mourir d'amour"* en conformité au Christ pascal, au don rédempteur de sa vie qui engendre l'Église. Ce thème thérésien s'articule étroitement avec celui de la solidarité universelle du chrétien dans la communion à la mort salvatrice du Christ, en vue de lui... de collaborer à son œuvre de salut."

[11] Jean Clapier, *Aimer jusqu'a mourir d'amour*, 505-506.

[12] André Combes, *St Thérèse and Suffering*, 94.

[13] André Combes, *St Thérèse and Suffering*, 94.

[14] P. Lucien-Marie de Saint Joseph, "Le Martyre d'Amour," 331: "Le don de soi le plus absolu qui soit. C'est un passage à la limite qui est dans la logique d'amour."

of the giving of her very self in a radical oblation.[15] She wanted to be consumed by the love of God until nothing remained and therefore called on God's Divine Love to overflow *"into her soul."*[16] She had been prepared by love and love would finally consume her, and she would truly die as a martyr of love.

First Motive Cause of Martyrdom

St Thomas says, "no act of itself is as meritorious as dying for Christ because a man is giving what is most dear, namely, his own life."[17] Thérèse makes the ultimate sacrifice; she gives her very life to Love without holding anything back. She would never have been able to do this if charity had not reached its heights by being perfected by the gift of wisdom. Through the gift of wisdom, in the evening of her life, Jesus conforms His *Little Flower* most profoundly and

---

[15] Jean Clapier, *Aimer jusqu'à mourir d'amour*, 511: "Si Thérèse se reçoit entièrement de Dieu, de la spiration de son propre amour, c'est parce qu'elle offre tout à Dieu, jusqu'au souffle de sa propre vie. Et si tout est offert à Dieu, jusqu'à sa propre personne, c'est parce que Thérèse cède, sans aucune restriction, à l'aimantation de Dieu manifestée dans le don de son Fils et qu'elle consent librement à aimer jusqu'au degré ultime de sa *kenosis* : l'oblation pascale."

[16] Àngel de les Gavarres, *Thérèse: The Little Child of God's Mercy*, 309.

[17] *Super Ep. ad Hebr.*, cap. 11, lec. 8, n. 645: "Nullus autem actus quantum est de se, est ita meritorius, sicut quo quis moritur propter Christum, quia dat illud quod habet charius, scilicet vitam propriam."

most perfectly to His cruciform Love. Earlier in this chapter, a proposed objection was answered concerning the operation of the gift of fortitude and the gift of wisdom at the moment of Thérèse's Confirmation. A further objection may also be proposed when one considers martyrdom and the operation of the gifts of fortitude and wisdom. One may object that martyrdom concerns the gift of fortitude rather than the gift of wisdom. Of course, this is true if we consider the strength that is needed to endure martyrdom. However, when a person dies as a *martyr of love,* there is obviously a great level of *love* involved, just as there is when a person dies as a bloody martyr; the person who dies as a martyr of love is operating from the heights of charity. St Thomas explains:

> A virtuous act may be considered ... in comparison with its *first motive cause,* which is the *love of charity,* and it is in this respect that an act comes to belong to the perfection of life, since, as the Apostle says (Colossians 3:14), that "charity. . . is the bond of perfection." Now, of all virtuous acts martyrdom is the greatest proof of the perfection of charity: since a man's love for a thing is proved to be so much the greater, according as that which he despises for its sake is more dear to him, or that which he chooses to suffer for its sake is more odious. But it is evident that of all the goods of the present life man loves life itself most, and on the other hand he hates death more than anything, especially when it is accompanied by the pains of bodily torment, ...And from this point of view it is clear that martyrdom is the most perfect of human acts in respect of its genus, as being the sign of the greatest

charity, according to John 15:13: "Greater love than this no man hath, that a man lay down his life for his friends."[18]

It is charity that inclines a person to undergo a martyr's death, and it is due to the virtue of charity that martyrdom is meritorious. Hence, without charity a true act of martyrdom could never exist.[19] Giving up one's life would be of no value if it was not rooted in love because it is not death in itself which makes martyrdom a virtuous act. St Thomas says

---

[18] *ST* II-II, q. 124, a. 3. St Thomas explains that martyrdom must be voluntary: "A reward is due to martyrdom, not in respect of the exterior infliction, but because it is suffered voluntarily: since we merit only through that which is in us" (*ST supplementum*, III q. 96, a. 6, ad 2). Therefore the "merit of martyrdom is... in the voluntary endurance of death, namely in the fact that a person willingly suffers being put to death" (*ST* II-II, q. 124, a. 4, ad 4). "Christ as God delivered Himself up to death by the same will and action as that by which the Father delivered Him up; but as man He gave Himself up by a will inspired of the Father" (*ST* III, q. 47, a. 3, ad 2). Thérèse had also been inspired with the will to offer herself as an oblation to the Father and she freely offers herself as a sacrifice to the Father in union with Christ.

[19] *ST* II-II, q. 124, a. 2, ad 2: "Charity inclines one to the act of martyrdom, as its first and chief motive cause, being the virtue commanding it, whereas fortitude inclines thereto as being its proper motive cause, being the virtue that elicits it. Hence martyrdom is an act of charity as commanding, and of fortitude as eliciting. For this reason also it manifests both virtues. It is due to charity that it is meritorious, like any other act of virtue: and for this reason it avails not without charity." Aquinas says: "Now the human mind's movement to the fruition of the Divine good is the proper act of charity, whereby all the acts of the other virtues are ordained to this end, since all the other virtues are commanded by charity. Hence the merit of life everlasting pertains first to charity, and secondly, to the other virtues, inasmuch as their acts are commanded by charity" (*ST* I-II, q. 114, a. 4).

"endurance of death is not praiseworthy in itself, but only in so far as it is directed to some good consisting in an act of virtue, such as faith or the love of God."[20] Thérèse wants to imitate her Spouse who's "enduring of the Passion was most acceptable to God, as coming from charity."[21] The ultimate perfection and pre-eminent example of charity is manifested most truly and most purely by the imitation of Christ crucified. Thérèse, in order to be more fully conformed to Jesus, wants to give up her very life in one final act of love, like her Spouse who died in one final act of Love. Only when charity is perfected by the gift of wisdom is the cruciform love of Christ on the Cross made manifest.

The Church does not officially recognise souls who die as martyrs of love by giving them the title "martyr." However, this does not trouble these souls; they never even give this a second thought. What is important to them is the "quality of love" – to exercise the love of a martyr – that is their essential desire.[22] St Thomas explains that charity is the "root of all merit; [therefore] the work proceeding from greater charity is more meritorious."[23] Thus, we cannot say that the

---

[20] *ST* II-II, q. 124, a. 3. Cf. P. Lucien-Marie de Saint Joseph, "Le Martyre d'Amour," 332.
[21] *ST* III, q. 48, a. 3.
[22] P. Lucien-Marie de Saint Joseph, "Le Martyre d'Amour," 333-334: "Que l'Église ne puisse en faire une reconnaissance officielle, cela ne trouble pas l'âme qui n'a jamais pensé à une telle éventualité. Ce que l'âme veut c'est une qualité d'amour, telle qu'éventuellement il se traduise sans hésiter par l'acception de la mort violente. Exercer l'amour pour Dieu comme martyre, même sans l'être en fait, voilà ce qui était l'essentiel du désir de l'âme. Dieu l'aura exaucée par d'autres voies."
[23] St Thomas Aquinas, *Super Ep. ad Hebr.*, cap. 11, lec. 8, n. 645: "Si vero consideretur radix omnis meriti, quae est charitas, I Cor. XIII,

death of those who die as *martyrs of love* is less meritorious than those who endure bloody martyrdom. Martyrdom of love is of no less value to the Lord since it is offered with great charity. In fact, St Francis de Sales in his book *Treatise on the Love of God* explains, "All the elect...died in the habit of holy love; but further, some died even in the exercise of it, others for this love, and others, by this same love. But what belongs to the sovereign degree of love is, that some die of love."[24] In other words to die of love according to St Francis de Sales, belongs to a preeminent degree of charity; in order for a person to die as a *martyr of love,* charity has reached its heights with the help of the gift of wisdom.

Transforming Union

A person who dies as a *martyr of love* has reached the stage of the transforming union; between this soul and God, there is only a very thin veil which is keeping the soul from flying off to heaven. When the soul dies as a *martyr of love,* the very thin veil is broken through *love.* We know that when St Thérèse speaks of

---

v. 2, sic opus procedens ex maiori charitate, est magis meritorium."

In a letter to Monsieur l' Abbé, Thérèse speaks about martyrdom of the heart and its value. Thérèse says that martyrdom of the heart is not necessarily "less fruitful than the pouring out of one's blood" (*GC* II, LT 213, 1042). Note: Martyrdom of the heart is not synonymous with martyrdom of love.

[24] St Francis de Sales, *Treatise on the Love of God,* translated by Henry Benedict Mackey (Rockford, IL: Tan Books and Publishers, Inc., 1997), bk VII chapter XI.

martyrdom of love, she is familiar with the writings of St John of the Cross who describes this type of martyrdom. In a conversation with Mother Agnes, Thérèse quotes the following words from St John of the Cross:

> "Tear through the veil of this sweet encounter!" I've always applied these words to the death of love that I desire. Love will not wear out the veil of my life; it will tear it suddenly.
>
> With what longing and what consolation I repeated from the beginning of my religious life these other words of St John of the Cross: "It is of the highest importance that the soul practice love very much in order that, being consumed rapidly, she may be scarcely retained here on earth but promptly reach the vision of her God face to face."[25]

---

[25] *LC*, July 27, 5, 113. St John of the Cross explains that the person that has reached the state of union "knows full well that it is characteristic of God to take to Himself, before their time, souls that love Him ardently, perfecting them in a short while by means of that love, which in any event they would have gained at their own pace. This is what the Wise Man said: *He pleased God and was loved; and living among sinners he was translated and carried away lest evil should change his understanding or affection deceive his soul. Perfected in a short time, he fulfilled a long time. Because his soul was pleasing to God, He therefore made haste to take him out of the midst,* etc. [Wis. 4:10-11, 13-14] These are the words of the Wise Man in which it will be seen how rightly and adequately the soul uses the expression 'tear through,' for the Holy Spirit uses the words 'carry away' and 'make haste,' which indicate something apart from all delay. God's making haste signifies the haste by which He perfected in a short time the love of the just man, and 'carry away' reflects to a premature death" (St John of the Cross, *Living Flame of Love*, stanza 1, 34, 593-594). Cf., Guy Gaucher, *John and Thérèse*:

She exclaims, "Oh! yes, I desire heaven! 'Tear the veil of this sweet encounter,' Oh, my God!"[26] St John of the Cross explains that a person who wants to die as a martyr of love greatly desires that the flame of love will finally tear through the "veil of mortal life."[27] The soul feels "that it is all inflamed in the divine union ... it seems, because it is so vigorously transformed in God, so sublimely possessed by Him ... that it is singularly close to beatitude – so close that only a thin veil separates it."[28] Thérèse had been led to the heights of sanctity and had already reached the transforming union.[29] She knows that she has reached a very high degree of sanctity; and she continues to ask the Lord to slay her with His Love. Thérèse asks the Lord to tear the thin veil which keeps her from seeing God face to face in heaven. She desires that God take her to Himself; these words finally do become a reality for Thérèse. St John of the Cross explains:

Flames of Love, translated by Alexandra Plettenberg-Serban English (New York: Alba House, 1999), 134-135.

[26] *LC*, September 2, 8, 181.

[27] St John of the Cross, *Living Flame of Love*, stanza 1, 1, 580.

[28] St John of the Cross, *Living Flame of Love*, stanza 1, 1, 579.

[29] Cf. Jamart, *Spiritual Doctrine of St. Thérèse*, 247-253; Miller, 159-190; Gabriel de Sainte Marie-Madeleine, OCD, "St. Thérèse's 'Little Way' and the Teachings of St. John of the Cross," 82-84. Garrigou-Lagrange explains: "The lives of some great servants of God especially dedicated to reparation, to immolation for the salvation of souls or to the apostolate by interior suffering, make one think... of a prolongation of the night of the spirit even after their entrance into the transforming union. In such cases, this trial would no longer be chiefly purificatory; it would be above all reparative" (*Three Ages of the Interior Life*, vol. II, 503). For an excellent explanation of Thérèse's Trial of Faith see Fredrick Miller's book, *The Trial of Faith of St. Thérèse of Lisieux*.

> The enamored soul desires this tearing so that it may suffer no delay by waiting for its life to be destroyed naturally, or cut off at such and such a time. The force of love and the disposition the soul sees in itself make it desire and beg that the veil of life be torn immediately by a supernatural encounter and impetus of love.[30]

St Francis de Sales describes what happens when a soul dies as a martyr of love:

> ... love not only wounds the soul, so as to make her languish, but even pierces her through, delivering its blow right in the middle of the heart, and so fatally, that it drives the soul out of the body – which happens thus. The soul, powerfully drawn by the divine sweetness of her beloved, to correspond on her side with his sweet attractions, forcibly and to the best of her power springs out towards this longed-for beloved who attracts her, and, not being able to draw her body after her, rather than stay with it in this miserable life, she quits it and gets clear; flying alone, as a fair dove, into the delicious bosom of her heavenly spouse. She throws herself upon her beloved, and her beloved draws and ravishes her to himself. And as the bridegroom leaves father and mother to cleave to his dearly beloved, so this chaste bride forsaketh the flesh to unite herself to her beloved. Now this is the most violent effect of love in a soul, and one which requires first a great off stripping of all such affections as keep the heart attached either to the world or to the body, so that as fire, having by little and little separated an essence from its mass, and

---

[30] St John of the Cross, *Living Flame of Love*, stanza 1, 34, 593-594. Cf. Guy Gaucher, John *and Thérèse: Flames of Love*, 134-135.

> wholly purified it, at length brings out the quintessence — even so holy love having withdrawn man's heart from all humours, inclinations, and passions, as far as may be, does at length purge out the soul, to the end that by this death, precious in the divine eyes, she may pass to eternal glory.[31]

When a person dies a martyr of love, God wounds the soul, tears through the veil of this mortal life, and carries the soul to its heavenly Spouse. Martyrdom of love is much more about receiving than it is about enduring; it is receiving "without being able to contain."[32] It is love that will be the "active agent" in Thérèse's final martyrdom.[33] Thus, Thérèse's role in her martyrdom is "essentially passive. She offer[s] herself, without resistance, to that Love which set her alight, burned and consumed her at every moment."[34] She is accepted as a victim, a martyr of Divine Love; and therefore, she becomes a living witness of God's love and generosity to all those who offer themselves to God's merciful love. She is a witness of what God can do in the soul who does not put any obstacle in

---

[31] St Francis de Sales, *Treatise on the Love of God,* bk VII chapter XI.

[32] Conrad de Meester, *The Power of Confidence,* 172. St Francis de Sales explains that St Teresa of Avila "revealed after her death that she had died of an impetuous assault of love, which had been so violent that nature not being able to support it, the soul had departed towards the beloved object of its affections" (*Treatise on the Love of God,* bk VII chapter XI).

[33] Àngel de les Gavarres, *Thérèse: The Little Child of God's Mercy,* 313.

[34] Àngel de les Gavarres, *Thérèse: The Little Child of God's Mercy,* 309.

the way of His Divine inspirations.[35] In Thérèse's intense love for the Cross and her constant desire to work for the salvation of souls, she desired to give her life as a perfect offering to God. Thus, she gave to her Lord the most beautiful offering that she was able to offer.[36] Thérèse died for love and from love; she was a witness to God's merciful love.

The Desire to Die as a Martyr of Love and the Gift of Wisdom

Through the gift of wisdom, we can have a quasi-experiential knowledge of the goodness of God's will. St Thomas explains:

> ... knowledge of God's will or goodness is affective or experimental and thereby a man experiences in himself the taste of God's sweetness, and complacency in God's will.[37]

---

[35] André Combes, *The Spirituality of St. Thérèse*, 58. The word martyr has the same meaning as witness. St Thomas Aquinas, *Super I Ep. ad Thess.*, 2-2. St Thomas says: "The sufficient motive for martyrdom is not only confession of the faith, but any other virtue, not civic but infused, that has Christ for its end. For one becomes a witness of Christ by any virtuous act, inasmuch as the works which Christ perfects in us bear witness to His goodness" (*ST* III, q. 96, a. 6, ad 9). Thérèse dies as a martyr of love and therefore as a witness to God's Love.

[36] André Combes, *St. Thérèse and Suffering*, 124.

[37] *ST* II-II, q. 97, a. 2, ad 2. The Thomistic meaning of the word *complacency* means satisfaction, or delight. See Roy J. Deferrari, *A Lexicon of St Thomas Aquinas*.

This connatural knowing gives us a taste or savour of the goodness of God and conformity to His will. Through the operation of the gift of wisdom, Thérèse often experiences a connatural type of knowing which helps her to understand the heart of her Spouse; she feels that through this experiential knowledge, Jesus inspires desires within her heart that are in conformity to His will:

> I have frequently noticed that Jesus doesn't want me to lay up *provisions*; He nourishes me at each moment with a totally new food; I find it within me without my knowing how it is there. I believe it is Jesus himself hidden in the depths of my poor little heart: He is giving me the grace of acting within me, making me think of all He desires me to do at the present moment.[38]

In one of her prayers, she writes:

> I am certain then, that you will grant my desires: *I feel* it, O my God, the more you want to give, the more you make us desire. *I feel* within my heart immense desires and it is with confidence I ask you to come and take possession of my soul.[39]

The desire to die as a martyr of love is not simply a desire which came from the heart of Thérèse alone; rather it is a desire which has been placed in her heart by Jesus Himself. God inspires Thérèse with the desire to die as a martyr of love, and she has absolute confidence that God will accept her offering because she believes it to be inspired by Him. She says,

---

[38] Ms A 76r, 165.
[39] *Prayers* 6, 58 (emphasis added).

> The holy martyrs will be careful not to be idle. Incomparable palms and fiery arrows will be arranged with touching care along the entire route of the royal procession. They want to render homage to the martyrdom of love which is to consume the life of the joyful bride in a short time.[40]

Thérèse has no doubt that God always makes all her desires conform to His will. She exclaims: "Ah! The Lord is so good to me that it is quite impossible for me to fear Him. He has always given me what I desire or rather He has made me desire what He wants to give me."[41] In this, "the presence of the gift of wisdom is plainly discernible."[42] This connatural way of knowing seems to be how God continually guides Thérèse. She says, "How merciful is the way God has guided me. *Never* has He given me the desire for anything which He has not given me."[43] Thérèse has absolute confidence that God will do His Will in and through her if she remains open to His grace. She has complete trust in her Spouse: "I am not at all worried about the future; I am sure God will do His will, it is the only grace I desire."[44]

Desire for Martyrdom Fulfilled

As stated earlier in this chapter, when Thérèse was younger, she was on a trip to Rome with her father

---

[40] *GC* II, LT 182, 927.
[41] Ms C 31r, 250.
[42] Miller, *Trial of Faith*, 174.
[43] Ms A 71r, 152.
[44] *GC* II, LT 221, 1072.

and sister, and she visited the Colosseum. She describes her experience: "My heart was beating hard when my lips touched the dust stained with the blood of the first Christians. I asked for the grace of being a martyr for Jesus and felt that my prayer was answered!"[45] Even though Thérèse would not die as a bloody martyr like the martyrs in the Colosseum, she does die a martyr – a martyr of love. St John of the Cross explains how God does indeed fulfil the longings of those who desire to die as a martyr even though they do not actually die as a bloody martyr. In his work *The Ascent of Mount Carmel* he writes:

> A soul has intense desires to be a martyr. God answers, "you shall be a martyr"; and He bestows deep interior consolation and confidence in the truth of this promise. Regardless of the promise, this person in the end does not die a martyr; yet the promise will have been true. Why, then, was there no literal fulfilment? Because the promise will be fulfilled in its chief, essential meaning: the bestowal of the essential love and reward of a martyr. God truly grants the soul the essence of both its desire and His promise, because the formal desire of the soul was not a manner of death, but the service of God through martyrdom and the exercise of a martyr's love for Him. The manner of death in itself is of no value without this love, and God bestows martyrdom's love and reward perfectly by other means. Even though the individual does not die a martyr, he is profoundly satisfied, since God has fulfilled his desire.

---

[45] Ms A 61r, 131.

> When these aspirations and other similar ones born of love are unfulfilled in the way one expected, they are fulfilled in another, far better way, and render more honor to God than was thought of in making the request ... Since numerous saints desired various particular favors from God, yet did not receive them in this life, it is of faith that as their desire was just and good it was fulfilled perfectly in heaven. Consequently, if God makes the promise in this life, "your desire shall be fulfilled," it will come true, even though in a different way.[46]

All the saints that have desired martyrdom have been "under the influence" of the gift of wisdom.[47] Thérèse longed for her martyrdom and this desire never left her. At first she desired bloody martyrdom but then she understood that God desired to grant her not bloody martyrdom, but that she die as a martyr of love. Thérèse had reached the heights of perfection and her desire to die of love was an effect of the gift of wisdom.

The desire for martyrdom is of no little importance in the spiritual life; this includes the desire for either physical martyrdom or the martyrdom of love. Concerning bloody martyrdom, St Thomas explains that a person's desire "to suffer martyrdom may possibly proceed from a greater charity than another [person's] act of martyrdom."[48] He writes:

> ... since in the act of suffering martyrdom there is a very great difficulty, the will to suffer martyrdom

---

[46] St John of the Cross, *The Ascent of Mount Carmel*, bk II, ch. 19, 13, 168-169. Cf. Guy Gaucher, *John and Thérèse: Flames of Love*, 143.
[47] Martinez, Sanctifier, 193.
[48] *ST* III, q. 96, a. 6, ad 3.

does not reach the degree of merit due to actual martyrdom by reason of its difficulty: although, indeed it may possibly attain to a higher reward, if we consider the root of merit since the will of one man to suffer martyrdom may possibly proceed from a greater charity than another man's act of martyrdom. Hence one who is willing to be a martyr may by his will merit an essential reward equal to or greater than that which is due to an actual martyr.[49]

This can certainly be extended to desiring to die as a martyr of love; by desiring to die as a martyr of love we may merit an essential reward even if we do not actually die as a martyr of love. But it is unlikely one's desire will proceed from a greater charity than one who actually dies a martyr of love; nevertheless, in order for one to merit an essential reward an authentic desire alone can suffice.

Thérèse had desired martyrdom of love and longed to have this desire fulfilled. God does assure Thérèse that she will die as a martyr – in one of her poems entitled *Jesus, My Beloved, Remember!...* she writes:

> Remember, Jesus, Word of Life,
> How you loved me and even died for me.
> I also want to love you to folly.
> I also want to live and die for You.
> You know, O my God! all that I desire
> Is to make you loved and one day be a martyr.
> I want to die of love.

---

[49] *ST* III, q. 96, a. 6, ad 3.

> Lord, my desire,
> Remember.[50]

Thérèse's desire will finally be answered. Jesus will take His *Little Flower* to Himself at a very young age, through the *martyrdom of love*; the *Little Flower* will die as a *victim of His Divine Love.*

True Love for Jesus and the Authentic Desire for Martyrdom

Thérèse's desire to die a death of love cannot be properly understood unless it is looked at in view of her relationship with and love for Jesus. She always acted in union with and for Jesus. It is the passion of Jesus and His death on the Cross which is the foundation of Thérèse's whole desire to love to the point of dying for love.[51] In 1 John we read: "In this we have known the charity of God, because he hath laid down his life for us" (1 Jn 3:16). "True love always involves sacrifice, and if love is void of sacrifice, it may be because it is far from perfect. By God's design, true love and sacrifice are inextricably linked.[52] The summit of the mystical life "cannot exist without love

---

[50] PN 24, 26, 129. This poem was written for Sister Geneviève; however, it also seems to be echoing the wishes and desires of Thérèse.

[51] Jean Clapier, *Aimer jusqu'à mourir d'amour*, 508: "Il est clair que son désir de souffrir et de mourir ne peut être correctement compris sinon dans sa relation mystique à Jésus, son amour pour Jésus; car il s'agit toujours d'un souffrir et d'un mourir pour Jésus, en union avec Jésus."

[52] Martinez, *Sanctifier*, 102.

of the Cross, and love of the Cross does not exist without the contemplation of the mystery of the redemption, of the mystery of Christ dying for love of us."[53] The soul that is travelling along the rough road that leads to union with God desires to be crucified with Christ;[54] martyrdom is seen as a great treasure. St Thérèse in her poem *Living on Love* expresses what loving God and attaining full union with Him requires when she says:

> Living on Love is not setting up one's tent
> At the top of Tabor.
> It's climbing Calvary with Jesus,
> It's looking at the Cross as a treasure!...[55]

Longing to Die to be with Christ

The person who reaches the state of the perfect has been "transformed by the gift of wisdom."[56] Souls

---

[53] Garrigou Lagrange, *Three Ages of the Interior Life,* vol. II, 467-468.

[54] Martinez, *Sanctifier*, 105. P. Lucien-Marie de Saint Joseph points out that the only truly authentic desire for martyrdom must be based on a genuine understanding of suffering out of love so that the desire to give to God a complete gift of self outweighs any desire to suffer: "Seul l'amour peut véritablement restaurer l'ordre compromis par le péché et seul il donne sa valeur à la souffrance comme il lui confère le mérite. Or c'est précisément dans le développement de la logique de l'amour que vient s'inscrire le désir authentique du martyre et non dans celle de la recherche morbide de la souffrance…Or nous disons que l'important est que le facteur don de soi ait le pas sur le facteur désir de la souffrance" ("Le Martyre d'Amour," 330-332).

[55] PN 17, 4, 90.

[56] Garrigou Lagrange, *Christian Perfection and Contemplation,* 308.

who have reached this stage will often have the desire to leave this world and be fully united with God in heaven.[57] St Thomas says: "there are two impulses in man, the impulse of nature and that of grace: of nature, not to die …and the impulse of grace, which charity follows, is to love God and neighbor. This impulse to love God moves us to be with Christ."[58] This desire is due to the soul's wanting to be more perfectly united to God. The only way that it can live in full and complete union with God is to die,[59] because "one cannot live simultaneously in glory and in the mortal flesh."[60] Hence, the person who desires to die as a martyr of love desires full and complete union with God in heaven.

Martyrdom of love is a death in the Lord, but a

---

[57] Garrigou Lagrange, *Christian Perfection and Contemplation*, 41. Arintero, points out that if a person has a longing to die (if it is God's will), and if he or she desires to suffer and endure many reproaches for the sake of God, this is a true sign that this person has reached "true union" with God (*Mystical Evolution and Vitality of the Church*, vol. II, 162).

[58] St Thomas Aquinas, *Super Ep. ad Phil.*, cap 1, lec. 3, n. 35: "In homine enim duplex est motus, naturae scilicet et gratiae. Naturae ad non moriendum. II Cor. V, 4: *nolumus expoliari, sed supervestiri*, et cetera. Io. ult.: *et alius ducet te quo tu non vis*, et cetera. Et gratiae, quam suggeret caritas, quae movet ad dilectionem Dei et proximi. Hic affectus ad dilectionem Dei movet, ut simus cum Christo."

[59] Renault, Emmanuel, OCD, "Le désir de mourir chez Thérèse d'Avila," in Saint Thérèse d'Avila, *Colloque de Venasque* (Éditions du Carmel, Septembre 1982), 188: "En définitive, son désir de mourir était l'envers de son désir de voir Dieu, ou plus exactement la condition nécessaire pour réaliser l'union parfaite d'amour avec Lui, et donc en réalité un désir de vivre en plénitude."

[60] St John of the Cross, *Spiritual Canticle*, stanza 11, 9, 451, [Phil.1:23].

death which properly speaking is an entering into the fullness of life with Christ who gives life. For the disciple of Christ, death becomes the opportunity for the consummation of love and above all an assumption of the redemptive death of Christ.[61] To die in Christ is to live with Christ. This desire for death is not an unhealthy desire, but one that is founded on an intense love for Christ and the desire to be more fully united to Him; death in Christ will bring the fullness of life. Therefore, "the Christian can experience a desire for death like St. Paul's: 'My desire is to depart and be with Christ.'"[62] When Thérèse is close to death, she says: "I am not dying I am entering into life."[63] And in one of her plays, she expresses the words of St Joan of Arc, which no doubt also express her own desires:

> I want nothing more than to die for Your love. I wish to die in order to begin to live. I wish to die to be united with Jesus.[64]

The Soul Desires Only God's Will

As Thérèse's love blossoms, her will tends more and

---

[61] Jean Clapier, *Aimer jusqu'à mourir d'amour*, 505-506 : "Le désire de *"mourir d'amour"* est intérieur à celui de *mouriren-Christ* en vue d'être pleinement unie au Christ, déterminée à assumer les conséquences ultimes d'une fidèle *sequela Christi*. La mort d'amour thérèsienne se présente comme une mort vécue dans l'amour extrême du Christ manifesté à l'heure de son sacrifice pascal."
[62] *CCC* 1011.
[63] *CCC* 1011. St Thérèse of Lisieux, *Last Conversations*.
[64] *Plays, Joan of Arc Accomplishing Her Mission*, scene 9, 183.

more towards God until she reaches perfect conformity to His will. Love of God and conformity to His Will go hand in hand – one cannot develop without the other. In his encyclical *Deus Caritas Est*, Benedict XVI describes the relationship between the devout soul and God:

> ... the one becomes similar to the other, and this leads to a community of will and thought. The love-story between God and man consists in the very fact that this communion of thought and sentiment, and thus our will and God's will increasingly coincide.[65]

Thérèse desires to enter into the fullness of life; however, if God wants her to remain on earth, she would prefer to do what He wills: "I don't want to die more than to live; that is, if I had the choice, I would prefer to die. But since it's God who makes the choices for me, I prefer what He wills. It's what He does that I love."[66] The soul that has reached such a high degree of holiness is content to remain on earth if that is what God desires, or to depart this life and to be with God if that is His will.[67] As St John of the Cross says: "In

---

[65] Benedict XVI, *Deus Caritas Est*, 39.
[66] LC, May 27, 4, 50-51. Cf. Gaucher, *John and Thérèse: Flames of Love*, 136.
[67] St Catherine of Siena, *Dialogue of St. Catherine of Siena*, translated by Algar Thorold (Rockford, Illinois: Tan Books and Publishers, Inc., 1974), 180-181. God the Father speaking to St Catherine describes the soul that has reached the state of the perfect: " as their will is not their own, but becomes one with Mine, they are contented to remain, if I desire them to remain, with their pain, for the greater praise and glory of My Name and the salvation of souls. So that in nothing are they in discord with My Will; but they run their course with ecstatic desire, clothed in Christ crucified,

life and in death she is conformed to the will of God."[68] Thérèse expresses precisely these sentiments: "I will be content to die or to live, for I will only what God wills; everything is for His love."[69] Even when Thérèse was very sick and nearing death she said, "If I were told I was going to be cured, don't believe I'd be dejected; I would be happy, just as much as I would be to die."[70] And in a poem she calls *My Joy!* Thérèse writes:

---

and keeping by the Bridge of His doctrine, glorying in His shame and pains. Inasmuch as they appear to be suffering they are rejoicing, because the enduring of many tribulations is to them a relief in the desire which they have for death, for oftentimes the desire and the will to suffer pain mitigates the pain caused them by their desire to quit the body. These not only endure with patience, as I told thee they did, who are in the third state, but they glory, through My Name, in bearing much tribulation. In bearing much tribulation they find pleasure, and not having it they suffer pain, fearing that I reward not their well-doing or that the sacrifice of their desires is not pleasing to Me; but when I permit to them many tribulations they rejoice, seeing themselves clothed with the suffering and shame of Christ crucified. Wherefore were it possible for them to have virtue without toil they would not want it. They would rather delight in the Cross, with Christ, acquiring it with pain, than in any other way obtain Eternal Life. Why? Because they are inflamed and steeped in the Blood, where they find the blaze of My charity, which charity is a fire proceeding from Me, ravishing their heart and mind and making their sacrifices acceptable" (*Dialogue*, 180-181).

[68] St John of the Cross, *Spiritual Canticle*, stanza 20 and 21, 11, 492.
[69] *LC*, June 5, 271. Recalled in a letter from Sr Marie of the Eucharist to M. Guérin.
[70] *LC*, August 17, 287. Recalled in a letter from Sr Marie of the Eucharist to M. Guérin. Even when Thérèse is in tremendous pain and suffering she says "my pilgrimage seems to be unable to end. Far from complaining about it I rejoice that God permits me to suffer still for His love" (*GC* II, LT 263, 1173).

> Lord, I'm willing to live a long time more
> If that is your desire.
> I'd like to follow you to Heaven
> If that would make you happy.
> Love, that fire from the Homeland,
> Never ceases to consume me.
> What do life and death matter to me?
> Jesus, my joy, it's to love you![71]

When Mother Agnes asked Thérèse if it pained her that she was still not going to heaven, she said, "Little Mother, you still don't understand me? See, all my sentiments are expressed in this stanza of one of my little hymns":

> For long on earth would I remain
> If Thou, O Lord, didst will,
> Or join at once Thy heavenly train
> Jesus, thy love, that heavenly fire,
> Consuming joyfully,
> Joins life and death as if the same –
> Thy love is all I see.[72]

Thérèse had such a fervent desire to do the will of God; all that she did and all that she suffered was for love of God. She can truly repeat the words of St John of the Cross who describes souls that are in love with God when he says, "My Beloved, all that is rough and toilsome I desire for your sake, and all that is sweet and pleasant I desire for your sake."[73] She abandoned

---

[71] PN 45, 7, 186. Cf. Guy Gaucher, *John and Thérèse: Flames of Love*, 136.

[72] *LC*, August 5, 285. Recalled in a letter from Mother Agnes of Jesus to M. and Mme Guérin.

[73] St John of the Cross, *Spiritual Canticle*, stanza 28, 10, 523.

herself completely into the hands of God, and said that this was her joy: "I would not be so cheerful as I am if God were not showing me that the only joy on earth is to accomplish His will."[74] She explains:

> If my soul had not been filled in advance with abandonment to God's will, if it had been necessary that it let itself be submerged by these feelings of joy and sadness that succeed each other so quickly on this earth, this would have been bitter pain, and I could not have borne it. But these changes only touch the surface of my soul.[75]

Thérèse believes that "perfection consists in doing [God's] will, in being what He wills us to be."[76] She exclaims: "Oh! how sweet is the way of Love! How I want to apply myself to doing the will of God always with the greatest self-surrender!"[77] Thérèse's perfect conformity to the will of God is the effect of the gifts of the Holy Spirit, and in particular the effect of the gift of wisdom on charity. No one can express the words that Thérèse has expressed unless he or she has truly attained a high degree of union with God.

---

[74] *GC* II, LT 255, 1146.
[75] *LC*, July 10, 13, 87.
[76] Ms A 2v 14. Cf., Combes, "Thomas and Thérèse," 170. St Teresa of Avila also says perfection consists in being perfectly conformed to the will of God (*Interior Castle*, II Mansions, ch. 1, 8, 301).
[77] Ms A 84v, 181.

The Flame of Love Within the Heart of Thérèse

Thérèse has been transformed by the operation of the gift of wisdom and has reached the heights of perfection.[78] Her relationship with the Lord continues to blossom, and her soul continues to be inflamed with the fire of love for her beloved Spouse. Thérèse is content to die young or to continue earthly life until old age; however, one desire always remains – that she die as a martyr of love. She says, "I would want to be sick all my life if this pleases God, and I even consent to my life being very long; the only favour I desire is that it be broken through love."[79] Thérèse expresses explicitly her desire to die as a martyr of love: "I no longer have any great desire except that of loving to the point of dying of love."[80] She further expresses this in her poem *Living on Love* when she says,

> Dying of Love is what I hope for.
> When I shall see my bonds broken,
> My God will be my Great Reward.
> I don't desire to possess other goods.

---

[78] St Thomas says that a person can reach spiritual perfection "even in childhood" (*ST* I, q. 72, a. 8, ad 2). Sister Marie of the Sacred Heart speaking about the perfection of Thérèse even at a young age said: "She has matured early and Jesus wants to gather her up for the delights of heaven. If you knew all she has told us, all her little thoughts –they are wonderful and bear the stamp of wisdom and sanctity." Guy Gaucher, OCD, *The Passion of Thérèse of Lisieux* (New York: The Crossroad Publishing Company, 2000), 161.
[79] Ms C 8r-8v, 215.
[80] Ms C 7v, 214.

> I want to be set on fire with his Love.
> I want to see Him, to unite myself to Him
> forever.
> This is my Heaven...that is my destiny
> Living on Love!!!.... [81]

Thérèse's heart burns with love for God; she describes this as a sweet martyrdom: "Allow me, then, during my exile, the delights of love. Allow me to taste the sweet bitterness of my martyrdom."[82] She exclaims in one of her poems:

> Your Love is my only martyrdom.
> The more I *feel* it burning within me,
> The more my soul desires you...
> Jesus, make me die
> Of Love for You!!![83]

Thérèse wants to be "taken to the summit of the *mountain of Love*."[84] She understands that if she is to die of love, she also has to continually live a life abounding in love.[85] So she continually asks God to inflame her with the fire of His Love. In her poem entitled *Living on Love!* she writes:

> Dying of Love is a truly sweet martyrdom,
> And that is the one I wish to suffer.
> O Cherubim! Tune your lyre,
> For I sense my exile is about to end!...
> Flame of Love, consume me unceasingly.

---

[81] PN 17, 15, 92.
[82] Ms B 4v, 197.
[83] PN 31, R.6, 151 (emphasis added).
[84] GC I, LT 110, 652.
[85] Àngel de les Gavarres, *Thérèse: The Little Child of God's Mercy*, 330.

> Life of an instant, your burden is so heavy to me!
> Divine Jesus, make my dream come true:
> To die of Love!…
>
> Dying of Love is what I hope for,
> When I shall see my bonds broken,
> My God will be my Great Reward.
> I don't desire to possess other goods.
> I want to be set on fire with his Love.
> I want to see Him, to unite myself to Him forever.
> That is my Heaven… that is my destiny:
> Living on Love!!!…[86]

When a person truly loves God and desires to reach the very heights of perfection, God "descends upon the soul in mercy, impressing and infusing His love and grace in her, making her beautiful and lifting her so high as to make her a partaker of the very divinity."[87] The Holy Spirit transforms the soul enveloping it with His Love and divinises it;[88] thus, these souls "already enjoy a foretaste of glory by

---

[86] PN 17, 14-15, 92. In her book *My Sister Saint Thérèse*, Sister Geneviève of the Holy Face, Celine Martin says this poem "was composed in its entirety during one of Thérèse's hours of Adoration before the Blessed Sacrament at 'les Quarante-Heures' in February 1895. It would not, therefore, be temerarious to believe that it was written under supernatural promptings and, as such, comprises the sum of the Saint's aspirations" (*My Sister Saint Thérèse*, 86-87).

[87] St John of the Cross, *Spiritual Canticle*, stanza, 32, 4, 535.

[88] Gabriel de Sainte Marie-Madeleine, "Les Sommets de la Vie d'Amour," 279.

reason of that intimate and secret union by which they are gradually being deified."⁸⁹

Love Finally Takes Her Life

Thérèse senses that she will soon be going to God her great reward; and even though she is prepared to remain on earth for many years she feels that it is God's will that she reach the homeland in the springtime of her life. In letters to a missionary she writes, "How happy I am to die! Yes ... I am happy to die because I feel that such is God's will, and that much more than here below I shall be useful to souls who are dear to me, to your own in particular."⁹⁰ In another place, she writes, "Never have I asked God to die young, this would have appeared to me as cowardliness; but He, from my childhood, saw fit to give me the intimate conviction that my course here below would be short. It is, then, the thought alone of accomplishing the Lord's will that makes up all my joy."⁹¹

Thérèse was very happy to die because she felt that this was God's will for her, and that her offering had been willed by God and accepted by Him. In a letter to her three blood sisters, she writes:

> My mind takes flight to Eternity, time is about to end! ...I do not long for the life of this world, my

---

⁸⁹ Ven. Arintero, *Mystical Evolution and Vitality of the Church*, vol. II, 189.
⁹⁰ *GC* II, LT 253, 1139.
⁹¹ *GC* II, LT 258, 1152.

> heart is thirsting for the waters of eternal life! ... In a little while my soul will leave the earth, will end its exile, will terminate its combat.... I am ascending to heaven .... I am touching the homeland, I am carrying off the victory!... I am about to enter into the abode of the elect, to see beauties that the eye of man has never seen, to listen to harmonies the ear has never heard, to enjoy delights the heart has never tasted....[92]

Through the operation of the gift of wisdom, Thérèse had tasted the goodness of the Lord; she would soon fly off to her rest, where she would taste in abundance the eternal delights of God forever in heaven.

Love finally will take Thérèse's life. Even though she was very sick with tuberculosis, she had no doubt it was love that would consume her life. She says, "I do not count on the illness, it is too slow a leader. I *count only on love*. Ask Good Jesus that all the prayers being offered for me may serve to increase the Fire which must consume me."[93] One could object that Thérèse did not die from love; rather her life was taken, through tuberculosis. The response to such an objection can be found in the writings of St John of the Cross:

> It should be known that the death of persons who have reached this state is far different in its cause and mode than the death of others, even though it is similar in natural circumstances. If the death of other people is caused by sickness or old age, the death of these persons is not so induced, in spite of

---

[92] *GC* II, LT 245, 1129.
[93] *GC* II, LT 243, 1121.

their being sick or old; their soul is not wrested from them unless by some impetus and encounter of love, far more sublime than previous ones, of greater power, and more valiant, since it tears through this veil and carries off the jewel, which is the soul.[94]

St John of the Cross describes this death of love as being something very beautiful:

> The death of such persons is very gentle and very sweet, sweeter, and more gentle than was their whole spiritual life on earth. For they die with the most sublime impulses and delightful encounters of love, resembling the swan whose song is much sweeter at the moment of death. Accordingly, David affirmed that the death of the saints is precious in the sight of the Lord. [Ps. 115:15][95]

Thérèse was suffering so intensely before her death that Mother Agnes said to her, "My poor little child, you're like the martyrs in the amphitheatre; we can no longer do anything for you!"[96] In light of such intense suffering, is it possible to conclude that Thérèse was dying the death of love described by St John of the Cross? This key question can be resolved by taking a closer look at her death itself. It is true that until the very moment of her death Thérèse experienced both

---

[94] St John of the Cross, *Living Flame of Love*, stanza 1, 30, 591-592.
[95] St John of the Cross, *Living Flame of Love*, stanza 1, 30, 592. Guy Gaucher notes that Thérèse had St John of the Cross's work *Living Flame of Love* at her bedside and when Mother Agnès asked how the sisters would know that Thérèse was actually dying of love this is one of the texts that she marked with a little Cross (*John and Thérèse: Flames of Love*, 133-134).
[96] LC, September 28, 2, 201.

exterior suffering and interior trials. She suffered immensely and a lot of the time she appeared to be in agony. Yet, in the last few moments before her death, she was manifestly changed. Thérèse had no concern as to whether her death of love would be accompanied by great delights; her only desire was to love God and imitate the Lord, and that her life be broken through love. She says:

> Do not be troubled, little sisters, if I suffer very much and if you see in me as I have already said to you no sign of joy at the moment of death. Our Lord really died as a Victim of Love, and see what His agony was! … Our Lord died on the Cross in anguish, and yet His was the most beautiful death of love. To die of love does not mean to die in transports. I tell you frankly, it appears to me that this is what I am experiencing.[97]

Thérèse lived the mystery of the Cross. In her final agony she shared in a most profound way the suffering of her Beloved Spouse. When Thérèse says that "to die of love does not mean to die in transports," she means it is not to die "in transports of sensible joy."[98] St John Paul II in His apostolic letter *Novo Millennio Ineunte*, writes:

> Not infrequently the saints have undergone something akin to Jesus' experience on the Cross in the paradoxical blending of bliss and pain. These souls imitate the spotless Lamb, the Only-begotten Son, who on the Cross was both blissful and

---

[97] *Story of a Soul*, Epilogue, 269; LC, July 4, 2, 73.
[98] Gabriel of St Mary Magdalen, "St. Thérèse's 'Little Way' and the Teachings of St. John of the Cross," 81.

afflicted. In the same way, Thérèse of Lisieux lived her agony in communion with the agony of Jesus, "experiencing" in herself the very paradox of Jesus' own bliss and anguish.[99]

Thérèse expresses this mystery when she describes our Lord's agony in the garden: "Our Lord enjoyed all the delights of the Trinity when He was in the garden of Olives, and still His agony was none the less cruel. It's a mystery, but I assure you that I understand something about it by what I'm experiencing."[100]

Mother Agnes says to Thérèse, "How I sense your agony! And yet it's a month ago that you were saying beautiful things about the death of love." Thérèse answers, "What I was saying then, I would say right now."[101] Mother Agnes also recalls a conversation that she had with Thérèse:

> I was recalling for her what St. John of the Cross said on the death of those who were consumed by love. She sighed and said: "I shall have to say that 'joy and transports' are at the bottom of my heart.

---

[99] St John Paul II, Novo *Millennio Ineunte*, 27. In the same section John Paul II writes "In the Dialogue of Divine Providence, God the Father shows Catherine of Siena how joy and suffering can be present together in holy souls: 'Thus the soul is blissful and afflicted: afflicted on account of the sins of its neighbour, blissful on account of the union and the affection of charity which it has inwardly received. These souls imitate the spotless Lamb, my Only-begotten Son, who on the Cross was both blissful and afflicted.'"

[100] *LC*, July 6, 4, 75.

[101] *LC*, August 15, 1, 148.

But it wouldn't be so encouraging to souls if they didn't believe I suffered very much."[102]

From Thérèse's own account, it seems clear that she experienced the mystery of both suffering and delight in her final days. The following testimony given by Sister Agnes of Jesus who was present at Thérèse's death also gives us an accurate account of Thérèse's final moments:

> Her face had regained the lily-white complexion it always had in full health; her eyes were fixed above, brilliant with peace and joy. She made certain beautiful movements with her head, as though someone had divinely wounded her with an arrow of love, then had withdrawn the arrow to wound again ... Sister Marie of the Eucharist approached with a candle to get a closer view of that sublime look. In the light of the candle, there didn't appear any movement in her eyelids. This ecstasy lasted almost the space of a Credo, and she gave her last breath.[103]

Thérèse had received anointing of the sick on 30 September and then Viaticum for her journey.[104] As *God's Little Flower* was about to breathe her last, she uttered her last words: "Oh! I love Him! ... My God, I love you!"[105]

> These last words of the Saint are the key of her whole doctrine, to her interpretation of the Gospel, the act of love, expressed in her last breath was as

---

[102] *LC,* August 15, 1, 148.
[103] *LC,* September 30, 206-207.
[104] *GC* II, LT 263, 1173.
[105] *Story of a Soul,* Epilogue, 271.

it were, the continuous breathing of her soul, the beating of her heart. The simple words *"Jesus, I love you"* are at the heart of all her writings.[106]

---

[106] Benedict XVI, General Audience, "St. Thérèse of Lisieux," St. Peter's Square, 6 April 2011.

Conclusion

The focus of the present work has been the operation of the pre-eminent gift of the Holy Spirit (which bears the name of *wisdom*) by which we taste and savour Divine things through a connatural experience. The operation of this gift has been clearly differentiated from the intellectual virtue which bears the same name, *wisdom*, and which is not the subject of the present study. As the Angelic Doctor teaches,[1] there are two modalities by which we can know. One way is "by discourse in its various forms" which is "purely intellectual,"[2] and this corresponds to the intellectual virtue of wisdom. The other way is by "intimate experience,"[3] which we receive "on account of a certain *connaturality*."[4] This second way of knowing comes "from the very depths of love,"[5] and corresponds to the gift of wisdom.

The gift of wisdom perfects the theological virtue of charity "by giving it the divine modality it lacks as long as charity is subject to human reason, even illumined by faith."[6] Through the gift of wisdom, the virtue of charity is perfected by giving it a "savoury experience of God and supernatural mysteries."[7] This "intimate way" of experiencing God "is a taste, love,

---

[1] *ST* II-II, q.45, a. 2.
[2] Martinez, *Sanctifier*, 152-53.
[3] Martinez, *Sanctifier*, 152-53. Cf. John of St Thomas, *Gifts of the Holy Ghost*, 125.
[4] *ST* II-II, q. 45, a. 2.
[5] Martinez, *Sanctifier*, 152-53.
[6] Royo and Aumann, Theology of Christian Perfection, 531.
[7] Royo and Aumann, Theology of Christian Perfection, 531.

delight, or internal contact of the will with spiritual things."[8] By way of the gift of wisdom we really do taste, because we know God through an "experience of the heart" and taste the object which is loved, namely God.[9] Consequently, we are able to say, "Taste and see that the Lord is good" (Psalm 34:8). This experience, which is an effect of the operation of the gift of wisdom, conforms the person to Christ. Indeed, "grace and charity, as well as the gift of wisdom, make us deiform."[10]

This work has demonstrated that through the operation of the gift of wisdom, a person – in this case St Thérèse of Lisieux – is more and more conformed to Christ. This conformity to Christ is manifested in particular by way of a desire to suffer. Of course this desire to suffer is not for the sake of suffering itself, but precisely for love of God and the salvation of souls. Through the operation of the gift of wisdom, as St Thomas says, the bitter becomes sweet and the labour rest.[11] In this book, I have endeavoured to describe the gift of wisdom and how through the operation of this gift, the soul is made *deiform*; the more that this gift is operating, the more the person becomes conformed to Christ. Hence, there is a profound link between the operation of the gift of wisdom (when it is operating in a very high degree) and the desire to suffer in conformity to Christ.

Having followed St Thomas' teaching on the gift of wisdom, and then having highlighted the operation of

---

[8] John of St Thomas, *Gifts of the Holy Ghost*, 125.
[9] Gabriel of St Mary Magdalen, *Divine Intimacy*, 937.
[10] Torrell, *Spiritual Master*, 127.
[11] *ST* II-II, q. 45, a. 3, ad 3.

this gift in the life of St Thérèse, it is clear that the work of St Thomas is not only speculative but also very practical. St Thomas' theology gives us the essential principles that are necessary to help us understand the working of the Holy Spirit in the life of a soul that is open to the grace of God. St Thomas' teaching on the life of grace and the whole supernatural organism provides a solid foundation from which to understand Spiritual Theology. By faithfully following his teaching a person can avoid falling into a vague sentimental view of the spiritual life.[12] One is given the essential teachings which are necessary in order to remain faithful to the teaching of the Church.

By following St Thomas' teaching on the gift of wisdom and by using his principles to examine the life of St Thérèse of Lisieux, one can see clearly that Thérèse has reached a remarkable degree of sanctity, due to the effect of the operation of the gift of wisdom on charity. The gift of wisdom perfects and refines Thérèse's love for God until her heart is all aflame with the fire of Divine love. Through the operation of the gift of wisdom, Thérèse knows, judges, and tastes the things of God; she has a connatural knowing of Divine things, which is the hallmark of the gift of wisdom. Through this gift, Jesus teaches Thérèse in the secret of her heart, and she contemplates the truths and mysteries of the faith with precision and depth. Through the operation of this precious gift, Thérèse judges all things in life – in a sense from a divine point of view – and God reveals to Thérèse the immensity of

---

[12] Cf. *Christian Perfection and Contemplation*, 4. "Pope Benedict XV congratulated the editor of *La vie spirituelle* for making this doctrine known," (15 September 1921).

His infinite love and mercy, a love and mercy that He wants to share with everyone. Due to the operation of the gift of wisdom, Thérèse is also constantly aware of the Trinity dwelling in her soul, and she is always filled with a deep and unshakable peace.

Thérèse is completely abandoned to the action of God's grace working in her life. As she grows in perfection through the effect of the gift of wisdom on charity, she becomes progressively more and more conformed to her Beloved Spouse. She desires nothing more than to follow God's will utterly and completely. The gift of wisdom brings Thérèse to the point of desiring to die as a martyr of love. This is the central effect of the gift of wisdom in the life of St Thérèse. With all her heart, she desires that in one act of perfect love, she will be able to offer herself as an oblation of love to the Father, following in the footsteps of her Beloved Lord and Saviour.

Thérèse goes through various stages in her spiritual journey, in which the effects of the gift of wisdom are clearly manifested. One of these effects is her desire to suffer; as she grows in this desire, she even finds sweetness in suffering, desiring to imitate her crucified Lord more and more. Through the gift of wisdom, a soul begins to see and judge things from a divine point of view rather than a human point of view and begins to see and penetrate what the limited human intellect cannot understand. It begins to look on suffering in a different light; for the Holy Spirit gives His beloved souls a profound penetration into the mystery of suffering so that they see the true and immense value of the Cross. Thérèse's profound love of the Cross speaks volumes about the immense love she has for the Lord. Without the operation of the gift of wisdom, Thérèse could never have found sweetness in suffering; such sentiments would be impossible.

This sweetness, this intense love of the Cross, comes when the soul has reached a high degree of union with Christ and the person, in a sense, sees through the eyes of God. The Cross is sweet to Thérèse because of the grace of the Holy Spirit and the gift of wisdom. It is only by the grace of the Holy Spirit and the operation of this gift that the desire to undergo hardship and even to find sweetness in suffering can be understood. The love of holy souls can grow so strong from the effect of this gift on charity that not only do they desire to follow and imitate their crucified Lord, but they even find sweetness in suffering. Through the gift of wisdom, Thérèse is able to penetrate and understand the mystery of the Cross and all its riches, so that suffering becomes sweet and desirable to her. Of course, she understands that this suffering must be united to love, since it is only love which can transform suffering. Finding sweetness in suffering is not something which is inconsistent with Thérèse's *Little Way*, for she never asks God for extra suffering. Rather, she accepts all suffering which comes her way with love and an unreserved acceptance of everything the Lord desires to give her – she is completely abandoned to the will of God.

Thérèse desires only the will of God, whatever that entails; she is happy to remain on earth until an old age and undergo suffering for love of Christ, or to depart this life at a young age. One desire, however, which never leaves Thérèse is the desire to die as a martyr of love. Through the operation of the gift of wisdom, Thérèse reaches the very summit of love. She has been brought to such a high degree of sanctity and has become so inflamed with a love for God, that her love cannot be contained. She desires to be utterly conformed to her cruciform Christ and give her whole life in one final offering of complete and perfect love. Thérèse wants to give all to Love and therefore she desires that God will finally take her life in one act of perfect love. In doing so, Thérèse will be able to give the ultimate sacrifice; she will give her very life to Love without holding anything back. Thérèse would never have been inclined to do this if charity had not reached its heights by being perfected by the gift of wisdom; but her love has become so strong that only the ultimate sacrifice of love can satisfy the flame of love which burns so strongly within her heart.

The desire to die as a martyr of love is not all that is required to be able to die in this way. For the soul that dies a martyr of love has reached the transforming union, and only a thin veil separates that soul from God. In the martyrdom of love, God carries a soul to Himself through one final wound of love which tears the thin veil that has kept the soul from flying off to God. Thus, when a person dies as a martyr of love, charity has reached its heights, the soul has already reached the transforming union with the help of the gift of wisdom, and a final wound of love carries the soul to God.

Not everyone will be called to die as a martyr of love; however, everyone is called to the heights of sanctity and union with God. The operation of the gift of wisdom in the life of a soul is not something extraordinary; rather, it is the normal development of baptismal grace. The soul that remains faithful to the working of the Holy Spirit and that gives itself wholly to God without reserve can reach the very heights of perfection. The gift of wisdom can have such a profound effect on the life of a soul that it can bring a person to the stage of the transforming union. It is indeed one of the most beautiful gifts that we could hope for, short of the Beatific Vision. As it leads us to the heights of sanctity, it produces such a love for God in our soul that after tasting the goodness of the Lord, nothing on this earth can compare. In fact, this gift is so exquisite that when it is operating with abundance in a soul, the sweetness of the Lord is so irresistible that the soul would be content to fly away from this place of exile and be united even more fully with the Lord face to face in heaven. So sweet is this gift, that the love it produces in a soul can indeed carry a soul through many a trial and hardship. The bitter becomes sweet, the labour rest, and peace – deep peace – remains in the depth of the soul.

BIBLIOGRAPHY

PRIMARY SOURCES – ST THOMAS AQUINAS

St Thomas Aquinas. *Commento alle Sentenze di Pietro Lombardo*. Vol. 6. Traduzione di P. Lorenzo Perotto. Bologna, Italia: Edizioni Studio Domenicano, 2000.

_____. *Commentary on the Gospel of John*, Chapters 1-8. Translated by Fabian R. Larcher, OP. Latin/English Edition of the Works of St. Thomas Aquinas, vol. 35. Lander, WY: The Aquinas Institute for the Study of Sacred Doctrine, 2013.

_____. *Commentary on the Gospel of John*, Chapters 9-21. Translated by Fabian R. Larcher, OP. Latin/English Edition of the Works of St. Thomas Aquinas, vol. 36. Lander, WY: The Aquinas Institute for the Study of Sacred Doctrine, 2013.

_____. *Commentary of the Gospel of Matthew, Chapters 1-12*. Translated by Jeremy Holmes and Beth Mortensen. Latin/English Edition of the Works of St Thomas Aquinas, vol. 33. Lander, WY: The Aquinas Institute for the Study of Sacred Doctrine, 2013.

_____. *Commentary on Isaiah*, Translated by Louis St. Hilaire, Steubenville, Ohio, Emmaus Academic, 2021.

———. *Commentary on the Letters of Saint Paul to the Corinthians.* Translated by Fabian R. Larcher, OP, Beth Mortensen, and Daniel Keating. Latin/English Edition of the Works of St Thomas Aquinas, vol. 38. Lander, WY: The Aquinas Institute for the Study of Sacred Doctrine, 2012.

———. *Commentary on the Letters of Saint Paul to the Philippians, Colossians, Thessalonians, Timothy, Titus, and Philemon.* Translated by Fabian R. Larcher, OP. Latin/English Edition of the Works of St. Thomas Aquinas, vol. 40. Lander, WY: The Aquinas Institute for the Study of Sacred Doctrine, 2012.

———. *Commentary on the Letter of Saint Paul to the Hebrews.* Translated by Fabian Larcher, OP. Latin/English Edition of the Works of St Thomas Aquinas, vol. 41. Lander, WY: The Aquinas Institute for the Study of Sacred Doctrine, 2012.

———. *Commentary on the Letters of Saint Paul to the Galatians and Ephesians.* Translated by Fabian R. Larcher, OP, and Matthew L. Lamb. Latin/English Edition of the Works of St. Thomas Aquinas, vol. 39. Lander, WY: The Aquinas Institute for the Study of Sacred Doctrine, 2012.

———. *Commentary on the Letter of Saint Paul to the Romans.* Translated by Fabian R. Larcher, OP. Latin/English Edition of the Works of St. Thomas Aquinas, vol. 37. Lander, WY: The Aquinas Institute for the Study of Sacred Doctrine, 2012.

_____. *The Light of Faith, The Compendium of Theology*. Translated by Cyril Vollert, S.J. Manchester, NH: Sophia Institute Press, 1993.

_____. *Summa Theologiae*. Translated by the Fathers of the English Dominican Province. New York: Benziger Bros., 1948.

_____. *S. Thomae Aquinatis Opera Omnia*. Volumes 1-7. Rome: Edited by R. Busa, S.J., 1980.

SECONDARY SOURCES – ST THOMAS AQUINAS

Ashley, Benedict, OP. *Thomas Aquinas: The Gifts of the Spirit*. New York: New City Press, 1995.

Aumann, Jordan, OP. *Spiritual Theology*. London: Sheed and Ward, 1980.

Bonino, Serge-Thomas, OP. "The Role of the Apostles in the Communication of Revelation according to *Lectura super Ioannem* of St. Thomas Aquinas." In *Reading John with Saint Thomas*. Edited by Dauphinais, Michael and Matthew Levering. *Theological Exegesis and Speculative Theology*. Washington, D.C.: The Catholic University of America Press, 2005.

Brennan, Robert Edward, OP. *The Seven Horns of the Lamb, A Study of the Gifts Based on Saint Thomas*

Aquinas. Milwaukee: The Bruce Publishing Company, 1966.

Chenu, Marie-Dominique, OP. *Aquinas and His Role in Theology.* Translated by Paul Philibert. Collegeville, MN: The Liturgical Press, 2002.

Deferrari, Roy J., Mary Inviolata Barry, and Ignatius McGuiness. *A Lexicon of St. Thomas Aquinas.* Washington, D.C.: Catholic University of America Press, 1948.

Fatula, Mary Ann, OP. *Thomas Aquinas, Preacher and Friend.* Collegeville, MN: The Liturgical Press, 1993.

Garrigou-Lagrange, Reginald, OP. *Christian Perfection and Contemplation.* Translated by Sister Mary Timothea Doyle, OP. Rockford, IL: Tan Books and Publishers, Inc., 2003.

_____. *Grace.* Translated by the Dominican Nuns, Corpus Christi Monastery, California. St. Louis, MO: B. Herder Book Co., 1952.

_____. *The Three Ages of the Interior Life.* 2 Volumes. Translated by Sister Mary. Timothea Doyle, OP. Rockford, IL: Tan Books and Publishers, Inc., 1989.

_____. *The Love of God and the Cross of Jesus.* Vol. I.

Translated by Sister Jeanne Marie. St. Louis, MO: B. Herder Book Co., 1948.

_____. *The Three Conversions of the Spiritual Life*. Rockford, IL: Tan Books and Publishers, Inc., 2002.

Giertych, Wojciech, OP. *The New Law as a Rule for Acts*, Dissertatio ad Lauream in Facultate S. Theologiae apud Pontificiam Universitatem S. Thomae de Urbe, Romae, 1989.

Heath, Thomas, OP. "The Gift of Wisdom." Appendix 4 to Summa Theologiae. Vol.35. London: Blackfriars, 1972.

John of St. Thomas. *The Gifts of The Holy Ghost*. Translated from the Latin by Dominic Hughes, OP. New York: Sheed and Ward, 1951.

Labourdette, Marie-Michel, OP. *Cours de Théologie moral, dela grâce*. Vol. VI (I-II, q. 109-114), Toulouse: Studium Saint Thomas d'Aquin, 1958-1962.

Marín, Antonio Royo OP. *The Great Unknown: The Holy Ghost and His Gifts*. Carmel, N.Y.: Western Hemisphere Cultural Society, 1991.

Maritain, Jacques, *The Range of Reason.* New York: Charles Scribner's Sons, 1953.

McArthur, Ronald. "St. Thomas and the Formation of the Catholic Mind." In *The Ever-Illuminating Wisdom of St. Thomas Aquinas*. The Wethersfield Institute. San Francisco: Ignatius Press, 1999.

O'Connor, Edward, CSC. "The Gifts of the Holy Spirit." Appendices 1-5 to *Summa Theologiae*. Vol. 24. London: Blackfrairs,1974.

Ramirez, Jacobus M., OP. *De Donis Spiritus Sancti deque Vita Mystica*. Madrid: Instituto De Filosofia "Luis Vives", 1974.

Royo, Antonio OP. and Jordan Aumann OP. *The Theology of Christian Perfection*. Dubuque, Iowa: The Priory Press, 1962.

Spezzano, Daria E. "The Grace of the Holy Spirit, the Virtue of Charity and the Gift of Wisdom: Deification in Thomas Aquinas' Summa Theologiae," (Ph.D. diss., University of Notre Dame, 2011).

Tanquerey, Reverend Adolphe, SS., DD. *The Spiritual life*. Translated by Herman Brandersis, SS., AM. New York: Desclee & Co., 1930.

Torrell, Jean-Pierre, OP. *Saint Thomas Aquinas: The Person and his Work*. Vol. I. Translated by Robert Royal. Washington, D.C.: The Catholic University of America Press, 2003.

_____. *Saint Thomas Aquinas*: *Spiritual Master*. Vol. II. Translated by Robert Royal. Washington, DC.: The Catholic University of America Press, 2003.

Tugwell, Simon, OP. *The Beatitudes*: *Soundings in the Christian Tradition*. Springfield, IL: Templegate Publishers, 1980.

PRIMARY SOURCES – ST THÉRÈSE OF LISIEUX

Thérèse de Lisieux, St. *Her Last Conversations*. Translated from the Original Manuscripts by John Clarke, OCD. Washington, D.C.: ICS Publications, 1977.

_____. *Letters of St. Thérèse of Lisieux. General Correspondence*. Vol. I. Translated from the Original Manuscripts by John Clarke, OCD. Washington, D.C.: ICS Publications, 1982.

_____. *Letters of St. Thérèse of Lisieux, General Correspondence*. Vol. II. Translated from the Original Manuscripts by John Clarke, OCD. Washington, D.C. : ICS Publications, 1988.

_____. *Oeuvres Complètes*. Paris : Les Éditions du Cerf et Desclée De Brouwer, 2006.

_____. *Story of a Soul*, 3rd ed. Translated from the Original Manuscripts by John Clarke, OCD. Washington, D.C.: ICS Publications, 1996.

_____. *The Plays of Saint Thérèse of Lisieux.* Translated by Susan Conroy and David J. Dwyer. Washington, D.C.: ICS Publications, 2008.

_____. *The Poetry of Saint Thérèse of Lisieux.* Translated by Donald Kinney, OCD. Washington, D.C.: ICS Publications, 1996.

_____. *The Prayers of Saint Thérèse of Lisieux.* Translated by Aletheia Kane, OCD. Washington, D.C.: ICS Publications, 1997.

SECONDARY SOURCES – ST THÉRÈSE OF LISIEUX

Arintero, Juan G., OP, Ven. *The Mystical Phenomena. The Mystical Life of Saint Thérèse of the Child Jesus.* Translated from the Original Spanish text by Jose L. Morales, Ph.D. Spanish original published in Salamanca: Spain Editorial Fides, 1926. English translation: 1973.

Budnik, Mary Ann. "Heroic Parents – Models for Our Times." In Franciscan Friars of the Immaculate. In *Saint Thérèse Doctor of the Little Way.* New Bedford, MA: The Academy of the Immaculate, 1997.

Carroll, Eamon. "Thérèse and the Mother of God." In Sullivan, John, OCD., Editor. *Experiencing Saint Thérèse Today.* Carmelite Studies V. Washington, D.C.: ICS Publications, 1990.

Clapier Jean, OCD. *Aimer jusqu'à mourir d'amour: Thérèse de Lisieux et le mystère pascal par Jean Clapier.* Paris: Les Éditions Du Cerf, 2003.

Combes André. *St. Thérèse and Suffering: The Spirituality of St. Thérèse in Essence.* Translated by Msgr. Philip E. Hallett. Dublin: M.H. Gill and Son, Ltd., 1951.

_____. *The Spirituality of St. Thérèse (An Introduction).* Translated by Monsignor Philip E. Hallet. Dublin: M.H. Gill and Son, Ltd., 1950.

Conrad De Meester, OCD. *The Power of Confidence.* Translated by Susan Conroy. New York: Alba House, 1998.

Franciscan Friars of the Immaculate. *Saint Thérèse: Doctor of the Little Way.* New Bedford, MA: The Academy of the Immaculate, 1997.

Gaucher, Guy, OCD. *The Passion of Thérèse of Lisieux.* Translated by Sr Anne Marie Brennan, OCD. New York: The Crossroad Publishing Company, 2000.

_____. *John and Thérèse: Flames of Love.* Translated by Alexandra Plettenberg-Serban. New York: Alba House, 1999.

_____. *The Story of a life: St Thérèse of Lisieux.* Translated by Sr Anne Marie Brennan, OCD. San Francisco: Harper and Row Publishers, 1987.

Gavarres, Àngel de les. *Thérèse: The Little Child of God's Mercy.* Translated by Michael Gaughran. Washington, D.C.: ICS Publications, 1999.

Geneviève of the Holy Face, Sister (Céline Martin). *My Sister Saint Thérèse.* Authorized Translation by The Carmelite Sisters of New York of Conseils et Souvenirs. Rockford, IL: Tan Books and Publishers, Inc., 1997.

Görres, Ida Friederike. *The Hidden Face.* Translated by Richard and Clara Winston. London: Burns & Oates, 1959.

Griffin, Michael D., O C D. *Welcome to Carmel.* Hubertus, WI: Teresian Charism Press, 1998.

Guitton, Jean. *The Spiritual Genius of Saint Thérèse of Lisieux.* Translated by Felicity Leng. Kent: Burns & Oates, 1997.

Jamart, François, OCD. *Complete Spiritual Doctrine of St. Thérèse of Lisieux.* Translated by Walter Van De Putte, CSSP. New York: St. Paul Publications, 1961.

Liagre, Louis, CSSp. *A Retreat with Saint Thérèse.* Translated by Dom P. J. Owen, OSB. Westminister, MD: The Newman Press, 1961.

Little Catechism of the Act of Oblation of St. Thérèse of the Child Jesus. Translated by Michael Collins, A.M. In collaboration with Carmel of Kilmacud Co., Dublin. Westminster, MD: The Newman Press, 1949.

Marie-Eugène of the Child Jesus, OCD. Bl. *Under the Torrent of His Love: Thérèse of Lisieux a Spiritual Genius.* Translated by Sister Mary Thomas Noble, OP. New York: Alba House, 1994.

Miller, Fredrick L. *The Trial of Faith of St. Thérèse of Lisieux.* New York: Alba House, 1998.

O'Mahony, Christopher. *St. Thérèse of Lisieux by Those Who Knew Her.* Dublin: Veritas Publications, Co., 1975.

Piat, Stéphane-Joseph, OFM. *Céline.* Translated by The Carmelite Sisters of the Eucharist of Colchester, CT. San Francisco: Ignatius Press, 1997.

Rohrbach, Peter. T. "Thérèse de Lisieux, St." *New Catholic Encyclopedia.* Second Edition. Vol. 13.

Sackville-West, Vita. *The Eagle and the Dove.* London: Michael Joseph Ltd., 1943.

Scarpellini, Don Giuseppe. *Santa Teresa di Gesù Bambino e la scoperta del Volto Santo.* Rimini, Italy: Mostra a cura di Scarpellini Don Giuseppe.

Schmidt, Herbert. *St. Thérèse: A Martyr of Love*. Copyright Rev. Herbert Schmidt, 1989.

Sheen, Fulton. *St. Thérèse: A Treasured Love Story*. Irving TX: Basilica Press, 2007.

MAGISTERIAL TEACHING

Benedict XVI. *Deus Caritas Est*. Vatican City: Libreria Editrice Vaticana, 2006.

———. *Spe Salvi*. Vatican City: Libreria Editrice Vaticana, 2007.

———. General Audience. St Peter's Square, 2 June 2010. "St Thomas Aquinas." Vatican City: Libreria Editrice Vaticana, 2010.

———. General Audience. St Peter's Square, 6 April 2011. "St Thérèse of Lisieux." Vatican City: Libreria Editrice Vaticana, 2011.

Catechism of the Catholic Church. New York: Doubleday, 1995.

Francis. *Amoris Lutetia*. Vatican City: Libreria Editrice Vaticana 2016.

———. *L'Osservatore Romano*, Weekly ed. in English, n. 41, 9 October 2013.

Flannery, Austin, OP. ed. *Vatican Council II.* Vol. I. *The Conciliar and Post Conciliar Documents.* New Rev. ed. Dublin, Ireland: Dominican Publications.

John Paul II, St. *Dives in Misericordia.* Vatican City: Libreria Editrice Vaticana, 1980.

———. *Salvifici Doloris.* Vatican City: Libreria Editrice Vaticana, 1984.

———. *Dominum et Vivificantem.* Vatican City: Libreria Editrice Vaticana, 1986.

———. *Fides et Ratio.* Vatican City: Libreria Editrice Vaticana, 1998.

———. "Regina Coeli," Pentecost, 9 April 1989. https://www.vatican.va/liturgical_year/pentecost documents/hf_jp-ii_reg_19890409_en.html.

———. *Divini Amoris Scientia.* Vatican City: Libreria Editrice Vaticana, 1997.

———. *Novo Millennio Ineunte.* Vatican City: Libreria Editrice Vaticana, 2001.

Leo XIII. *Divinum Illud Munus.* Vatican City: Libreria Editrice Vaticana, 1897.

———. *Aeterni Patris.* Vatican City: Libreria Editrice Vaticana, 1879.

Paul VI, St. *Gaudete in Domino.* Vatican City: Libreria Editrice Vaticana,1975.

Piux X, St. *Pascendi Dominici Gregis.* Vatican City: Libreria Editrice Vaticana, 1907.

———. Apostolic Letter, *In praecipius* to the Roman Academy of St. Thomas, I, 124. https://stpaulcenter.com/aquinas-the-biblical-approach-of-the-model-catholic-theologian/.

Pius XI. *Studiorum Ducem*, 1923. https://www.papalencyclicals.net/pius11/p11stud.htm or https://www.ewtn.com/catholicism/library/on-st-thomas-aquinas-3526.

CHURCH FATHERS

Augustine, St. *Commentary on the Lord's Sermon on the Mount.* Translated by Denis J. Kavanagh, OSA. Washington D.C.: The Catholic University of America Press in association with Consortium Books, 1951.

Gregory the Great, St. *The Moralia in Job.* Vol. 1, Parts I and II. Ex Fontibus Co., 2012.

OTHER WORKS

Arintero, Juan G., OP. Ven. *Stages in Prayer*. Translated by Kathleen Pond. London: Blackfriars, 1957.

_____. *The Mystical Evolution in the Development and Vitality of the Church*. Vol. I. Translated by Jordan Aumann, OP. St. Louis, MO: B. Herder Book Co, 1949.

_____. *The Mystical Evolution in the Development and Vitality of the Church*. Vol. II. Translated by Jordan Aumann, OP. St. Louis MO: B. Herder Book Co., 1951.

Arminjon, Charles. *The End of the Present World and the Mysteries of the Future life*. Translated by Martin Research Associates. Illinios: Martin Books Edition, 1968.

Aumann Jordan, OP. *Christian Spirituality in the Catholic Tradition*. London: Sheed and Ward, Ltd., 1985.

Bouyer, Louis. *Introduction to Spirituality*. Translated by Mary Perkins Ryan. Collegeville, MN: Liturgical Press, 1961.

Carmelite Missal, Proper of the Liturgy of the Hours. Rome: Institutum Carmelitanum, 1993.

Catherine of Siena. *The Dialogue of St. Catherine of Siena*. Translated from the Original Italian Edition by Algar Thorold. Rockford, IL: Tan Books and Publishers, Inc., 1974.

Congar, Yves, OP. *I Believe in the Holy Spirit*. Vol. II and Vol. III. Translated by David Smith. New York: The Seabury Press, 1983.

Dubay, Thomas, SM. *Fire Within*. San Francisco: Ignatius Press, 1989.

Francis de Sales, St. *Treatise on the Love of God*. Translated by Henry Benedict Mackey, OSB. Rockford, IL: Tan Books and Publishers, Inc., 1997.

Gabriel of St. Mary Magdalen, OCD. *Divine Intimacy*. Translated from the 7th Italian Edition by the Discalced Carmelite Nuns of Boston. Boston: Published by Msgr Wm. J. Doheny, CSC, 1981.

Gardeil, Antione, OP. *The Gifts of the Holy Ghost in the Dominican Saints*. Translated by Anselm M. Townsend, OP. Milwaukee: The Bruce Publishing Company, 1937.

_____. *Le Saint-Esprit dans la vie chrétienne*. Juvisy (Seine-et-Oise): Cerf, 1934.

Jean-Pierre de Caussade, SJ. *Abandonment to Divine Providence*. Translated and Introduced by John Beevers. New York: Doubleday Books, 1975.

John of the Cross, St. *The Collected Works*. Translated by Kieran Kavanaugh, OCD. and Otilio Rodriguez, OCD. Washington, D.C.: ICS Publications, 1991.

Maritain, Jacques. *The Range of Reason*. New York: Charles Scribner's Sons, 1953.

Marie Eugène of the Child Jesus, OCD, Bl. *I Want to See God*, Vol. I. Translated by Sister M. Verda Clare, Maria Press, Inc., 2000.

_____. *I am a Daughter of the Church*. Vol. II. Translated by Sister M. Verda Clare, CSC. Allen, TX: Christian Classics, 1998.

Martinez, Rev. Luis M. *The Sanctifier*. Translated by Sister M. Aquinas, OSU. Boston: Pauline Books and Media, 1985.

Pinckaers, Servais, OP. *The Sources of Christian Ethics*. Translated from the third edition by Sr. May Thomas Noble, OP. Edinburgh: T&T Clark, 1995.

Sackville-West, Vita. *The Eagle and the Dove*. London: Michael Joseph Ltd., 1943.

Stein, Edith, St. *The Science of the Cross*. In *The Collected Works of Edith Stein*. Vol. VI. Translated by Josephine Koeppel, OCD. Washington, D.C.: ICS Publications, 2002.

Teresa of Avila, St. *The Collected Works.* Vol. I-III. Translated by Kieran Kavanaugh, OCD, and Otilio Rodriguez, OCD. Washington, D.C.: ICS Publications, 1980.

Thomas à Kempis. *The Imitation of Christ.* Translated by Leo Sherley-Price. London: Penguin Books, 1952.

Vonier, Anscar, OSB. *The Spirit and the Bride.* London: Burns, Oates and Washbourne, Ltd., 1935.

Wiseman, James A., OSB. "Myticism." In *The New Dictionary of Catholic Spirituality.* Edited by Michael Downey. Collegeville, MN: The Liturgical Press, 1993.

ARTICLES

Aumann, Jordan, OP. "Mystical Experience, the Infused Virtues and the Gifts." *Angelicum* 58 (1981): 33-54.

_____. *"Spiritual Theology in the Thomistic Tradition."* Angelicum 51(1974): 571–598.

Camillus, Father, OCD. "The Act of Oblation to Merciful Love." *Spiritual Life.* Vol. XII, no. 2, Summer Issue. Discalced Carmelite Fathers of the Province of the Immaculate Heart of Mary, Washington Province (1966): 111- 118.

Dedek, John F. "Quasi Experimentalis, A Historical Approach to the Meaning of St. Thomas." *Theological Studies* 22 (1961): 357-390.

Gabriel de Sainte Marie-Madeleine, OCD. "Les Sommets dela Vie D'Amour." *Angelicum* 14 (19-37): 264-280.

———. "St. Thérèse's 'Little Way' and the Teachings of St. John of the Cross." *Spiritual Life*, Vol. 2, no. 2, June (1956): 74-92.

Gardini, Fabio, OP. "The Growth Process of Christian Prayer Life." *Angelicum* 69 (1992): 389-421.

Giertych, Wojciech, OP. "Why are there so few Thomist Saints?" *Angelicum*, Rome, February–March, Special Issue, A joint Project of the Journal Angelicum and the Angelicum-STOQ (2009): 987-998.

Lucien-Marie, P. de Saint-Joseph, "Le Martyre d'Amour." *Etudes Carmélitaines Limites De L'Humain, Desclée de Brouwer* (1953): 328-339.

Philipe de la Trinité, "Le Thomisme de Sainte Thérèse de l'Enfant-Jésus en matière de Rédemption," VT 8 (1962): 1-8.

Renault Emmanuel, OCD. "Le désire de mourir chez Thérèse d'Avila." *Saint Thérèse d'Avila, Colloque De Venasque*. Éditions du Carmel, Centre Notre-

Dame De Vie Spiritualité (Septembre 1982): 184-193.

Sarrasin Claude. "La Contemplation de Saint Thérèse de l'Enfant-Jésus." *Thérèse au Milieu des Docteurs, Colloque avec Thérèse de l'Enfant-Jésus* 19-22. Septembre 1997 à Notre de Vie, Venasque Éditions du Carmel (1998): 39-49.

Tugwell, Simon, OP. "Jean Pierre de Caussade, Saint Thérèse of Lisieux." *Doctrine and Life,* Vol. 33, No. 1 (1983): 336-345.

Claritas Spiritual Theology®
London
claritas-st.com